Mastering Spring 5.0

Master reactive programming, microservices, Cloud Native
applications, and more

This book is based on Spring Version 5.0 RC1

Ranga Rao Karanam

BIRMINGHAM - MUMBAI

Mastering Spring 5.0

First published: June 2017

Production reference: 1240617

Published by Packt Publishing Ltd.
Livery Place
35 Livery Street
Birmingham
B3 2PB, UK.

ISBN 978-1-78712-317-5

www.packtpub.com

Credits

Author
Ranga Rao Karanam

Reviewer
Jarosław Krochmalski

Commissioning Editor
Kunal Parikh

Acquisition Editor
Denim Pinto

Content Development Editor
Siddhi Chavan

Technical Editor
Supriya Thabe

Copy Editor
Stuti Srivastava

Project Coordinator
Prajakta Naik

Proofreader
Safis Editing

Indexer
Rekha Nair

Graphics
Abhinash Sahu

Production Coordinator
Shraddha Falebhai

About the Author

Ranga Rao Karanam is a programmer, trainer, and architect. His areas of interest include Cloud Native Applications, microservices, evolutionary design, high-quality code, DevOps, BDD, TDD, and refactoring. He loves consulting for start-ups on developing scalable, component-based Cloud Native applications, and following modern development practices such as BDD, continuous delivery, and DevOps. He loves the freedom the Spring Framework brings to developing enterprise Java applications.

Ranga started *in28minutes* with the vision of creating high-quality courses on developing Cloud Native Java applications. He is looking forward to enhancing his already considerable success--75,000 students on Udemy and 35,000 subscribers on YouTube.

Ranga likes to play cricket and go hiking. His dream is to spend a year hiking the Himalayas.

My family and best friends – thank you for everything!

About the Reviewer

Jarosław Krochmalski is a passionate software designer and developer who specializes in the financial business domain. He has over 12 years of experience in software development. He is a clean-code and software craftsmanship enthusiast. He is a Certified ScrumMaster and a fan of Agile. His professional interests include new technologies in web application development, design patterns, enterprise architecture, and integration patterns. He likes to experiment with NoSQL and cloud computing. Jaroslaw has been working with IDEA since its first release and has observed the IDE grow and mature. He has been designing and developing software professionally since 2000 and has been using Java as his primary programming language since 2002. In the past, he worked for companies such as Kredyt Bank (KBC) and Bank BPS on many large-scale projects, such as international money orders, express payments, and collection systems. He currently works as a consultant for the Danish company 7N as an infrastructure architect for the Nykredit bank. You can reach him via Twitter at @jkroch or by email at jarek@finsys.pl.

He has authored the books, *IntelliJ Idea Essentials*, *Developing with Docker*, and *Docker and Kubernetes for Java Developers* by Packt, and he has reviewed another book by Packt, *Spring Essentials*.

Hello to all my friends in Finsys, 7N, and Nykredit — keep up the good work!

www.PacktPub.com

For support files and downloads related to your book, please visit www.PacktPub.com.

Did you know that Packt offers eBook versions of every book published, with PDF and ePub files available? You can upgrade to the eBook version at www.PacktPub.com and as a print book customer, you are entitled to a discount on the eBook copy. Get in touch with us at service@packtpub.com for more details.

At www.PacktPub.com, you can also read a collection of free technical articles, sign up for a range of free newsletters and receive exclusive discounts and offers on Packt books and eBooks.

https://www.packtpub.com/mapt

Get the most in-demand software skills with Mapt. Mapt gives you full access to all Packt books and video courses, as well as industry-leading tools to help you plan your personal development and advance your career.

Why subscribe?

- Fully searchable across every book published by Packt
- Copy and paste, print, and bookmark content
- On demand and accessible via a web browser

Customer Feedback

Table of Contents

Preface

Spring 5.0 is due to arrive with a myriad of new and exciting features that will change the way we've used the framework so far. This book will show you this evolution--from solving the problems of testable applications to building distributed applications on the Cloud. The book begins with an insight into the new features in Spring 5.0, and shows you how to build an application using Spring MVC. You will then get a thorough understanding of how to build and extend microservices using the Spring Framework. You will also understand how to build and deploy Cloud applications. You will realize how application architectures have evolved from monoliths to those built around microservices. The advanced features of Spring Boot will also be covered and displayed through powerful examples.

By the end of this book, you will be equipped with the knowledge and best practices to develop applications with the Spring Framework.

What this book covers

Chapter 1, *Evolution to Spring Framework 5.0*, takes you through the evolution of the Spring Framework, ranging from its initial versions to Spring 5.0. Initially, Spring was used to develop testable applications using dependency injection and core modules. Recent Spring Projects, such as Spring Boot, Spring Cloud, Spring Cloud Data Flow--deal with application infrastructure and moving applications to Cloud. We get an overview of different Spring modules and projects.

Chapter 2, *Dependency Injection*, dives deep into dependency injection. We will look at different kinds of dependency injection methods available in Spring, and how auto-wiring makes your life easy. We will also take a quick look into unit testing.

Chapter 3, *Building a Web Application with Spring MVC*, gives a quick overview of building a web application with Spring MVC.

Chapter 4, *Evolution toward Microservices and Cloud-Native Applications*, explains the evolution of application architectures in the last decade. We will understand why microservices and Cloud Native applications are needed and get a quick overview of the different Spring projects that help us build Cloud-Native applications.

Chapter 5, *Building Microservices with Spring Boot*, discusses how Spring Boot takes away the complexity in creating production-grade Spring-based applications. It makes it easy to get started with Spring-based projects and provides easy integration with third-party libraries. In this chapter, we will take the students on a journey with Spring Boot. We will start with implementing a basic web service and then move on to adding caching, exception handling, HATEOAS, and internationalization, while making use of different features from the Spring Framework.

Chapter 6, *Extending Microservices*, focuses on adding more advanced features to the microservices that we built in Chapter 4, *Evolution toward Microservices and Cloud-Native Applications*.

Chapter 7, *Advanced Spring Boot Features*, takes a look at the advanced features in Spring Boot. You will learn how to monitor a microservice with a Spring Boot Actuator. Then, you will deploy the microservice to Cloud. You will also learn how to develop more effectively with the developer tools provided by Spring Boot.

Chapter 8, *Spring Data*, discusses the Spring Data module. We will develop simple applications to integrate Spring with JPA and Big Data technologies.

Chapter 9, *Spring Cloud*, discusses the distributed systems in the Cloud that have common problems, configuration management, service discovery, circuit breakers, and intelligent routing. In this chapter, you will learn how Spring Cloud helps you develop solutions for these common patterns. These solutions should work well on the Cloud as well as developer local systems.

Chapter 10, *Spring Cloud Data Flow*, talks about the Spring Cloud Data Flow, which offers a collection of patterns and best practices for microservices-based distributed streaming and batch data pipelines. In this chapter, we will understand the basics of Spring Cloud Data Flow and use it to build basic data flow use cases.

Chapter 11, *Reactive Programming*, explores programming with asynchronous data streams. In this chapter, we will understand Reactive programming and take a quick look at the features provided by the Spring Framework.

Chapter 12, *Spring Best Practices*, helps you understand best practices in developing enterprise applications with Spring related to unit testing, integration testing, maintaining Spring configuration, and more.

Chapter 13, *Working with Kotlin in Spring*, introduces you to a JVM language gaining quick popularity--Kotlin. We will discuss how to setup a Kotlin project in Eclipse. We will create a new Spring Boot project using Kotlin and implement a couple of basic services with unit and integration testing.

What you need for this book

To be able to run examples from this book, you will need the following tools:

- Java 8
- Eclipse IDE
- Postman

We will use Maven embedded into Eclipse IDE to download all the dependencies that are needed.

Who this book is for

This book is for experienced Java developers who knows the basics of Spring, and wants to learn how to use Spring Boot to build applications and deploy them to the Cloud.

Conventions

In this book, you will find a number of text styles that distinguish between different kinds of information. Here are some examples of these styles and an explanation of their meaning.

Code words in text, database table names, folder names, filenames, file extensions, pathnames, dummy URLs, and user input are shown as follows: "Configure `spring-boot-starter-parent` in your `pom.xml` file".

A block of code is set as follows:

```
<properties>
  <mockito.version>1.10.20</mockito.version>
</properties>
```

Any command-line input or output is written as follows:

```
mvn clean install
```

New terms and **important words** are shown in bold. Words that you see on the screen, for example, in menus or dialog boxes, appear in the text like this: "Provide the details and click on **Generate Project**."

Warnings or important notes appear in a box like this.

Tips and tricks appear like this.

Reader feedback

Feedback from our readers is always welcome. Let us know what you think about this book—what you liked or disliked. Reader feedback is important for us as it helps us develop titles that you will really get the most out of.

To send us general feedback, simply e-mail feedback@packtpub.com, and mention the book's title in the subject of your message.

If there is a topic that you have expertise in and you are interested in either writing or contributing to a book, see our author guide at www.packtpub.com/authors.

Customer support

Now that you are the proud owner of a Packt book, we have a number of things to help you to get the most from your purchase.

Downloading the example code

You can download the example code files for this book from your account at http://www.packtpub.com. If you purchased this book elsewhere, you can visit http://www.packtpub.com/support and register to have the files e-mailed directly to you.

You can download the code files by following these steps:

1. Log in or register to our website using your e-mail address and password.
2. Hover the mouse pointer on the **SUPPORT** tab at the top.
3. Click on **Code Downloads & Errata**.
4. Enter the name of the book in the **Search** box.
5. Select the book for which you're looking to download the code files.

6. Choose from the drop-down menu where you purchased this book from.
7. Click on **Code Download**.

Once the file is downloaded, please make sure that you unzip or extract the folder using the latest version of:

- WinRAR / 7-Zip for Windows
- Zipeg / iZip / UnRarX for Mac
- 7-Zip / PeaZip for Linux

The code bundle for the book is also hosted on GitHub at `https://github.com/PacktPubl ishing/Mastering-Spring-5.0`. We also have other code bundles from our rich catalog of books and videos available at `https://github.com/PacktPublishing/`. Check them out!

Errata

Although we have taken every care to ensure the accuracy of our content, mistakes do happen. If you find a mistake in one of our books—maybe a mistake in the text or the code—we would be grateful if you could report this to us. By doing so, you can save other readers from frustration and help us improve subsequent versions of this book. If you find any errata, please report them by visiting `http://www.packtpub.com/submit-errata`, selecting your book, clicking on the **Errata Submission Form** link, and entering the details of your errata. Once your errata are verified, your submission will be accepted and the errata will be uploaded to our website or added to any list of existing errata under the Errata section of that title.

To view the previously submitted errata, go to `https://www.packtpub.com/books/conten t/support`and enter the name of the book in the search field. The required information will appear under the **Errata** section.

Piracy

Piracy of copyrighted material on the Internet is an ongoing problem across all media. At Packt, we take the protection of our copyright and licenses very seriously. If you come across any illegal copies of our works in any form on the Internet, please provide us with the location address or website name immediately so that we can pursue a remedy.

Please contact us at `copyright@packtpub.com` with a link to the suspected pirated material.

We appreciate your help in protecting our authors and our ability to bring you valuable content.

Questions

If you have a problem with any aspect of this book, you can contact us at `questions@packtpub.com`, and we will do our best to address the problem.

1
Evolution to Spring Framework 5.0

The first version of Spring Framework 1.0 was released in March 2004. For more than a decade and a half, Spring Framework remained the framework of choice to build Java applications.

In the relatively young and dynamic world of Java frameworks, a decade is a long time.

In this chapter, we start with understanding the core features of Spring Framework. We will look at why the Spring Framework became popular and how it adapted to remain the framework of choice. After taking a quick look at the important modules in the Spring Framework, we will jump into the world of Spring Projects. We will end the chapter by looking at the new features in Spring Framework 5.0.

This chapter will answer the following questions:

- Why is Spring Framework popular?
- How has Spring Framework adapted to the evolution of application architectures?
- What are the important modules in Spring Framework?
- Where does Spring Framework fit in the umbrella of Spring Projects?
- What are the new features in Spring Framework 5.0?

Spring Framework

The Spring website (`https://projects.spring.io/spring-framework/`) defines Spring Framework as follows: *The Spring Framework provides a comprehensive programming and configuration model for modern Java-based enterprise applications.*

Spring Framework is used to wire enterprise Java applications. The main aim of Spring Framework is to take care of all the technical plumbing that is needed in order to connect the different parts of an application. This allows programmers to focus on the crux of their jobs--writing business logic.

Problems with EJB

Spring Framework was released in March 2004. When the first version of Spring Framework was released, the popular way of developing an enterprise application was using **Enterprise Java Beans (EJB)** 2.1.

Developing and deploying EJBs was a cumbersome process. While EJBs made the distribution of components easier, developing, unit testing, and deploying them was not easy. The initial versions of EJBs (1.0, 2.0, 2.1) had a complex **Application Programmer Interface (API)**, leading to a perception (and truth in most applications) that the complexity introduced far outweighed the benefits:

- Difficult to unit test. Actually, difficult to test outside the EJB Container.
- Multiple interfaces need to be implemented with a number of unnecessary methods.
- Cumbersome and tedious exception handling.
- Inconvenient deployment descriptors.

Spring Framework was introduced as a lightweight framework aimed at making developing Java EE applications simpler.

Why is Spring Framework popular?

The first version of Spring Framework was released in March 2004. In the subsequent decade and a half, the use and popularity of Spring Framework only grew.

The important reasons behind the popularity of Spring Framework are as follows:

- Simplified unit testing--because of dependency injection
- Reduction in plumbing code
- Architectural flexibility
- Keeping up with changing times

Let's discuss each of these in detail.

Simplified unit testing

Earlier versions of EJBs were very difficult to unit test. In fact, it was difficult to run EJBs outside the container (as of version 2.1). The only way to test them was to deploy them in a container.

Spring Framework brought in the concept of **Dependency Injection** (**DI**). We will discuss dependency injection in complete detail in Chapter 2, *Dependency Injection*.

The dependency injection enables unit testing by making it easy to replace the dependencies with their mocks. We do not need to deploy the entire application to unit test it.

Simplifying unit testing has multiple benefits:

- Programmers are more productive
- Defects are found earlier so they are less costly to fix
- Applications have automated unit tests, which can run in **Continuous Integration** builds, preventing future defects

Reduction in plumbing code

Before Spring Framework, typical J2EE (or Java EE, as it is called now) applications contained a lot of plumbing code. For example: getting a database connection, exception handling code, transaction management code, logging code, and a lot more.

Let's take a look at a simple example of executing a query using prepared statement:

```
PreparedStatement st = null;
try {
      st = conn.prepareStatement(INSERT_TODO_QUERY);
      st.setString(1, bean.getDescription());
      st.setBoolean(2, bean.isDone());
      st.execute();
   }
catch (SQLException e) {
      logger.error("Failed : " + INSERT_TODO_QUERY, e);
  } finally {
            if (st != null) {
        try {
        st.close();
        } catch (SQLException e) {
        // Ignore - nothing to do..
        }
      }
   }
```

In the preceding example, there are four lines of business logic and more than 10 lines of plumbing code.

With Spring Framework, the same logic can be applied in a couple of lines:

```
jdbcTemplate.update(INSERT_TODO_QUERY,
bean.getDescription(), bean.isDone());
```

How does Spring Framework do this magic?

In the preceding example, Spring JDBC (and Spring, in general) converts most checked exceptions into unchecked exceptions. Typically, when a query fails, there is not a lot we can do--other than to close the statement and fail the transaction. Instead of implementing exception handling in every method, we can have centralized exception handling and inject it in using Spring **Aspect-Oriented Programming (AOP)**.

Spring JDBC removes the need to create all the plumbing code involved in getting a connection, creating a prepared statement, and so on. The `jdbcTemplate` class can be created in the Spring context and injected into the **Data Access Object (DAO)** class wherever it is needed.

Similar to the preceding example, Spring JMS, Spring AOP, and other Spring modules help in reducing a lot of plumbing code.

Spring Framework lets the programmer focus on the primary job of a programmer-- writing business logic.

Avoiding all the plumbing code also has another great benefit--reduced duplication in code. Since all code for transaction management, exception handling, and so on (typically, all your cross-cutting concerns) is implemented at one place, it is easier to maintain.

Architectural flexibility

Spring Framework is modular. It is built as a set of independent modules built on top of the core Spring modules. Most of the Spring modules are independent--you can use one of them without having to use others.

Let's look at a few examples:

- In the web layer, Spring offers a framework of its own--Spring MVC. However, Spring has great support for Struts, Vaadin, JSF, or any web framework of your choice.
- Spring Beans can provide lightweight implementation for your business logic. However, Spring can be integrated with EJBs as well.
- In the data layer, Spring simplifies JDBC with its Spring JDBC module. However, Spring has great support for any of your preferred data layer frameworks--JPA, Hibernate (with or without JPA), or iBatis.
- You have the option of implementing your cross-cutting concerns (logging, transaction management, security, and so on) with Spring AOP. Or, you can integrate with a fully fledged AOP implementation such as AspectJ.

Spring Framework does not want to be the jack-of-all-trades. While focusing on its core job of reducing coupling between different parts of the application and making them testable, Spring provides great integration with frameworks of your choice. This means you have flexibility in your architecture--if you do not want to use a specific framework, you can easily replace it with another.

Keep up with changing times

The first version of Spring Framework focused on making applications testable. However, as time moved on, there were new challenges. Spring Framework managed to evolve and stay ahead of the curve with the flexibility and modules that are offered. A couple of examples are listed as follows:

- Annotations were introduced in Java 5. Spring Framework (version 2.5 – Nov 2007) was ahead of Java EE in introducing an annotation-based controller model for Spring MVC. Developers using Java EE had to wait until Java EE 6 (Dec 2009 – 2 years) before having comparable functionality.
- Spring Framework introduced a number of abstractions ahead of Java EE to keep the application decoupled from specific implementation. Caching API provides a case in point. Spring provided a transparent caching support in Spring 3.1. Java EE came up with *JSR-107* for JCache (in 2014)--support for which was provided in Spring 4.1.

Another important thing Spring brings in is the umbrella of Spring Projects. Spring Framework is just one of the many projects under Spring Projects. We will discuss the different Spring Projects in a separate section. The following examples illustrate how Spring managed to stay ahead of times with new Spring Projects:

- **Spring Batch** defines a new approach to building Java Batch applications. We had to wait until Java EE 7 (June 2013) to have comparable batch application specification in Java EE.
- As architecture evolved toward Cloud and microservices, Spring came up with new Cloud-oriented Spring Projects. Spring Cloud helps in simplifying the development and deployment of microservices. Spring Cloud Data Flow provides orchestrations around microservice applications.

Spring modules

The modularity of Spring Framework is one of the most important reasons for its widespread used. Spring Framework is highly modular with more than 20 different modules--having clearly defined boundaries.

The following figure shows different Spring modules--organized by the layer of application they are typically used in:

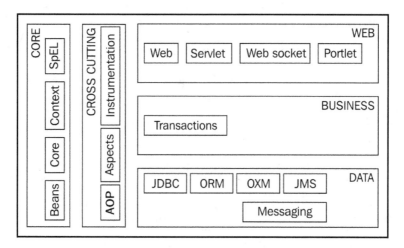

We will start with discussing the Spring Core Container before moving on to other modules grouped by the application layer they are typically used in.

Spring Core Container

Spring Core Container provides the core features of Spring Framework--dependency injection, **IoC** (**Inversion of Control**) container, and the application context. We will learn more about DI and IoC Container in `Chapter 2`, *Dependency Injection*.

Important core Spring modules are listed in the following table:

Module/Artifact	Use
spring-core	Utilities used by other Spring modules.
spring-beans	Support for Spring beans. In combination with spring-core provides the core feature of Spring Framework--dependency injection. Includes implementation of BeanFactory.
spring-context	Implements ApplicationContext, which extends BeanFactory and provides support to load resources and internationalization, among others.
spring-expression	Extends **EL** (**Expression Language** from JSP) and provides a language for bean property (including arrays and collections) access and manipulations.

Cross-cutting concerns

Cross-cutting concerns are applicable to all application layers--logging and security, among others. **AOP** is typically used to implement cross-cutting concerns.

Unit tests and integration tests fit this category since they are applicable to all layers.

Important Spring modules related to cross-cutting concerns are listed as follows:

Module/Artifact	Use
spring-aop	Provides basic support for Aspect-Oriented Programming--with method interceptors and pointcuts.
spring-aspects	Provides integration with the most popular and fully featured AOP framework, AspectJ.
spring-instrument	Provides basic instrumentation support.
spring-test	Provides basic support for unit testing and integration testing.

Web

Spring provides its own MVC framework, Spring MVC, other than providing great integration with popular web frameworks such as Struts.

Important artifacts/modules are listed as follows:

- **spring-web**: Provides basic web features, such as multi-part file upload. Provides support for integration with other web frameworks, such as Struts.
- **spring-webmvc**: Provides a fully featured web mvc framework--Spring MVC, which includes features to implement REST services as well.

We will cover Spring MVC and develop web applicaitions and rest services with it in Chapter 3, *Building Web Application with Spring MVC* and Chapter 5, *Building Microservices with Spring Boot*.

Business

The business layer is focused on executing the business logic of the applications. With Spring, business logic is typically implemented in **Plain Old Java Object** (**POJO**).

Spring Transactions (spring-tx) provides declarative transaction management for POJO and other classes.

Data

The data layer in applications typically talks to the database and/or the external interfaces. Some of the important Spring modules related to the data layer are listed in the following table:

Module/Artifact	Use
spring-jdbc	**Provides abstraction around JDBC to avoid boilerplate code.**
spring-orm	Provides integration with ORM frameworks and specifications-- JPA and Hibernate, among others.
spring-oxm	Provides an object to XML mapping integration. Supports frameworks such as JAXB, Castor, and so on.
spring-jms	Provides abstraction around JMS to avoid boilerplate code.

Spring Projects

While Spring Framework provides the base for core features of enterprise applications (DI, web, data), other Spring Projects explore integration and solutions to other problems in the enterprise space--deployment, Cloud, Big Data, Batch and Security, among others.

Some of the important Spring Projects are listed as follows:

- Spring Boot
- Spring Cloud
- Spring Data
- Spring Batch
- Spring Security
- Spring HATEOAS

Spring Boot

Some of the challenges while developing microservices and web applications are as follows:

- Making framework choices and deciding compatible framework versions
- Providing mechanisms for externalizing configuration--properties that can change from one environment to another
- Health checks and monitoring--providing alerts if a specific part of the application is down
- Deciding the deployment environment and configuring the application for it

Spring Boot solves all these problems out of the box by taking an *opinionated view* of how applications have to be developed.

We will look at Spring Boot in depth in two chapters--Chapter 5, *Building Microservices with Spring Boot* and Chapter 7, *Advanced Spring Boot Features*.

Spring Cloud

It is not an exaggeration to say *The world is moving to the Cloud*.

Cloud Native microservices and applications are the order of the day. We will discuss this in detail in Chapter 4, *Evolution toward Microservices and Cloud-Native Applications*.

Spring is taking rapid strides toward making application development for the Cloud simpler with Spring Cloud.

Spring Cloud provides solutions for common patterns in distributed systems. Spring Cloud enables developers to quickly create applications that implement common patterns. Some of the common patterns implemented in Spring Cloud are listed as follows:

- Configuration management
- Service discovery
- Circuit breakers
- Intelligent routing

We will discuss Spring Cloud and its varied range features in more detail in Chapter 9, *Spring Cloud*.

Spring Data

There are multiple sources of data in today's world--SQL (relational) and a variety of NOSQL databases. Spring Data tries to provide a consistent data-access approach to all these different kinds of databases.

Spring Data provides integration with a varied range of specifications and/or data stores:

- JPA
- MongoDB
- Redis
- Solr
- Gemfire
- Apache Cassandra

Some of the important features are listed as follows:

- Provides abstractions around repository and object mappings--by determining queries from method names
- Simple Spring integration
- Integration with Spring MVC controllers
- Advanced automatic auditing features--created by, created date, last changed by, and last changed date

We will discuss Spring Data in more detail in `Chapter 8`, *Spring Data*.

Spring Batch

Enterprise applications today process large volumes of data using batch programs. The needs of these applications are very similar. Spring Batch provides solutions for high-volume batch programs with high performance requirements.

Important features in Spring Batch are as follows:

- The ability to start, stop, and restart jobs--including the ability to restart failed jobs from the point where they failed
- The ability to process data in chunks
- The ability to retry steps or to skip steps on failure
- Web-based administration interface

Spring Security

Authentication is the process of identifying the user. **Authorization** is the process of ensuring that a user has access to perform the identified action on the resource.

Authentication and authorization are critical parts of Enterprise applications, both web applications and web services. Spring Security provides declarative authentication and authorization for Java based applications.

Important features in Spring Security are as follows:

- Simplified authentication and authorization
- Great integration with Spring MVC and Servlet APIs
- Support to prevent common security attacks--**cross-site forgery request** (**CSRF**) and Session Fixation
- Modules available for integration with SAML and LDAP

We will discuss how to secure web applications with Spring Security in `Chapter 3`, *Building Web Application with Spring MVC*.

We will discuss how to secure REST Services with Basic and OAuth authentication mechanisms using Spring Security in `Chapter 6`, *Extending Microservices*.

Spring HATEOAS

HATEOAS stands for **Hypermedia as The Engine of Application State**. Though it sounds complex, it is quite a simple concept. Its main aim is to decouple the server (the provider of the service) from the client (the consumer of the service).

The service provider provides the service consumer with information about what other actions can be performed on the resource.

Spring HATEOAS provides a HATEOAS implementation--especially for the REST services implemented with Spring MVC.

Important features in Spring HATEOAS are as follows:

- Simplified definition of links pointing to service methods, making the links less fragile
- Support for JAXB (XML-based) and JSON integration
- Support for service consumer (client side)

We will discuss how to use HATEOAS in `Chapter 6`, *Extending Microservices*.

New features in Spring Framework 5.0

Spring Framework 5.0 is the first major upgrade in Spring Framework, almost four years after Spring Framework 4.0. In this time frame, one of the major developments has been the evolution of the Spring Boot project. We will discuss the new features in Spring Boot 2.0 in the next section.

One of the biggest features of Spring Framework 5.0 is **Reactive Programming**. Core reactive programming features and support for reactive endpoints are available out of the box with Spring Framework 5.0. The list of important changes includes the following:

- Baseline upgrades
- JDK 9 runtime compatibility
- Usage of JDK 8 features in the Spring Framework code
- Reactive programming support
- A functional web framework
- Java modularity with Jigsaw
- Kotlin support
- Dropped features

Baseline upgrades

Spring Framework 5.0 has JDK 8 and Java EE 7 baseline. Basically, it means that previous JDK and Java EE versions are not supported anymore.

Some of the important baseline Java EE 7 specifications for Spring Framework 5.0 are listed as follows:

- Servlet 3.1
- JMS 2.0
- JPA 2.1
- JAX-RS 2.0
- Bean Validation 1.1

There are many changes to the minimum supported versions of several Java frameworks. The following list contains some of the minimum supported versions of prominent frameworks:

- Hibernate 5
- Jackson 2.6
- EhCache 2.10
- JUnit 5
- Tiles 3

The following list shows the supported server versions:

- Tomcat 8.5+
- Jetty 9.4+
- WildFly 10+
- Netty 4.1+ (for web reactive programming with Spring Web Flux)
- Undertow 1.4+ (for web reactive programming with Spring Web Flux)

Applications using earlier versions of any of the preceding specifications/frameworks need to be upgraded at least to the previously listed versions before they can use Spring Framework 5.0.

JDK 9 runtime compatibility

JDK 9 is expected to be released mid-2017. Spring Framework 5.0 is expected to have runtime compatibility with JDK 9.

Usage of JDK 8 features in Spring Framework code

The Spring Framework 4.x baseline version is Java SE 6. This means that it supports Java 6, 7, and 8. Having to support Java SE 6 and 7 puts constraints on the Spring Framework code. The framework code cannot use any of the new features in Java 8. So, while the rest of the world upgraded to Java 8, the code in Spring Framework (at least the major parts) was restricted to using earlier versions of Java.

With Spring Framework 5.0, the baseline version is Java 8. Spring Framework code is now upgraded to use the new features in Java 8. This will result in more readable and performant framework code. Some of the Java 8 features used are as follows:

- Java 8 default methods in core Spring interfaces
- Internal code improvements based on Java 8 reflection enhancements
- Use of functional programming in the framework code--lambdas and streams

Reactive programming support

Reactive programming is one of the most important features of Spring Framework 5.0.

Microservices architectures are typically built around event-based communication. Applications are built to react to events (or messages).

Reactive programming provides an alternate style of programming focused on building applications that react to events.

While Java 8 does not have built-in suppport for reactive programming, there are a number of frameworks that provide support for reactive programming:

- **Reactive Streams**: Language-neutral attempt to define reactive APIs.
- **Reactor**: Java implementation of Reactive Streams provided by the Spring Pivotal team.
- **Spring WebFlux**: Enables the development of web applications based on reactive programming. Provides a programming model similar to Spring MVC.

We will discuss Reactive Programming and how you can implement it with Spring Web Flux in Chapter 11, *Reactive Programming*.

Functional web framework

Building on top of the reactive features, Spring 5 also provides a functional web framework.

A functional web framework provides features to define endpoints using functional programming style. A simple hello world example is shown here:

```
RouterFunction<String> route =
route(GET("/hello-world"),
request -> Response.ok().body(fromObject("Hello World")));
```

A functional web framework can also be used to define more complex routes, as shown in the following example:

```
RouterFunction<?> route = route(GET("/todos/{id}"),
request -> {
   Mono<Todo> todo = Mono.justOrEmpty(request.pathVariable("id"))
   .map(Integer::valueOf)
   .then(repository::getTodo);
   return Response.ok().body(fromPublisher(todo, Todo.class));
  })
 .and(route(GET("/todos"),
 request -> {
   Flux<Todo> people = repository.allTodos();
   return Response.ok().body(fromPublisher(people, Todo.class));
 }))
.and(route(POST("/todos"),
request -> {
  Mono<Todo> todo = request.body(toMono(Todo.class));
  return Response.ok().build(repository.saveTodo(todo));
}));
```

A couple of important things to note are as follows:

- `RouterFunction` evaluates the matching condition to route requests to the appropriate handler function
- We are defining three endpoints, two GETs, and one POST, and mapping them to different handler functions

We will discuss Mono and Flux in more detail in Chapter 11, *Reactive Programming*.

Java modularity with Jigsaw

Until Java 8, the Java platform was not modular. A couple of important problems resulted out of this:

- **Platform Bloat**: Java modularity has not been a cause of concern in the last couple of decades. However, with **Internet of Things (IOT)** and new lightweight platforms such as Node.js, there is an urgent need to address the bloat of the Java platform. (Initial versions of JDK were less than 10MB in size. Recent versions of JDK need more than 200 MB.)

- **JAR Hell**: Another important concern is the problem of JAR Hell. When Java ClassLoader finds a class, it will not see whether there are other definitions for the class available. It immediately loads the first class that is found. If two different parts of the application need the same class from different jars, there is no way for them to specify the jar from which the class has to be loaded.

Open System Gateway initiative (OSGi) is one of the initiatives, started way back in 1999, to bring modularity into Java applications.

Each module (referred to as bundle) defines the following:

- **imports**: Other bundles that the module uses
- **exports**: Packages that this bundle exports

Each module can have its own life cycle. It can be installed, started, and stopped on its own.

Jigsaw is an initiative under **Java Community Process (JCP)**, started with Java 7, to bring modularity into Java. It has two main aims:

- Defining and implementing a modular structure for JDK
- Defining a module system for applications built on the Java platform

Jigsaw is expected to be part of Java 9 and Spring Framework 5.0 is expected to include basic support for Jigsaw modules.

Kotlin support

Kotlin is a statically typed JVM language that enables code that is expressive, short, and readable. Spring framework 5.0 has good support for Kotlin.

Consider a simple Kotlin program illustrating a data class, as shown here:

```
import java.util.*
data class Todo(var description: String, var name: String, var
targetDate : Date)
fun main(args: Array<String>) {
  var todo = Todo("Learn Spring Boot", "Jack", Date())
  println(todo)
    //Todo(description=Learn Spring Boot, name=Jack,
    //targetDate=Mon May 22 04:26:22 UTC 2017)
  var todo2 = todo.copy(name = "Jill")
  println(todo2)
    //Todo(description=Learn Spring Boot, name=Jill,
    //targetDate=Mon May 22 04:26:22 UTC 2017)
```

```
        var todo3 = todo.copy()
        println(todo3.equals(todo)) //true
    }
```

In fewer than 10 lines of code, we created and tested a data bean with three properties and the following functions:

- `equals()`
- `hashCode()`
- `toString()`
- `copy()`

Kotlin is strongly typed. But there is no need to specify the type of each variable explicitly:

```
val arrayList = arrayListOf("Item1", "Item2", "Item3")
// Type is ArrayList
```

Named arguments allow you to specify the names of arguments when calling methods, resulting in more readable code:

```
var todo = Todo(description = "Learn Spring Boot",
name = "Jack", targetDate = Date())
```

Kotlin makes functional programming simpler by providing default variables (`it`) and methods such as `take`, `drop`, and so on:

```
var first3TodosOfJack = students.filter { it.name == "Jack"
  }.take(3)
```

You can also specify default values for arguments in Kotlin:

```
import java.util.*
data class Todo(var description: String, var name: String, var
targetDate : Date = Date())
fun main(args: Array<String>) {
   var todo = Todo(description = "Learn Spring Boot", name = "Jack")
}
```

With all its features making the code concise and expressive, we expect Kotlin to be a language to be learned for the .

We will discuss more about Kotlin in `Chapter 13`, *Working with Kotlin in Spring*.

Dropped features

Spring Framework 5 is a major Spring release with substantial increase in the baselines. Along with the increase in baseline versions for Java, Java EE and a few other frameworks, Spring Framework 5 removed support for a few frameworks:

- Portlet
- Velocity
- JasperReports
- XMLBeans
- JDO
- Guava

If you are using any of the preceding frameworks, it is recommended that you plan a migration and stay with Spring Framework 4.3--which has support until 2019.

Spring Boot 2.0 new features

The first version of Spring Boot was released in 2014. The following are some of the important updates expected in Spring Boot 2.0:

- The baseline JDK version is Java 8
- The baseline Spring Version is Spring Framework 5.0
- Spring Boot 2.0 has support for Reactive Web programming with WebFlux

Minimum supported versions of some important frameworks are listed as follows:

- Jetty 9.4
- Tomcat 8.5
- Hibernate 5.2
- Gradle 3.4

We will discuss Spring Boot extensively in `Chapter 5`, *Building Microservices with Spring Boot* and `Chapter 7`, *Advanced Spring Boot Features*.

Summary

Over the course of the last decade and a half, Spring Framework has dramatically improved the experience of developing Java Enterprise applications. With Spring Framework 5.0, it brings in a lot of features while significantly increasing the baselines.

In the subsequent chapters, we will cover dependency injection and understand how we can develop web applications with Spring MVC. After that, we will move into the world of microservices. In Chapters 5, *Building Microservices with Spring Boot*, Chapter 6, *Extending Microservices*, and Chapter 7, *Advanced Spring Boot Features*, we will cover how Spring Boot makes the creation of microservices simpler. We will then shift our attention to building applications in the Cloud with Spring Cloud and Spring Cloud Data Flow.

2
Dependency Injection

Any Java class we write depends on other classes. The other classes a class depends on are its dependencies. If a class directly creates instances of dependencies, a tight coupling is established between them. With Spring, the responsibility of creating and wiring objects is taken over by a new component called the **IoC container**. Classes define dependencies and the Spring **Inversion of Control** (**IoC**) container creates objects and wires the dependencies together. This revolutionary concept, where the control of creating and wiring dependencies is taken over by the container, is famously called IoC or **dependency injection** (**DI**).

In this chapter, we start with exploring the need for DI. We use a simple example to illustrate the use of DI. We will understand the important advantages of DI--easier maintainability, less coupling and improved testability. We will explore the DI options in Spring. We will end the chapter by looking at the standard DI specification for Java **Contexts and Dependency Injection** (**CDI**) and how Spring supports it.

This chapter will answer the following questions:

- What is dependency injection?
- How does proper use of dependency injection make applications testable?
- How does Spring implement DI with annotations?
- What is a component scan?
- What is the difference between Java and XML application contexts?
- How do you create unit tests for Spring contexts?
- How does mocking make unit testing simpler?

- What are the different bean scopes?
- What is CDI and how does Spring support CDI?

Understanding dependency injection

We will look at an example to understand dependency injection. We will write a simple business service that talks to a data service. We will make the code testable and see how proper use of DI makes the code testable.

The following is the sequence of steps we will follow:

1. Write a simple example of a business service talking to a data service. When a business service directly creates an instance of a data service, they are tightly coupled to one another. Unit testing will be difficult.
2. Make code loosely coupled by moving the responsibility of creating the data service outside the business service.
3. Bring in the Spring IoC container to instantiate the beans and wire them together.
4. Explore the XML and Java configuration options that Spring provides.
5. Explore Spring unit testing options.
6. Write real unit tests using mocking.

Understanding dependencies

We will start with writing a simple example; a business service talking to another data service. Most Java classes depend on other classes. These are called **dependencies** of that class.

Take a look at an example class BusinessServiceImpl, as follows:

```
public class BusinessServiceImpl {
  public long calculateSum(User user) {
    DataServiceImpl dataService = new DataServiceImpl();
    long sum = 0;
    for (Data data : dataService.retrieveData(user)) {
      sum += data.getValue();
    }
    return sum;
  }
}
```

Typically, all well-designed applications have multiple layers. Every layer has a well-defined responsibility. The business layer contains the business logic. The data layer talks to the external interfaces and/or databases to get the data. In the preceding example, the `DataServiceImpl` class gets some data related to the user from the database. `BusinessServiceImpl` class is a typical business service, talking to the data service `DataServiceImpl` for data and adding business logic on top of it (in this example, the business logic is very simple: calculate the sum of data returned by the data service).

`BusinessServiceImpl` depends on `DataServiceImpl`. So, `DataServiceImpl` is a dependency of `BusinessServiceImpl`.

Focus on how `BusinessServiceImpl` creates an instance of `DataServiceImpl`.

```
DataServiceImpl dataService = new DataServiceImpl();
```

`BusinessServiceImpl` creates an instance by itself. This is tight coupling.

Think for a moment about unit testing; how do you unit test the `BusinessServiceImpl` class without involving (or instantiating) the `DataServiceImpl` class? It's very difficult. One might need to do complicated things such as reflection to write a unit test. So, the preceding code is not testable.

 A piece of code (a method, a group of methods, or a class) is testable when you can easily write a simple unit test for it. One of the approaches used in unit testing is to mock the dependencies. We will discuss mocking in more detail later.

Here's a question to think about: how do we make the preceding code testable? How do we reduce tight coupling between `BusinessServiceImpl` and `DataServiceImpl`?

The first thing we can do is to create an interface for `DataServiceImpl`. Instead of using the direct class, we can use the newly created interface of `DataServiceImpl` in `BusinessServiceImpl`.

The following code shows how to create an interface:

```
public interface DataService {
  List<Data> retrieveData(User user);
}
```

Let's update the code in `BusinessServiceImpl` to use the interface:

```
DataService dataService = new DataServiceImpl();
```

Using interfaces helps in creating loosely coupled code. We can replace the wire with any implementation of an interface into a well-defined dependency.

For example, consider a business service that needs some sorting.

The first option is to use the sorting algorithm directly in the code, for example, bubble sort. The second option is to create an interface for the sorting algorithm and use the interface. The specific algorithm can be wired in later. In the first option, when we need to change the algorithm, we will need to change the code. In the second option, all that we need to change is the wiring.

We are now using the `DataService` interface, but `BusinessServiceImpl` is still tightly coupled as it is creating an instance of `DataServiceImpl`. How can we solve that?

How about `BusinessServiceImpl` not creating an instance of `DataServiceImpl` by itself? Can we create an instance of `DataServiceImpl` elsewhere (we will discuss who will create the instance later) and give it to `BusinessServiceImpl`?

To enable this, we will update the code in `BusinessServiceImpl` to have a setter for `DataService`. The `calculateSum` method is also updated to use this reference. The updated code is as follows:

```java
public class BusinessServiceImpl {
  private DataService dataService;
  public long calculateSum(User user) {
    long sum = 0;
    for (Data data : dataService.retrieveData(user)) {
      sum += data.getValue();
    }
    return sum;
  }
  public void setDataService(DataService dataService) {
    this.dataService = dataService;
  }
}
```

Instead of creating a setter for the data service, we could have also created a `BusinessServiceImpl` constructor accepting a data service as an argument. This is called a **constructor injection**.

You can see that `BusinessServiceImpl` can now work with any implementation of `DataService`. It is not tightly coupled with a specific implementation: `DataServiceImpl`.

To make the code even more loosely coupled (as we start writing the tests), let's create an interface for `BusinessService` and have `BusinessServiceImpl` updated to implement the interface:

```
public interface BusinessService {
   long calculateSum(User user);
}
public class BusinessServiceImpl implements BusinessService {
   //.... Rest of code..
}
```

Now that we have reduced coupling, one question remains still; who takes the responsibility for creating instance of the `DataServiceImpl` class and wiring it to the `BusinessServiceImpl` class?

That's exactly where the Spring IoC container comes into the picture.

The Spring IoC container

The Spring IoC container creates the beans and wires them together according to the configuration setup created by the application developer.

The following questions need to be answered:

- **Question 1**: How does the Spring IoC container know which beans to create? Specifically, how does the Spring IoC container know to create beans for the `BusinessServiceImpl` and `DataServiceImpl` classes?
- **Question 2**: How does the Spring IoC container know how to wire beans together? Specifically, how does the Spring IoC container know to inject the instance of the `DataServiceImpl` class into the `BusinessServiceImpl` class?
- **Question 3**: How does the Spring IoC container know where to search for beans? It is not efficient to search all packages in the classpath.

Before we can focus on creating a container, let's focus on questions 1 and 2; how to define what beans need to be created and how to wire them together.

Defining beans and wiring

Let's address the first question; how does the Spring IoC container know which beans to create?

We need to tell the Spring IoC container which beans to create. This can be done using `@Repository` or `@Component` or `@Service` annotations on the classes for which beans have to be created. All these annotations tell the Spring Framework to create beans for the specific classes where these annotations are defined.

A `@Component` annotation is the most generic way of defining a Spring bean. Other annotations have more specific context associated with them. `@Service` annotation is used in business service components. `@Repository` annotation is used in **Data Access Object** (**DAO**) components.

We use `@Repository` annotation on `DataServiceImpl` because it is related to getting data from the database. We use `@Service` annotation on the `BusinessServiceImpl` class as follows, since it is a business service:

```
@Repository
public class DataServiceImpl implements DataService
@Service
public class BusinessServiceImpl implements BusinessService
```

Let's shift our attention to question 2 now--how does the Spring IoC container know how to wire beans together? The bean of the `DataServiceImpl` class needs to be injected into that of the `BusinessServiceImpl` class.

We can do that by specifying an `@Autowired` annotation on the instance variable of the `DataService` interface in the `BusinessServiceImpl` class:

```
public class BusinessServiceImpl {
  @Autowired
  private DataService dataService;
```

Now that we have defined the beans and their wiring, to test this, we need an implementation of `DataService`. We will create a simple, hardcoded implementation. `DataServiceImpl` returns a couple of pieces of data:

```
@Repository
public class DataServiceImpl implements DataService {
  public List<Data> retrieveData(User user) {
    return Arrays.asList(new Data(10), new Data(20));
  }
}
```

Now that we have our beans and dependencies defined, let's focus on how to create and run a Spring IoC container.

Creating a Spring IoC container

There are two ways to create a Spring IoC container:

- Bean factory
- Application context

Bean factory is the basis for all Spring IoC functionality--bean life cycle and wiring. Application context is basically a superset of Bean factory with the additional functionality typically needed in an enterprise context. Spring recommends that you use the application context in all scenarios, except when the additional few KBs of memory that the application context consumes are critical.

Let's use an application context to create a Spring IoC container. We can have either a Java configuration or an XML configuration for an application context. Let's start with using a Java application configuration.

Java configuration for the application context

The following example shows how to create a simple Java context configuration:

```
@Configuration
class SpringContext {
}
```

The key is the `@Configuration` annotation. This is what defines this as a Spring configuration.

One question remains; how does Spring IoC container know where to search for beans?

We need to tell the Spring IoC container the packages to search for by defining a component scan. Let's add a component scan to our earlier Java configuration definition:

```
@Configuration
@ComponentScan(basePackages = { "com.mastering.spring" })
 class SpringContext {
 }
```

We have defined a component scan for the `com.mastering.spring` package. It shows how all the classes we discussed until now are organized. All the classes we have defined until now are present in this package as follows:

A quick review

Let's take a moment and review all the things we have done until now to get this example working:

- We have defined a Spring configuration class `SpringContext` with the `@Configuration` annotation with a component scan for the `com.mastering.spring` package

- We have a couple of files (in the preceding package):
    - `BusinessServiceImpl` with the `@Service` annotation
    - `DataServiceImpl` with the `@Repository` annotation
- `BusinessServiceImpl` has the `@Autowired` annotation on the instance of `DataService`

When we launch up a Spring context, the following things will happen:

- It will scan the `com.mastering.spring` package and find the `BusinessServiceImpl` and `DataServiceImpl` beans.
- `DataServiceImpl` does not have any dependency. So, the bean for `DataServiceImpl` is created.
- `BusinessServiceImpl` has a dependency on `DataService`. `DataServiceImpl` is an implementation of the `DataService` interface. So, it matches the autowiring criteria. So, a bean for `BusinessServiceImpl` is created and the bean created for `DataServiceImpl` is autowired to it through the setter.

Launching the application context with Java configuration

The following program shows how to launch a Java context; we use the main method to launch the application context using `AnnotationConfigApplicationContext`:

```
public class LaunchJavaContext {
  private static final User DUMMY_USER = new User("dummy");
  public static Logger logger =
  Logger.getLogger(LaunchJavaContext.class);
  public static void main(String[] args) {
    ApplicationContext context = new
    AnnotationConfigApplicationContext(
    SpringContext.class);
    BusinessService service =
    context.getBean(BusinessService.class);
    logger.debug(service.calculateSum(DUMMY_USER));
  }
}
```

The following lines of code create the application context. We want to create an application context based on the Java configuration. So, we use `AnnotationConfigApplicationContext`:

```
ApplicationContext context = new
AnnotationConfigApplicationContext(
   SpringContext.class);
```

Once the context is launched, we will need to get the business service bean. We use the `getBean` method that passes the type of the bean (`BusinessService.class`) as an argument:

```
BusinessService service = context.getBean(BusinessService.class );
```

We are all set to launch the application context by running the `LaunchJavaContext` program.

The console log

The following are some of the important statements from the log once the context is launched using `LaunchJavaContext`. Let's quickly review the log to get a deeper insight into what Spring is doing:

The first few lines show the component scan in action:

```
Looking for matching resources in directory tree
[/target/classes/com/mastering/spring]

Identified candidate component class: file
[/in28Minutes/Workspaces/SpringTutorial/mastering-spring-
example-1/target/classes/com/mastering/spring/business/BusinessServiceImpl.
class]

Identified candidate component class: file
[/in28Minutes/Workspaces/SpringTutorial/mastering-spring-
example-1/target/classes/com/mastering/spring/data/DataServiceImpl.class]

defining beans [******OTHERS*****,businessServiceImpl,dataServiceImpl];
```

Spring now starts to create the beans. It starts with `businessServiceImpl`, but it has an autowired dependency:

```
Creating instance of bean 'businessServiceImpl'Registered injected element
on class [com.mastering.spring.business.BusinessServiceImpl]:
AutowiredFieldElement for private com.mastering.spring.data.DataService
com.mastering.spring.business.BusinessServiceImpl.dataService

Processing injected element of bean 'businessServiceImpl':
AutowiredFieldElement for private com.mastering.spring.data.DataService
com.mastering.spring.business.BusinessServiceImpl.dataService
```

Spring moves on to `dataServiceImpl` and creates an instance for it:

```
Creating instance of bean 'dataServiceImpl'
Finished creating instance of bean 'dataServiceImpl'
```

Spring autowires `dataServiceImpl` into `businessServiceImpl`:

```
Autowiring by type from bean name 'businessServiceImpl' to bean named
'dataServiceImpl'
Finished creating instance of bean 'businessServiceImpl'
```

The XML configuration for the application context

In the previous example, we used a Spring Java configuration to launch an application context. Spring also supports XML configuration.

The following example shows how to launch an application context with an XML configuration. This will have two steps:

- Defining the XML Spring configuration
- Launching the application context with the XML configuration

Defining the XML Spring configuration

The following example shows a typical XML Spring configuration. This configuration file is created in the `src/main/resources` directory with the name `BusinessApplicationContext.xml`:

```xml
<?xml version="1.0" encoding="UTF-8" standalone="no"?>
<beans>  <!-Namespace definitions removed-->
  <context:component-scan base-package ="com.mastering.spring"/>
</beans>
```

The component scan is defined using `context:component-scan`.

Launching an application context with the XML configuration

The following program shows how to launch an application context using the XML configuration. We use the main method to launch the application context using `ClassPathXmlApplicationContext`:

```
public class LaunchXmlContext {
    private static final User DUMMY_USER = new User("dummy");
    public static Logger logger =
    Logger.getLogger(LaunchJavaContext.class);
    public static void main(String[] args) {
        ApplicationContext context = new
        ClassPathXmlApplicationContext(
        "BusinessApplicationContext.xml");
        BusinessService service =
        context.getBean(BusinessService.class);
        logger.debug(service.calculateSum(DUMMY_USER));
    }
}
```

The following lines of code create the application context. We want to create an application context based on the XML configuration. So, we use `ClassPathXmlApplicationContext` to create an application context: `AnnotationConfigApplicationContext`.

```
ApplicationContext context = new
ClassPathXmlApplicationContext (SpringContext.class);
```

Once the context is launched, we will need to get a reference to the business service bean. This is very similar to what we did with the Java configuration. We use the `getBean` method, passing the type of the bean (`BusinessService.class`) as an argument.

We can go ahead and run the `LaunchXmlContext` class. You will notice that we get output very similar to that we get when run the context with the Java configuration.

Writing JUnit using the Spring context

In the previous sections, we looked at how to launch a Spring context from the main method. Now let's shift our attention to launching a Spring context from a unit test.

We can use `SpringJUnit4ClassRunner.class` as a runner to launch a Spring context:

```
@RunWith(SpringJUnit4ClassRunner.class)
```

We would need to provide the location of the context configuration. We will use the XML configuration that we created earlier. Here's how you can declare this:

```
@ContextConfiguration(locations = {
"/BusinessApplicationContext.xml" })
```

We can autowire a bean from the context into the test using the `@Autowired` annotation. BusinessService is autowired by the type:

```
@Autowired
private BusinessService service;
```

As of now, `DataServiceImpl`, which is wired in, returns `Arrays.asList(new Data(10), new Data(20))`. `BusinessServiceImpl` calculates the sum 10+20 and returns 30. We will assert for 30 in the test method using `assertEquals`:

```
long sum = service.calculateSum(DUMMY_USER);
assertEquals(30, sum);
```

Why do we introduce unit testing so early in the book?

Actually, we believe we are already late. Ideally, we would have loved to use **Test-driven development (TDD)** and write tests before code. In my experience, doing TDD leads to simple, maintainable, and testable code.

Unit testing has a number of advantages:

- A safety net against future defects
- Defects are caught early
- Following TDD leads to a better design
- Well-written tests act as documentation of code and functionality--especially those written using the BDD Given-When-Then style

The first test we will write is not really a unit test. We will load up all the beans in this test. The next test, written using mocking, will be a real unit test, where the functionality being unit tested is the specific unit of code being written.

The complete list of the test is as follows; it has one test method:

```
@RunWith(SpringJUnit4ClassRunner.class)
@ContextConfiguration(locations = {
  "/BusinessApplicationContext.xml" })
  public class BusinessServiceJavaContextTest {
  private static final User DUMMY_USER = new User("dummy");
  @Autowired
```

```
      private BusinessService service;

      @Test
      public void testCalculateSum() {
        long sum = service.calculateSum(DUMMY_USER);
        assertEquals(30, sum);
      }
  }
```

There is one problem with the **JUnit** that we wrote. It is not a true unit test. This test is using the real (almost) implementation of `DataServiceImpl` for the JUnit test. So, we are actually testing the functionality of both `BusinessServiceImpl` and `DataServiceImpl`. That's not unit testing.

The question now is this; how do we unit test `BusinessServiceImpl` without using a real implementation of `DataService`?

There are two options:

- Create a stub implementation of the data service, providing some dummy data in the `src\test\java` folder. Use a separate test context configuration to autowire the stub implementation instead of the real the `DataServiceImpl` class.
- Create a mock of `DataService` and autowire the mock into `BusinessServiceImpl`.

Creating a stub implementation would mean the creation of an additional class and an additional context. Stubs become more difficult to maintain, as we need more variations in data for the unit test.

In the next section, we will explore the second option of using a mock for unit testing. With the advances in mocking frameworks (especially **Mockito**) in the last few years, you will see that we would not even need to launch a Spring context to execute the unit test.

Unit testing with mocks

Let's start with understanding what mocking is. Mocking is creating objects that simulate the behavior of real objects. In the previous example, in the unit test, we would want to simulate the behavior of `DataService`.

Unlike stubs, mocks can be dynamically created at runtime. We will use the most popular mocking framework, Mockito. To understand more about Mockito, we recommend the Mockito FAQ at `https://github.com/mockito/mockito/wiki/FAQ`.

We will want to create a mock for `DataService`. There are multiple approaches to creating mocks with Mockito. Let's use the simplest among them--annotations. We use the `@Mock` annotation to create a mock for `DataService`:

```
@Mock
private DataService dataService;
```

Once we create the mock, we will need to inject it into the class under test, `BusinessServiceImpl`. We do that using the `@InjectMocks` annotation:

```
@InjectMocks
private BusinessService service =
new BusinessServiceImpl();
```

In the test method, we will need to stub the mock service to provide the data that we want it to provide. There are multiple approaches. We will use the BDD style methods provided by Mockito to mock the `retrieveData` method:

```
BDDMockito.given(dataService.retrieveData(
  Matchers.any(User.class)))
  .willReturn(Arrays.asList(new Data(10),
  new Data(15), new Data(25)));
```

What we are defining in the preceding code is called stubbing. As with anything with Mockito, this is extremely readable. When the `retrieveData` method is called on the `dataService` mock with any object of type `User`, it returns a list of three items with values specified.

When we use Mockito annotations, we would need to use a specific JUnit runner, that is, `MockitoJunitRunner`. `MockitoJunitRunner` helps in keeping the test code clean and provides clear debugging information in case of test failures. `MockitoJunitRunner` initializes the beans annotated with `@Mock` annotation and also validates the usage of framework after execution of each test method.

```
@RunWith(MockitoJUnitRunner.class)
```

The complete list of the test is as follows. It has one test method:

```
@RunWith(MockitoJUnitRunner.class)
public class BusinessServiceMockitoTest {
  private static final User DUMMY_USER = new User("dummy");
   @Mock
  private DataService dataService;
  @InjectMocks
  private BusinessService service =
  new BusinessServiceImpl();
```

```
@Test
public void testCalculateSum() {
  BDDMockito.given(dataService.retrieveData(
  Matchers.any(User.class)))
  .willReturn(
    Arrays.asList(new Data(10),
    new Data(15), new Data(25)));
    long sum = service.calculateSum(DUMMY_USER);
    assertEquals(10 + 15 + 25, sum);
  }
}
```

Container managed beans

Instead of a class creating its own dependencies, in the earlier example, we looked at how the Spring IoC container can take over the responsibility of managing beans and their dependencies. The beans that are managed by the container are called **Container Managed Beans**.

Delegating the creation and management of beans to the container has many advantages. Some of them are listed as follows:

- Since classes are not responsible for creating dependencies, they are loosely coupled and testable. This leads to good design and fewer defects.
- Since the container manages the beans, a few hooks around the beans can be introduced in a more generic way. Cross-cutting concerns, such as logging, caching, transaction management, and exception handling can be woven around these beans using **Aspect-Oriented Programming (AOP)**. This leads to more maintainable code.

Dependency injection types

In the previous example, we used a setter method to wire in the dependency. There are two types of dependency injections that are used frequently:

- The setter injection
- The constructor injection

The setter injection

The setter injection is used to inject the dependencies through setter methods. In the following example, the instance of DataService uses the setter injection:

```
public class BusinessServiceImpl {
  private DataService dataService;
  @Autowired
  public void setDataService(DataService dataService) {
    this.dataService = dataService;
  }
}
```

Actually, in order to use the setter injection, you do not even need to declare a setter method. If you specify @Autowired on the variable, Spring automatically uses the setter injection. So, the following code is all that you need for the setter injection for DataService:

```
public class BusinessServiceImpl {
  @Autowired
  private DataService dataService;
}
```

The constructor injection

The constructor injection, on the other hand, uses a constructor to inject dependencies. The following code shows how to use a constructor for injecting in `DataService`:

```
public class BusinessServiceImpl {
  private DataService dataService;
  @Autowired
  public BusinessServiceImpl(DataService dataService) {
    super();
    this.dataService = dataService;
  }
}
```

When you run the code with the preceding implementation of `BusinessServiceImpl`, you will see this statement in the log, asserting that autowiring took place using the constructor:

```
Autowiring by type from bean name 'businessServiceImpl' via
constructor to bean named 'dataServiceImpl'
```

Constructor versus setter injection

Originally, in XML-based application contexts, we used the constructor injection with mandatory dependencies and the setter injection with nonmandatory dependencies.

However, an important thing to note is that when we use `@Autowired` on a field or a method, the dependency is required by default. If no candidates are available for an `@Autowired` field, autowiring fails and throws an exception. So, the choice is not so clear anymore with Java application contexts.

Using the setter injection results in the state of the object changing during the creation. For fans of immutable objects, the constructor injection might be the way to go. Using the setter injection might sometimes hide the fact that a class has a lot of dependencies. Using the constructor injection makes it obvious, since the size of the constructor increases.

Spring bean scopes

Spring beans can be created with multiple scopes. The default scope is a singleton.

Since there is only one instance of a singleton bean, it cannot contain any data that is specific to a request.

The scope can be provided with the @Scope annotation on any spring bean:

```
@Service
@Scope("singleton")
public class BusinessServiceImpl implements BusinessService
```

The following table shows the different types of scopes available for beans:

Scope	Use
Singleton	By default, all beans are of the scope singleton. Only one instance of such beans is used per instance of the Spring IoC container. Even if there are multiple references to a bean, it is created only once per container. The single instance is cached and used for all subsequent requests using this bean. It is important to specify that the Spring singleton scope is one object per one Spring container. If you have multiple spring containers in a single JVM, then there can be multiple instances of the same bean. So, the Spring singleton scope is a little different from the typical definition of a singleton.
Prototype	A new instance is created every time a bean is requested from the Spring container. If a bean contains a state, it is recommended that you use the prototype scope for it.
request	Available only in Spring web contexts. A new instance of bean is created for every HTTP request. The bean is discarded as soon as the request processing is done. Ideal for beans that hold data specific to a single request.
session	Available only in Spring web contexts. A new instance of bean is created for every HTTP session. Ideal for data specific to a single user, such as user permissions in a web application.
application	Available only in Spring web contexts. One instance of bean per web application. Ideal for things such as application configuration for a specific environment.

Java versus XML configuration

With the advent of annotations in Java 5, there is widespread use of Java configuration for Spring based applications. What is the right choice to make if you have to choose between a Java-based configuration as opposed to an XML-based configuration?

Spring provides equally good support for Java and XML-based configuration. So, it's left to the programmer and their team to make the choice. Whichever choice is made, it is important to have consistency across teams and projects. Here are some things you might need to consider when making a choice:

- Annotations lead to shorter and simpler bean definitions.
- Annotations are closer to the code they are applicable on than the XML-based configuration.
- Classes using annotations are no longer simple POJOs because they are using framework-specific annotations.
- Autowiring problems when using annotations might be difficult to solve because the wiring is no longer centralized and is not explicitly declared.
- There might be advantages of more flexible wiring using Spring context XML if it is packaged outside the application packaging--WAR or EAR. This will enable us to have different setup for integration tests, for example.

The @Autowired annotation in depth

When `@Autowired` is used on a dependency, the application context searches for a matching dependency. By default, all dependencies that are autowired are required.

Possible results are as follows:

- **One match is found**: This is the dependency you are looking for
- **More than one match is found**: Autowiring fails
- **No match is found**: Autowiring fails

Cases where more than one candidate is found can be resolved in two ways:

- Use the `@Primary` annotation to mark one of the candidates as the one to be used
- Use `@Qualifier` to further qualify autowiring

The @Primary annotation

When the `@Primary` annotation is used on a bean, it becomes the primary one to be used when there is more than one candidate available to autowire a specific dependency.

In the case of the following example , there are two sorting algorithms available: QuickSort and MergeSort. If the component scan finds both of them, QuickSort is used to wire any dependencies on SortingAlgorithm because of the @Primary annotation:

```
interface SortingAlgorithm {
}
@Component
class MergeSort implements SortingAlgorithm {
  // Class code here
}
@Component
@Primary
class QuickSort implements SortingAlgorithm {
  // Class code here
}
```

The @Qualifier annotation

The @Qualifier annotation can be used to give a reference to a Spring bean. The reference can be used to qualify the dependency that needs to be autowired.

In the case of the following example, there are two sorting algorithms available: QuickSort and MergeSort. But since @Qualifier("mergesort") is used in the SomeService class, MergeSort, which also has a mergesort qualifier defined on it, becomes the candidate dependency selected for autowiring:

```
@Component
@Qualifier("mergesort")
class MergeSort implements SortingAlgorithm {
  // Class code here
}
@Component
class QuickSort implements SortingAlgorithm {
  // Class code here
}
@Component
class SomeService {
  @Autowired
  @Qualifier("mergesort")
  SortingAlgorithm algorithm;
}
```

Other important Spring annotations

Spring provides a great deal of flexibility in defining beans and managing the life cycle of a bean. There are a few other important Spring annotations that we will discuss in the table, as follows:

Annotations	Use
@ScopedProxy	Sometimes, we will need to inject a request or a session-scoped bean into a singleton-scoped bean. In such situations, the @ScopedProxy annotation provides a smart proxy to be injected into singleton-scoped beans.
@Component, @Service, @Controller, @Repository	@Component is the most generic way of defining a Spring bean. Other annotations have more specific contexts associated with them. • @Service is used in the business service layer • @Repository is used in the **data access object (DAO)** • @Controller is used in presentation components
@PostConstruct	On any spring bean, a post construct method can be provided using the @PostConstruct annotation. This method is called once the bean is fully initialized with dependencies. This will be invoked only once during a bean lifecycle.
@PreDestroy	On any spring bean, a predestroy method can be provided using the @PreDestroy annotation. This method is called just before a bean is removed from the container. This can be used to release any resources that are held by the bean.

Exploring Contexts and dependency injection

CDI is Java EE's attempt at bringing DI into Java EE. While not as fully-fledged as Spring, CDI aims to standardize the basics of how DI is done. Spring supports the standard annotations defined in *JSR-330*. For the most part, these annotations are treated the same way as Spring annotations.

Before we can use CDI, we will need to ensure that we have dependencies for CDI jars included. Here's the code snippet:

```
<dependency>
  <groupId>javax.inject</groupId>
  <artifactId>javax.inject</artifactId>
  <version>1</version>
</dependency>
```

In this table, let's compare the CDI annotations with the annotations provided by Spring Framework. It should be noted that `@Value`, `@Required`, and `@Lazy` Spring annotations have no equivalent CDI annotations.

CDI annotation	Comparison with Spring annotations
`@Inject`	Similar to `@Autowired`. One insignificant difference is the absence of the required attribute on `@Inject`.
`@Named`	`@Named` is similar to `@Component`. Identifies named components. In addition, `@Named` can be used to qualify the bean with a name similar to the `@Qualifier` Spring annotation. This is useful in situations when multiple candidates are available for the autowiring of one dependency.
`@Singleton`	Similar to the Spring annotation `@Scope("singleton")`.
`@Qualifier`	Similar to a similarly named annotation in Spring--`@Qualifier`

An example of CDI

When we use CDI, this is what the annotations on the different classes would look like. There is no change in how we create and launch the Spring application context.

CDI marks no differentiation between `@Repository`, `@Controller`, `@Service`, and `@Component`. We use `@Named` instead of all the preceding annotations.

In the example, we use `@Named` for `DataServiceImpl` and `BusinessServiceImpl`. We use `@Inject` to inject `dataService` into `BusinessServiceImpl` (instead of `@Autowired`):

```
@Named //Instead of @Repository
public class DataServiceImpl implements DataService
@Named //Instead of @Service
public class BusinessServiceImpl {
    @Inject //Instead of @Autowired
    private DataService dataService;
```

Summary

Dependency injection (or IoC) is the key feature of Spring. It makes code loosely coupled and testable. Understanding DI is the key to making the best use of Spring Framework.

In this chapter, we took a deep look at DI and the options Spring Framework provides. We also looked at examples of writing testable code and wrote a couple of unit tests.

In the next chapter, we will shift our attention toward Spring MVC, the most popular Java web MVC framework. We will explore how Spring MVC makes the development of web applications easier.

3
Building a Web Application with Spring MVC

Spring MVC is the most popular web framework used to develop Java web applications. The beauty of Spring MVC lies in its clean, loosely coupled architecture. With a clean definition of roles for controllers, handler mappings, view resolvers, and **Plain Old Java Object** (**POJO**) command beans, Spring MVC makes use of all the core Spring features--like dependency injection and autowiring--to make it simple to create web applications. With its support for multiple view technologies, it is extensible too.

While Spring MVC can be used to create REST services, we discuss that in `Chapter 5`, *Building Microservices with Spring Boot*.

In this chapter, we will focus on reviewing the basics of Spring MVC with simple examples.

In this chapter will cover the following topics:

- The Spring MVC architecture
- The roles played by DispatcherServlet, view resolvers, handler mappings and controllers
- Model attributes and session attributes
- Form binding and validation
- Integration with Bootstrap
- Basics of Spring Security
- Writing simple unit tests for controllers

Java web application architecture

The way we develop Java web applications has evolved during the last couple of decades. We will discuss the different architectural approaches to developing Java web applications and see where Spring MVC fits in:

- Model 1 architecture
- Model 2 or MVC architecture
- Model 2 with Front Controller

Model 1 architecture

Model 1 architecture is one of the initial architecture styles used to develop Java-based web applications. A few important details are as follows:

- JSP pages directly handled the requests from the browser
- JSP pages made use of the model containing simple Java beans
- In some applications of this architecture style, JSPs even performed queries to the database
- JSPs also handled the flow logic: which page to show next

The following picture represents typical Model 1 architecture:

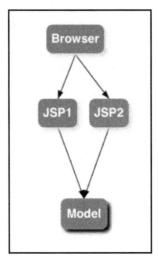

There are a lot of disadvantages in this approach, leading to quick shelving and the evolution of other architectures. A few important disadvantages are listed as follows:

- **Hardly any separation of concerns**: JSPs were responsible for retrieving data, displaying data, deciding which pages to show next (flow), and sometimes, even business logic as well
- **Complex JSPs**: Because JSPs handled a lot of logic, they were huge and difficult to maintain

Model 2 architecture

Model 2 architecture came in to solve the complexity involved with complex JSPs having multiple responsibilities. This forms the base for the MVC architecture style. The following image represents typical Model 2 architecture:

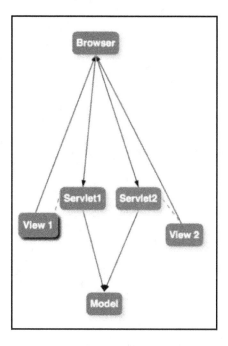

Model 2 architecture has a clear separation of roles between Model, View, and Controller. This leads to more maintainable applications. A few important details are as follows:

- **Model**: Represents the data to be used to generate a View.
- **View**: Uses the Model to render the screen.

- **Controller**: Controls the flow. Gets the request from the browser, populates the Model and redirects to the View. Examples are **Servlet1** and **Servlet2** in the preceding figure.

Model 2 Front Controller architecture

In the basic version of Model 2 architecture, the requests from the browser are handled directly by different servlets (or Controllers). In a number of business scenarios, one would want to do a few common things in servlets before we handle the request. An example would be to ensure that the logged-in user has the right authorization to execute the request. This is a common functionality that you would not want to be implemented in every servlet.

In Model 2 **Front Controller** architecture, all requests flow into a single controller called the Front Controller.

Picture below represents typical Model 2 Front Controller architecture:

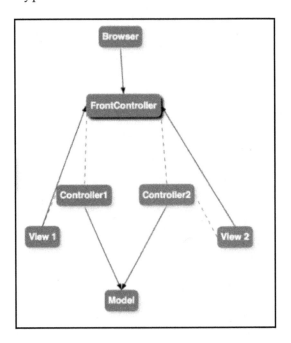

The following are some of the responsibilities of a typical Front Controller:

- It decides which Controller executes the request
- It decides which View to render
- It provides provisions to add more common functionality
- Spring MVC uses an MVC pattern with Front Controller. The Front Controller is called **DispatcherServlet**. We will discuss DispatcherServlet a little later.

Basic flows

Spring MVC uses a modified version of the Model 2 Front Controller architecture. Before we go into details about how Spring MVC works, we will focus on creating a few simple web flows using Spring MVC. In this section, we will create six typical web application flows using Spring MVC. The flows are listed as follows:

- **Flow 1**: Controller without a View; serving content on its own
- **Flow 2**: Controller with a View (a JSP)
- **Flow 3**: Controller with a View and using ModelMap
- **Flow 4**: Controller with a View and using ModelAndView
- **Flow 5**: Controller for a simple form
- **Flow 6**: Controller for a simple form with validation

At the end of every flow, we will discuss how to unit test the Controller.

Basic setup

Before we start with the first flow, we would need to get the application set up to use Spring MVC. In the next section, we will start by understanding how to set up Spring MVC in a web application.

We are using Maven to manage our dependencies. The following steps are involved in setting up a simple web application:

1. Add a dependency for Spring MVC.
2. Add DispatcherServlet to `web.xml`.
3. Create a Spring application context.

Adding dependency for Spring MVC

Let's start with adding the Spring MVC dependency to our `pom.xml`. The following code shows the dependency to be added in. Since we are using Spring BOM, we do not need to specify the artifact version:

```
<dependency>
  <groupId>org.springframework</groupId>
  <artifactId>spring-webmvc</artifactId>
</dependency>
```

DispatcherServlet is an implementation of the Front Controller pattern. Any request to Spring MVC will be handled by the Front Controller, that is, DispatcherServlet.

Adding DispatcherServlet to web.xml

To enable this, we would need to add DispatcherServlet to `web.xml`. Let's look at how to do that:

```
<servlet>
  <servlet-name>spring-mvc-dispatcher-servlet</servlet-name>
  <servlet-class>
    org.springframework.web.servlet.DispatcherServlet
  </servlet-class>
  <init-param>
    <param-name>contextConfigLocation</param-name>
    <param-value>/WEB-INF/user-web-context.xml</param-value>
  </init-param>
    <load-on-startup>1</load-on-startup>
</servlet>
<servlet-mapping>
  <servlet-name>spring-mvc-dispatcher-servlet</servlet-name>
  <url-pattern>/</url-pattern>
</servlet-mapping>
```

The first part is to define a servlet. We are also defining a context configuration location, `/WEB-INF/user-web-context.xml`. We will define a Spring context in the next step. In the second part, we are defining a servlet mapping. We are mapping a URL `/` to the DispatcherServlet. So, all requests will be handled by the DispatcherServlet.

Creating Spring context

Now that we have DispatcherServlet defined in `web.xml`, we can go ahead and create our Spring context. Initially, we will create a very simple context without really defining anything concrete:

```
<beans > <!-Schema Definition removed -->
    <context:component-scan
    base-package="com.mastering.spring.springmvc"  />
    <mvc:annotation-driven />
</beans>
```

We are defining a component scan for the `com.mastering.spring.springmvc` package so that all the beans and controllers in this package are created and auto-wired.

Using `<mvc:annotation-driven/>` initializes support for a number of features that Spring MVC supports such as:

- Request mapping
- Exception handling
- Data binding and validation
- Automatic conversion (for example, JSON) when the `@RequestBody` annotation is used

That's all the setup we need to be able to set up a Spring MVC application. We are ready to get started with the first flow.

Flow 1 - Simple controller flow without View

Let's start with a simple flow by showing some simple text that is output from a Spring MVC controller on screen.

Creating a Spring MVC controller

Let's create a simple Spring MVC controller as follows:

```
@Controller
public class BasicController {
  @RequestMapping(value = "/welcome")
  @ResponseBody
public String welcome() {
  return "Welcome to Spring MVC";
  }
}
```

A few important things to note here are as follows:

- `@Controller`: This defines a Spring MVC controller that can contain request mappings--mapping URLs to controller methods.
- `@RequestMapping(value = "/welcome")`: This defines a mapping of the URL `/welcome` to the `welcome` method. When the browser sends a request to `/welcome`, Spring MVC does the magic and executes the `welcome` method.
- `@ResponseBody`: In this specific context, the text returned by the `welcome` method is sent out to the browser as the response content. `@ResponseBody` does a lot of magic--especially in the context of REST services. We will discuss this in `Chapter 5`, *Building Microservices with Spring Boot*.

Running the web application

We are using Maven and Tomcat 7 to run this web application.

Tomcat 7 server launches up on port 8080 by default.

We can run the server by invoking the `mvn tomcat7:run` command.

Here is a screenshot of how this would look on the screen when the
`http://localhost:8080/welcome` URL is hit on the browser as in following screenshot:

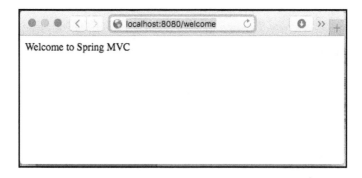

Unit testing

Unit testing is a very important part of developing maintainable applications. We will be
using the Spring MVC Mock framework to unit test the Controllers that we will write in this
chapter. We will add in a dependency on the Spring test framework to use the Spring MVC
Mock framework:

```
<dependency>
    <groupId>org.springframework</groupId>
    <artifactId>spring-test</artifactId>
    <scope>test</scope>
</dependency>
```

The approach we will be taking would involve the following:

1. Setting up the Controller to test.
2. Writing the test method.

Setting up the Controller to test

The controller we want to test is `BasicController`. The convention to create a unit test is a
class name with a suffix `Test`. We will create a test class named `BasicControllerTest`.

The basic setup is shown as follows:

```
public class BasicControllerTest {
  private MockMvc mockMvc;
  @Before
  public void setup() {
    this.mockMvc = MockMvcBuilders.standaloneSetup(
    new BasicController())
    .build();
  }
}
```

A few important things to note are as follows:

- mockMvc: This variable can be used across different tests. So, we define an instance variable of the MockMvc class.
- @Before setup: This method is run before every test in order to initialize MockMvc.
- MockMvcBuilders.standaloneSetup(new BasicController()).build(): This line of code builds a MockMvc instance. It initializes DispatcherServlet to serve requests to the configured controller(s), BasicController in this instance.

Writing the Test method

The complete Test method is shown in the following code:

```
@Test
public void basicTest() throws Exception {
  this.mockMvc
  .perform(
  get("/welcome")
  .accept(MediaType.parseMediaType
  ("application/html;charset=UTF-8")))
  .andExpect(status().isOk())
  .andExpect( content().contentType
  ("application/html;charset=UTF-8"))
  .andExpect(content().
   string("Welcome to Spring MVC"));
}
```

A few important things to note are as follows:

- `MockMvc mockMvc.perform`: This method executes the request and returns an instance of ResultActions that allows chaining calls. In this example, we are chaining the andExpect calls to check expectations.
- `get("/welcome").accept(MediaType.parseMediaType("application/html;charset=UTF-8"))`: This creates an HTTP get request accepting a response with the media type `application/html`.
- `andExpect`: This method is used to check expectations. This method will fail the test if the expectation is not met.
- `status().isOk()`: This uses ResultMatcher to check whether the response status is that of a successful request - 200.
- `content().contentType("application/html;charset=UTF-8")`: This uses ResultMatcher to check whether the content type of the response is as specified.
- `content().string("Welcome to Spring MVC")`: This uses ResultMatcher to check whether the response content contains the specified string.

Flow 2 - Simple controller flow with a View

In the previous flow, the text to show on the browser was hardcoded in the Controller. That is not a good practice. The content to be shown on the browser is typically generated from a View. The most frequently used option is a JSP.

In this flow, let's redirect from the Controller to a View.

Spring MVC controller

Similar to the previous example, let's create a simple Controller. Consider the example of a controller here:

```
@Controller
public class BasicViewController {
  @RequestMapping(value = "/welcome-view")
  public String welcome() {
    return "welcome";
  }
}
```

A few important things to note are as follows:

- `@RequestMapping(value = "/welcome-view")`: We are mapping an URL `/welcome-view`.
- `public String welcome()`: There is no `@RequestBody` annotation on this method. So, Spring MVC tries to match the string that is returned, `welcome`, to a view.

Creating a View - a JSP

Let's create `welcome.jsp` in the `src/main/webapp/WEB-INF/views/welcome.jsp` folder with the following content:

```
<html>
  <head>
    <title>Welcome</title>
  </head>
  <body>
    <p>Welcome! This is coming from a view - a JSP</p>
  </body>
</html>
```

This is a simple HTML with head, body, and some text in the body.

Spring MVC has to map the string returned from the `welcome` method to the real JSP at `/WEB-INF/views/welcome.jsp`. How does this magic happen?

View resolver

A view resolver resolves a View name to the actual JSP page.

The View name in this example is `welcome`, and we would want it to resolve to `/WEB-INF/views/welcome.jsp`.

A view resolver can be configured in the spring context `/WEB-INF/user-web-context.xml`. Here's the code snippet for that:

```
<bean class="org.springframework.web.
servlet.view.InternalResourceViewResolver">
 <property name="prefix">
   <value>/WEB-INF/views/</value>
 </property>
 <property name="suffix">
```

```
        <value>.jsp</value>
    </property>
  </bean>
```

A few important points to note:

- `org.springframework.web.servlet.view.InternalResourceViewResolver`: A view resolver supporting JSPs. `JstlView` is typically used. It also supports tiles with a TilesView.

- `<property name="prefix"> <value>/WEB-INF/views/</value> </property><property name="suffix"> <value>.jsp</value> </property>`: This maps the prefix and suffix to be used by view resolver. View resolver takes the string from the controller method and resolves to the view: prefix + viewname + `suffix`. So, the view name welcome is resolved to `/WEB-INF/views/welcome.jsp`.

Here is a screenshot of how this would look on the screen when the URL is hit:

Unit testing

A standalone setup of MockMvc Framework creates the bare minimum infrastructure required by DispatcherServlet. If provided with a view resolver, it can execute view resolution. However, it would not execute the view. So, during a unit test with the standalone setup, we cannot verify the content of the view. However, we can check whether the correct view is being delivered.

In this unit test, we want to set up `BasicViewController`, execute a get request to `/welcome-view`, and check whether the view name returned is `welcome`. In a future section, we will discuss how to execute the integration test, including the rendering of view. As far as this test is concerned, we restrict our purview to verifying the view name.

Setting up the Controller to test

This step is very similar to the previous flow. We want to test `BasicViewController`. We instantiate MockMvc using `BasicViewController`. We also configure a simple view resolver:

```
public class BasicViewControllerTest {
  private MockMvc mockMvc;
  @Before
  public void setup() {
    this.mockMvc = MockMvcBuilders.standaloneSetup
    (new BasicViewController())
    .setViewResolvers(viewResolver()).build();
  }
  private ViewResolver viewResolver() {
    InternalResourceViewResolver viewResolver =
    new InternalResourceViewResolver();
    viewResolver.setViewClass(JstlView.class);
    viewResolver.setPrefix("/WEB-INF/jsp/");
    viewResolver.setSuffix(".jsp");
   return viewResolver;
  }
}
```

Writing the Test method

The complete test method is shown as follows:

```
@Test
public void testWelcomeView() throws Exception {
  this.mockMvc
  .perform(get("/welcome-view")
  .accept(MediaType.parseMediaType(
  "application/html;charset=UTF-8")))
  .andExpect(view().name("welcome"));
}
```

A few important things to note are as follows:

- `get("/welcome-model-view")`: This executes the get request to the specified URL
- `view().name("welcome")`: This uses Result Matcher to check whether the view name returned is as specified

Flow 3 - Controller redirecting to a View with Model

Typically, in order to generate the view, we would need to pass some data to it. In Spring MVC, data can be passed to the view using a model. In this flow, we would set up a model with a simple attribute and use the attribute in the view.

Spring MVC controller

Let's create a simple Controller. Consider the following example controller:

```
@Controller
public class BasicModelMapController {
  @RequestMapping(value = "/welcome-model-map")
  public String welcome(ModelMap model) {
    model.put("name", "XYZ");
  return "welcome-model-map";
  }
}
```

A few important things to note are as follows:

- `@RequestMapping(value = "/welcome-model-map")`: The URI mapped is `/welcome-model-map`.
- `public String welcome(ModelMap model)`: The new parameter added is `ModelMap model`. Spring MVC will instantiate a model and make it available for this method. The attributes put into the model will be available for use in the view.
- `model.put("name", "XYZ")`: This adds an attribute with the `name` name and `XYZ` value to the model.

Creating a View

Let's create a view using the model attribute `name` that was set in the model in the controller. Let's create a simple JSP in the `WEB-INF/views/welcome-model-map.jsp` path:

```
Welcome ${name}! This is coming from a model-map - a JSP
```

One thing to note is this:

- ${name}: This uses the **Expression Language** (EL) syntax to access the attribute from the model.

Here is a screenshot of how this would look on the screen when the URL is hit:

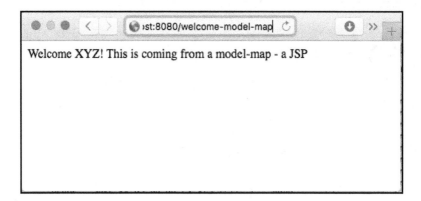

Unit testing

In this unit test, we want to set up BasicModelMapController, execute a get request to /welcome-model-map, and check whether the model has the expected attribute and whether the expected view name is returned.

Setting up the Controller to test

This step is very similar to the previous flow. We instantiate Mock MVC with BasicModelMapController:

```
this.mockMvc = MockMvcBuilders.standaloneSetup
  (new BasicModelMapController())
  .setViewResolvers(viewResolver()).build();
```

Writing the Test method

The complete Test method is shown in the following code:

```
@Test
public void basicTest() throws Exception {
  this.mockMvc
  .perform(
```

```
get("/welcome-model-map")
.accept(MediaType.parseMediaType
("application/html;charset=UTF-8")))
.andExpect(model().attribute("name", "XYZ"))
.andExpect(view().name("welcome-model-map"));
}
```

A few important things to note:

- get("/welcome-model-map"): Execute get request to the specified URL
- model().attribute("name", "XYZ"): Result Matcher to check if the model contains specified attribute **name** with specified value **XYZ**
- view().name("welcome-model-map"): Result Matcher to check if the view name returned is as specified

Flow 4 - Controller redirecting to a View with ModelAndView

In the previous flow, we returned a view name and populated the model with attributes to be used in the view. Spring MVC provides an alternate approach using ModelAndView. The controller method can return a ModelAndView object with the view name and appropriate attributes in the Model. In this flow, we will explore this alternate approach.

Spring MVC controller

Take a look at the following controller:

```
@Controller
public class BasicModelViewController {
  @RequestMapping(value = "/welcome-model-view")
   public ModelAndView welcome(ModelMap model) {
     model.put("name", "XYZ");
     return new ModelAndView("welcome-model-view", model);
   }
}
```

A few important things to note are as follows:

- `@RequestMapping(value = "/welcome-model-view")`: The URI mapped is `/welcome-model-view`.
- `public ModelAndView welcome(ModelMap model)`: Note that the return value is no longer a String. It is `ModelAndView`.
- `return new ModelAndView("welcome-model-view", model)`: Create a `ModelAndView` object with the appropriate view name and model.

Creating a View

Let's create a view using the model attribute `name` that was set in the model in the controller. Create a simple JSP in the `/WEB-INF/views/welcome-model-view.jsp` path:

```
Welcome ${name}! This is coming from a model-view - a JSP
```

Here is a screenshot of how this would look on the screen when the URL is hit:

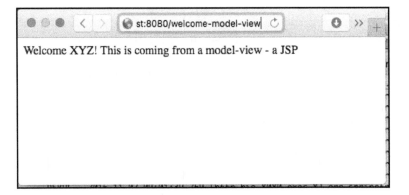

Unit testing

Unit testing for this flow is similar to the previous flow. We would need to check if the expected view name is returned.

Flow 5 - Controller redirecting to a View with a form

Now let's shift our attention to creating a simple form to capture input from the user.

The following steps will be needed:

- Create a simple POJO. We want to create a user. We will create a POJO User.
- Create a couple of Controller methods--one to display the form, and the other to capture the details entered in the form.
- Create a simple View with the form.

Creating a command or form backing object

POJO stands for Plain Old Java Object. It is usually used to represent a bean following the typical JavaBean conventions. Typically, it contains private member variables with getters and setters and a no-argument constructor.

We will create a simple POJO to act as a command object. Important parts of the class are listed as follows:

```
public class User {
    private String guid;
    private String name;
    private String userId;
    private String password;
    private String password2;
    //Constructor
    //Getters and Setters
    //toString
}
```

A few important things to note are as follows:

- This class does not have any annotations or Spring-related mappings. Any bean can act as a form-backing object.
- We are going to capture the name, user ID, and password in the form. We have a password confirmation field, password2, and unique identifier field guid.
- Constructor, getters, setters, and toString methods are not shown for brevity.

The Controller method to show the form

Let's start with creating a simple controller with a logger:

```
@Controller
public class UserController {
  private Log logger = LogFactory.getLog
  (UserController.class);
  }
```

Let's add the following method to the controller:

```
@RequestMapping(value = "/create-user",
method = RequestMethod.GET)
public String showCreateUserPage(ModelMap model) {
  model.addAttribute("user", new User());
  return "user";
}
```

Important things to note are as follows:

- `@RequestMapping(value = "/create-user", method = RequestMethod.GET)`: We are mapping a `/create-user` URI. For the first time, we are specifying a `Request` method using the method attribute. This method will be invoked only for HTTP Get Requests. HTTP `Get` Requests are typically used to show the form. This will not be invoked for other types of HTTP requests, such as Post.
- `public String showCreateUserPage(ModelMap model)`: This is a typical control method.
- `model.addAttribute("user", new User())`: This is used to set up the model with an empty form backing object.

Creating the View with a form

Java Server Pages is one of the view technologies supported by Spring Framework. Spring Framework makes it easy to create views with JSPs by providing a tag library. This includes tags for various form elements, binding, validation, setting themes and internationalizing messages. We will use the tags from the Spring MVC tag library as well as standard JSTL tag libraries to create our view in this example.

Let's start with creating the `/WEB-INF/views/user.jsp` file.

First, let's add the reference to the tag libraries to be used:

```
<%@ taglib uri="http://java.sun.com/jsp/jstl/core" prefix="c"%>
<%@ taglib uri="http://java.sun.com/jsp/jstl/fmt" prefix="fmt"%>
<%@ taglib uri="http://www.springframework.org/tags/form"
   prefix="form"%>
<%@ taglib uri="http://www.springframework.org/tags"
   prefix="spring"%>
```

The first two entries are for JSTL core and formatting tag libraries. We will use the Spring form tags extensively. We provide a `prefix` to act as a shortcut to refer to tags.

Let's create a form with one field first:

```
<form:form method="post" modelAttribute="user">
  <fieldset>
    <form:label path="name">Name</form:label>
    <form:input path="name"
    type="text" required="required" />
  </fieldset>
</form:form>
```

Important things to note are as follows:

- `<form:form method="post" modelAttribute="user">`: This is the `form` tag from the Spring form tag library. Two attributes are specified. Data in the form is sent using the post method. The second attribute, `modelAttribute`, specifies the attribute from the model that acts as the form backing object. In the model, we added an attribute with the name user. We use that attribute as `modelAttribute`.
- `<fieldset>`: This is the HTML element to group a set of related controls--labels, form fields, and validation messages.
- `<form:label path="name">Name</form:label>`: This is the Spring form tag to show a label. The path attribute specifies the field name (from bean) this label is applied to.
- `<form:input path="name" type="text" required="required" />`: This is the Spring form tag to create a text input field. The `path` attribute specifies the field name in the bean that this input field has to be mapped to. The required attribute indicates that this is a `required` field.

When we use the Spring form tags, the values from the form backing object (`modelAttribute="user"`) are bound automatically to the form, and on submitting the form, the values from the form are automatically bound to the form backing object.

A more complete list of the form tags including the name and user ID fields are listed as follows:

```
<form:form method="post" modelAttribute="user">
<form:hidden path="guid" />
<fieldset>
  <form:label path="name">Name</form:label>
  <form:input path="name"
   type="text" required="required" />
</fieldset>
<fieldset>
  <form:label path="userId">User Id</form:label>
  <form:input path="userId"
   type="text" required="required" />
</fieldset>
<!-password and password2 fields not shown for brewity-->
<input class="btn btn-success" type="submit" value="Submit" />
</form:form>
```

Controller get method to handle form submit

When the user submits the form, the browser sends an HTTP **POST** request. Now let's create a method to handle this. To keep things simple, we will log the content of the form object. The complete listing of the method is as follows:

```
@RequestMapping(value = "/create-user", method =
RequestMethod.POST)
public String addTodo(User user) {
  logger.info("user details " + user);
  return "redirect:list-users";
}
```

A few important details are as follows:

- `@RequestMapping(value = "/create-user", method = RequestMethod.POST)`: Since we want to handle the form submit, we use the `RequestMethod.POST` method.

- `public String addTodo(User user)`: We are using the form backing object as the parameter. Spring MVC will automatically bind the values from the form to the form backing object.
- `logger.info("user details " + user)`: Log the details of the user.
- return `redirect:list-users`: Typically, on submitting a form, we save the details of a database and redirect the user to a different page. Here, we are redirecting the user to `/list-users`. When we use `redirect`, Spring MVC sends an HTTP Response with status `302`; that is, `REDIRECT` to the new URL. The browser, on processing the `302` response, will redirect the user to the new URL. While the `POST/REDIRECT/GET` pattern is not a perfect fix for the duplicate form submission problem, it does reduce the occurrences, especially those that occur after the view is rendered.

The code for list users is pretty straightforward and is listed as follows:

```
@RequestMapping(value = "/list-users",
method = RequestMethod.GET)
public String showAllUsers() {
   return "list-users";
}
```

Unit testing

We will discuss unit testing when we add validations in the next flow.

Flow 6 - Adding validation to the previous flow

In the previous flow, we added a form. However, we did not validate the values in the form. While we can write JavaScript to validate the form content, it is always secure to do validation on the server. In this flow, let's add validation to the form that we created earlier on the server side using Spring MVC.

Spring MVC provides great integration with the Bean Validation API. *JSR 303* and *JSR 349* define specifications for the the Bean Validation API (version 1.0 and 1.1, respectively), and Hibernate Validator is the reference implementation.

Hibernate Validator dependency

Let's start with adding Hibernate Validator to our project pom.xml:

```xml
<dependency>
  <groupId>org.hibernate</groupId>
  <artifactId>hibernate-validator</artifactId>
  <version>5.0.2.Final</version>
</dependency>
```

Simple validations on the bean

The Bean Validation API specifies a number of validations that can be specified on attributes on the beans. Take a look at the following listing:

```java
@Size(min = 6, message = "Enter at least 6 characters")
private String name;
@Size(min = 6, message = "Enter at least 6 characters")
private String userId;
@Size(min = 8, message = "Enter at least 8 characters")
private String password;
@Size(min = 8, message = "Enter at least 8 characters")
private String password2;
```

An important thing to note are as follows:

- `@Size(min = 6, message = "Enter at least 6 characters")` : This specifies that the field should at least have six characters. If the validation does not pass, the text from the message attribute is used as a validation error message.

Other validations that can be performed using Bean Validation are as follows:

- `@NotNull`: It should not be null
- `@Size(min =5, max = 50)`: Maximum size of 50 characters and minimum of 5 characters.
- `@Past`: Should be a date in the past
- `@Future`: Should be a future date
- `@Pattern`: Should match the provided regular expression
- `@Max`: Maximum value for the field
- `@Min`: Minimum value for the field

Now let's focus on getting the controller method to validate the form on submits. The complete method listing is as follows:

```
@RequestMapping(value = "/create-user-with-validation",
method = RequestMethod.POST)
public String addTodo(@Valid User user, BindingResult result) {
  if (result.hasErrors()) {
    return "user";
  }
  logger.info("user details " + user);
  return "redirect:list-users";
}
```

Some important things are as follows:

- `public String addTodo(@Valid User user, BindingResult result)`: When the `@Valid` annotation is used, Spring MVC validates the bean. The result of the validation is made available in the `BindingResult` instance result.
- `if (result.hasErrors())`: Checks whether there are any validation errors.
- `return "user"`: If there are validation errors, we send the user back to the user page.

We need to enhance the `user.jsp` to show the validation messages in case of validation errors. The complete list for one of the fields is shown here. Other fields have to be similarly updated:

```
<fieldset>
  <form:label path="name">Name</form:label>
  <form:input path="name" type="text" required="required" />
  <form:errors path="name" cssClass="text-warning"/>
</fieldset>
```

`<form:errors path="name" cssClass="text-warning"/>`: This is the Spring form tag to display the errors related to the field name specified in the path. We can also assign the CSS class used to display the validation error.

Custom validations

More complex custom validations can be implemented using the `@AssertTrue` annotation. The following list an example method added to the `User` class:

```
@AssertTrue(message = "Password fields don't match")
private boolean isValid() {
    return this.password.equals(this.password2);
```

```
        }
```

`@AssertTrue(message = "Password fields don't match")` is the message to be shown if the validation fails.

Any complex validation logic with multiple fields can be implemented in these methods.

Unit testing

Unit testing for this part is focused on checking for validation errors. We will write a test for an empty form, which triggers four validation errors.

Controller setup

The controller setup is very simple:

```
this.mockMvc = MockMvcBuilders.standaloneSetup(
new UserValidationController()).build();
```

The Test method

The complete `Test` method is listed as follows:

```
@Test
public void basicTest_WithAllValidationErrors() throws Exception {
  this.mockMvc
    .perform(
      post("/create-user-with-validation")
      .accept(MediaType.parseMediaType(
      "application/html;charset=UTF-8")))
      .andExpect(status().isOk())
      .andExpect(model().errorCount(4))
      .andExpect(model().attributeHasFieldErrorCode
      ("user", "name", "Size"));
}
```

Some points to note here are as follows:

- `post("/create-user-with-validation")`: Creates an HTTP POST request to the specified URI. Since we are not passing any request parameters, all attributes are null. This will trigger validation errors.

- `model().errorCount(4)`: Checks whether there are four validation errors on the model.
- `model().attributeHasFieldErrorCode("user", "name", "Size")`: Checks whether the `user` attribute has a field `name` with the validation error named `Size`.

An overview of Spring MVC

Now that we've looked at a few basic flows with Spring MVC, we will switch our attention to understanding how these flows work. How does the magic happen with Spring MVC?

Important features

When working with the different flows, we looked at some of the important features of the Spring MVC Framework. These include the following:

- Loosely coupled architecture with well-defined, independent roles for each of the objects.
- Highly flexible Controller method definitions. Controller methods can have a varied range of parameters and return values. This gives flexibility to the programmer to choose the definition that meets their needs.
- Allows the reuse of domain objects as form backing objects. Reduces the need to have separate form objects.
- Built-in tag libraries (Spring, spring-form) with localization support.
- Model uses a HashMap with key-value pairs. Allows integration with multiple view technologies.
- Flexible binding. Type mismatches while binding can be handled as validation errors instead of runtime errors.
- Mock MVC Framework to unit test controllers.

How it works

Key components in the Spring MVC architecture are shown in the following figure:

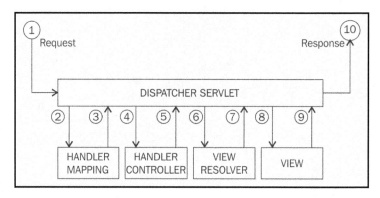

Let's look at an example flow and understand the different steps involved in executing the flow. We will take flow **4**, returning `ModelAndView` as the specific example. The URL of flow **4** is `http://localhost:8080/welcome-model-view`. The different steps are detailed as follows:

1. The browser issues a request to a specific URL. DispatcherServlet is the Front Controller, handling all requests. So, it receives the request.
2. Dispatcher Servlet looks at the URI (in the example, `/welcome-model-view`) and needs to identify the right controller to handle it. To help find the right controller, it talks to the handler mapping.
3. Handler mapping returns the specific handler method (in the example, the `welcome` method in `BasicModelViewController`) that handles the request.
4. DispatcherServlet invokes the specific handler method (`public ModelAndView welcome(ModelMap model)`).
5. The handler method returns the model and view. In this example, the ModelAndView object is returned.
6. DispatcherServlet has the logical view name (from ModelAndView; in this example, `welcome-model-view`). It needs to figure out how to determine the physical view name. It checks whether there are any view resolvers available. It finds the view resolver that was configured (`org.springframework.web.servlet.view.InternalResourceViewResolver`). It calls the view resolver, giving it the logical view name (in this example, `welcome-model-view`) as the input.

7. View resolver executes the logic to map the logical view name to the physical view name. In this example, `welcome-model-view` is translated to `/WEB-INF/views/welcome-model-view.jsp`.
8. DispatcherServlet executes the View. It also makes the Model available to the View.
9. View returns the content to be sent back to DispatcherServlet.
10. DispatcherServlet sends the response back to the browser.

Important concepts behind Spring MVC

Now that we have completed an example with Spring MVC, we are ready to understand the important concepts behind Spring MVC.

RequestMapping

As we've discussed in earlier examples, a `RequestMapping` is used to map a URI to a Controller or a Controller method. It can be done at class and/or method levels. An optional method parameter allows us to map the method to a specific request method (`GET`, `POST`, and so on).

Examples of request mapping

A few examples in the upcoming sections illustrate the variations.

Example 1

In the following example, there is only one `RequestMapping` in the `showPage` method. The `showPage` method will be mapped to `GET`, `POST`, and any other request types for URI `/show-page`:

```
@Controller
public class UserController {
  @RequestMapping(value = "/show-page")
  public String showPage() {
    /* Some code */
    }
}
```

Example 2

In the following example, there is a method defined on `RequestMapping--RequestMethod.GET`. The `showPage` method will be mapped only to the `GET` request for URI `/show-page`. All other request method types would throw "method not supported exception":

```
@Controller
public class UserController {
  @RequestMapping(value = "/show-page" , method =
  RequestMethod.GET)
  public String showPage() {
    /* Some code */
  }
}
```

Example 3

In the following example, there are two `RequestMapping` methods--one in the class and the other in the method. A combination of both `RequestMapping` methods is used to determine the URI. The `showPage` method will be mapped only to the `GET` request for the URI `/user/show-page`:

```
@Controller
@RequestMapping("/user")
public class UserController {
  @RequestMapping(value = "/show-page" , method =
  RequestMethod.GET)
  public String showPage() {
    /* Some code */
  }
}
```

Request Mapping methods - supported method arguments

The following are some of the types of arguments that are supported in Controller methods with Request Mapping:

Argument Type/Annotation	Use
`java.util.Map` / `org.springframework.ui.Model` / `org.springframework.ui.ModelMap`	Acts as the model (MVC) that will be the container for values that are exposed to the view.
Command or form objects	Used to bind request parameters to beans. Support for validation as well.
`org.springframework.validation.Errors` / `org.springframework.validation.BindingResult`	Result of validating the command or form object (the form object should be the immediately preceding method argument).
`@PreDestroy`	On any spring bean, a pre-destroy method can be provided using the `@PreDestroy` annotation. This method is called just before a bean is removed from the container. It can be used to release any resources that are held by the bean.
`@RequestParam`	The annotation to access specific HTTP request parameters.
`@RequestHeader`	The annotation to access specific HTTP request headers.

@SessionAttribute	The annotation to access attributes from HTTP Session.
@RequestAttribute	The annotation to access specific HTTP request attributes.
@PathVariable	The annotation allows access to variables from the URI template. /owner/{ownerId}. We will look at this in depth when we discuss microservices.

RequestMapping methods - supported return types

The RequestMapping methods support a varied range of return types. Thinking conceptually, a request mapping method should answer two questions:

- What's the view?
- What's the model that the view needs?

However, with Spring MVC, the view and model need not be explicitly declared at all times:

- If a view is not explicitly defined as part of the return type, then it is implicitly defined.
- Similarly, any model object is always enriched as detailed in the rules below.

Spring MVC uses simple rules to determine the exact view and model. A couple of important rules are listed as follows:

- **Implicit enriching of the Model**: If a model is part of the return type, it is enriched with command objects (including results from validation of the command objects). In addition, the results of methods with the @ModelAttribute annotations are also added to the model.

- **Implicit determination of the View**: If a view name is not present in the return type, it is determined using `DefaultRequestToViewNameTranslator`. By default, `DefaultRequestToViewNameTranslator` removes the leading and trailing slashes as well as the file extension from the URI; for example, the `display.html` becomes display.

The following are some of the return types that are supported on Controller methods with Request Mapping:

Return Type	What happens?
ModelAndView	The object includes a reference to the model and the view name.
Model	Only Model is returned. The view name is determined using `DefaultRequestToViewNameTranslator`.
Map	A simple map to expose a model.
View	A view with a model implicitly defined.
String	Reference to a view name.

View resolution

Spring MVC provides very flexible view resolution. It provides multiple view options:

- Integration with JSP, Freemarker.
- Multiple view resolution strategies. A few of them are listed as follows:
  - `XmlViewResolver`: View resolution based on an external XML configuration
  - `ResourceBundleViewResolver`: View resolution based on a property file
  - `UrlBasedViewResolver`: Direct mapping of the logical view name to a URL
  - `ContentNegotiatingViewResolver`: Delegates to other view resolvers based on the Accept request header
- Support for chaining of view resolvers with the explicitly defined order of preference.
- Direct generation of XML, JSON, and Atom using Content Negotiation.

Configuring JSP view resolver

The following example shows the commonly used approach to configure a JSP view resolver using `InternalResourceViewResolver`. The physical view name is determined using the configured prefix and suffix for the logical view name using `JstlView`:

```
<bean id="jspViewResolver" class=
  "org.springframework.web.servlet.view.
  InternalResourceViewResolver">
  <property name="viewClass"
    value="org.springframework.web.servlet.view.JstlView"/>
  <property name="prefix" value="/WEB-INF/jsp/"/>
  <property name="suffix" value=".jsp"/>
</bean>
```

There are other approaches using property and XML files for mapping.

Configuring Freemarker

The following example shows the typical approach used to configure a Freemarker view resolver.

First, the `freemarkerConfig` bean is used to load the Freemarker templates:

```
<bean id="freemarkerConfig"
  class="org.springframework.web.servlet.view.
  freemarker.FreeMarkerConfigurer">
  <property name="templateLoaderPath" value="/WEB-
  INF/freemarker/"/>
</bean>
```

The following bean definition shows how to configure a Freemarker view resolver:

```
<bean id="freemarkerViewResolver"
 class="org.springframework.web.servlet.view.
 freemarker.FreeMarkerViewResolver">
   <property name="cache" value="true"/>
   <property name="prefix" value=""/>
   <property name="suffix" value=".ftl"/>
</bean>
```

As with JSPs, the view resolution can be defined using properties or an XML file.

Handler mappings and Interceptors

In the version before Spring 2.5 (before there was support for Annotations), the mapping between a URL and a Controller (also called a handler) was expressed using something called a handler mapping. It is almost a historical fact today. The use of annotations eliminated the need for an explicit handler mapping.

HandlerInterceptors can be used to intercept requests to handlers (or **controllers**). Sometimes, you would want to do some processing before and after a request. You might want to log the content of the request and response, or you might want to find out how much time a specific request took.

There are two steps in creating a HandlerInterceptor:

1. Define the HandlerInterceptor.
2. Map the HandlerInterceptor to the specific handlers to be intercepted.

Defining a HandlerInterceptor

The following are the methods you can override in `HandlerInterceptorAdapter`:

- `public boolean preHandle(HttpServletRequest request, HttpServletResponse response, Object handler)`: Invoked before the handler method is invoked
- `public void postHandle(HttpServletRequest request, HttpServletResponse response, Object handler, ModelAndView modelAndView)`: Invoked after the handler method is invoked
- `public void afterCompletion(HttpServletRequest request, HttpServletResponse response, Object handler, Exception ex)`: Invoked after the request processing is complete

The following example implementation shows how to create a HandlerInterceptor. Let's start with creating a new class that extends `HandlerInterceptorAdapter`:

```
public class HandlerTimeLoggingInterceptor extends
HandlerInterceptorAdapter {
```

The `preHandle` method is invoked before the handler is called. Let's place an attribute on the request, indicating the start time of handler invocation:

```
@Override
public boolean preHandle(HttpServletRequest request,
  HttpServletResponse response, Object handler) throws Exception {
  request.setAttribute(
  "startTime", System.currentTimeMillis());
  return true;
}
```

The `postHandle` method is invoked after the handler is called. Let's place an attribute on the request, indicating the end time of the handler invocation:

```
@Override
public void postHandle(HttpServletRequest request,
HttpServletResponse response, Object handler,
ModelAndView modelAndView) throws Exception {
    request.setAttribute(
    "endTime", System.currentTimeMillis());
  }
```

The `afterCompletion` method is invoked after the request processing is complete. We will identify the time spent in the handler using the attributes that we set into the request earlier:

```
@Override
public void afterCompletion(HttpServletRequest request,
HttpServletResponse response, Object handler, Exception ex)
throws Exception {
  long startTime = (Long) request.getAttribute("startTime");
  long endTime = (Long) request.getAttribute("endTime");
  logger.info("Time Spent in Handler in ms : "
  + (endTime - startTime));
}
```

Mapping HandlerInterceptor to handlers

HandlerInterceptors can be mapped to specific URLs you would want to intercept. The following example shows an example XML context configuration. By default, the interceptor will intercept all handlers (**controllers**):

```
<mvc:interceptors>
  <bean class="com.mastering.spring.springmvc.
  controller.interceptor.HandlerTimeLoggingInterceptor" />
</mvc:interceptors>
```

We can configure precise URIs to be intercepted. In the following example, all handlers except those with URI mapping starting with /secure/are intercepted:

```
<mvc:interceptors>
  <mapping path="/**"/>
  <exclude-mapping path="/secure/**"/>
  <bean class="com.mastering.spring.springmvc.
    controller.interceptor.HandlerTimeLoggingInterceptor" />
</mvc:interceptors>
```

Model attributes

Common web forms contain a number of drop-down values--the list of states, the list of countries, and so on. These lists of values need to be available in the model so that the view can display the list. Such common things are typically populated into the model using methods that are marked with @ModelAttribute annotations.

There are two variations possible. In the following example, the method returns the object that needs to be put into the model:

```
@ModelAttribute
public List<State> populateStateList() {
  return stateService.findStates();
  }
```

The approach in this example is used to add multiple attributes to the model:

```
@ModelAttribute
public void populateStateAndCountryList() {
  model.addAttribute(stateService.findStates());
  model.addAttribute(countryService.findCountries());
  }
```

An important thing to note is that there is no limitation to the number of methods that can be marked with the @ModelAttribute annotation.

Model attributes can be made common across multiple controllers using Controller Advice. We will discuss Controller Advice later in this section.

Session attributes

All the attributes and values that we discussed until now are used within a single request. However, there might be values such as a specific web user configuration that might not change across requests. These kinds of values will typically be stored in an HTTP session. Spring MVC provides a simple type level (class level) annotation @SessionAttributes to specify the attributes that would be stored in the session.

Take a look at the following example:

```
@Controller
@SessionAttributes("exampleSessionAttribute")
public class LoginController {
```

Putting an attribute in the session

Once we define an attribute in the @SessionAttributes annotation, it is automatically added to the session if the same attribute is added to the model.

In the preceding example, if we put an attribute with the name exampleSessionAttribute into the model, it would be automatically stored into the session conversation state:

```
model.put("exampleSessionAttribute", sessionValue);
```

Reading an attribute from the session

This value can be accessed in other controllers by first specifying the @SessionAttributes annotation at a type level:

```
@Controller
@SessionAttributes("exampleSessionAttribute")
public class SomeOtherController {
```

The value of the session attribute will be directly made available to all model objects. So, it can be accessed from the model:

```
Value sessionValue =(Value)model.get("exampleSessionAttribute");
```

Removing an attribute from the session

It is important to remove values from the session when they are no longer needed. There are two ways in which we can remove values from the session conversational state. The first way is demonstrated in the following snippet. It uses the removeAttribute method available in the WebRequest class:

```
@RequestMapping(value="/some-method",method = RequestMethod.GET)
public String someMethod(/*Other Parameters*/
WebRequest request, SessionStatus status) {
  status.setComplete();
  request.removeAttribute("exampleSessionAttribute",
  WebRequest.SCOPE_SESSION);
   //Other Logic
}
```

This example shows the second approach using the cleanUpAttribute method in SessionAttributeStore:

```
@RequestMapping(value = "/some-other-method",
method = RequestMethod.GET)
public String someOtherMethod(/*Other Parameters*/
SessionAttributeStore store, SessionStatus status) {
  status.setComplete();
  store.cleanupAttribute(request, "exampleSessionAttribute");
  //Other Logic
}
```

InitBinders

Typical web forms have dates, currencies, and amounts. The values in the forms need to be bound to the form backing objects. Customization of how binding happens can be introduced using the @InitBinder annotation.

Customization can be done in a specific controller or a set of controllers using Handler Advice. This example shows how to set the default date format to use for form binding:

```
@InitBinder
protected void initBinder(WebDataBinder binder) {
  SimpleDateFormat dateFormat = new SimpleDateFormat("dd/MM/yyyy");
  binder.registerCustomEditor(Date.class, new CustomDateEditor(
  dateFormat, false));
}
```

The @ControllerAdvice annotation

Some of the functionality we defined at the controller level can be common across the application. For example, we might want to use the same date format across the application. So, `@InitBinder` that we defined earlier can be applicable across the application. How do we achieve that? `@ControllerAdvice` helps us make the functionality common across all Request Mappings by default.

For example, consider the Controller advice example listed here. We use a `@ControllerAdvice` annotation on the class and define the method with `@InitBinder` in this class. By default, the binding defined in this method is applicable to all request mappings:

```
@ControllerAdvice
public class DateBindingControllerAdvice {
  @InitBinder
  protected void initBinder(WebDataBinder binder) {
    SimpleDateFormat dateFormat = new
    SimpleDateFormat("dd/MM/yyyy");
    binder.registerCustomEditor(Date.class,
    new CustomDateEditor(
      dateFormat, false));
    }
  }
```

Controller advice can also be used to define common model attributes (`@ModelAttribute`) and common exception handling (`@ExceptionHandler`). All you would need to do is create methods marked with appropriate annotations. We will discuss exception handling in the next section.

Spring MVC - advanced features

In this section, we will discuss about advanced features related to Spring MVC, including the following:

- How do we implement generic exception handling for the web application?
- How do we internationalize messages?
- How do we write integration tests?

- How do we expose static content and integrate with frontend frameworks like Bootstrap?
- How do we secure our web application with Spring Security?

Exception handling

Exception handling is one of the critical parts of any application. It is very important to have a consistent exception handling strategy across the application. One of the popular misconceptions is that only bad applications need exception handling. Nothing can be further from the truth. Even well-designed, well-written applications need good exception handling.

Before the emergence of the Spring Framework, exception handling code was needed across application code due to the wide use of checked exceptions. For example, most of the JDBC methods threw checked exceptions, requiring a try catch to handle the exception in every method (unless you would want to declare that the method throws a JDBC exception). With Spring Framework, most of the exceptions were made unchecked exceptions. This made sure that, unless specific exception handling was needed, exception handling could be handled generically across the application.

In this section, we will look at couple of example implementations of exception handling as follows:

- Common exception handling across all controllers
- Specific exception handling for a Controller

Common exception handling across controllers

Controller advice can also be used to implement common exception handling across controllers.

Take a look at the following code:

```
@ControllerAdvice
public class ExceptionController {
  private Log logger =
  LogFactory.getLog(ExceptionController.class);
  @ExceptionHandler(value = Exception.class)
  public ModelAndView handleException
  (HttpServletRequest request, Exception ex) {
      logger.error("Request " + request.getRequestURL()
      + " Threw an Exception", ex);
```

```
        ModelAndView mav = new ModelAndView();
        mav.addObject("exception", ex);
        mav.addObject("url", request.getRequestURL());
        mav.setViewName("common/spring-mvc-error");
        return mav;
    }
}
```

Some things to note are as follows:

- `@ControllerAdvice`: Controller Advice, by default, is applicable to all controllers.
- `@ExceptionHandler(value = Exception.class)`: Any method with this annotation will be called when an exception of the type or the sub-type of the class specified(`Exception.class`) is thrown in the controllers.
- `public ModelAndView handleException (HttpServletRequest request, Exception ex)`: The exception that is thrown is injected into the Exception variable. The method is declared with a ModelAndView return type to be able to return a model with the exception details and an exception view.
- `mav.addObject("exception", ex)`: Adding the exception to the model so that the exception details can be shown in the view.
- `mav.setViewName("common/spring-mvc-error")`: The exception view.

The error view

Whenever an exception happens, `ExceptionController` redirects the user to the `ExceptionController` spring-mvc-error view after populating the model with exception details. The following snippet shows the complete jsp `/WEB-INF/views/common/spring-mvc-error.jsp`:

```
<%@ taglib prefix="c" uri="http://java.sun.com/jsp/jstl/core"%>
<%@page isErrorPage="true"%>
<h1>Error Page</h1>
 URL: ${url}
 <BR />
 Exception: ${exception.message}
<c:forEach items="${exception.stackTrace}"
    var="exceptionStackTrace">
    ${exceptionStackTrace}
</c:forEach>
```

Important things to note are as follows:

- `URL: ${url}`: Shows the URL from the model.
- `Exception: ${exception.message}`: Displays the exception message. The exception is populated into the model from `ExceptionController`.
- `forEach around ${exceptionStackTrace}`: Displays the stack trace from exception handling specific to `ExceptionController`.

Specific exception handling in a Controller

In some situations, there is a need for specific exception handling in a Controller. This situation can easily be handled by implementing a method annotated with `@ExceptionHandler(value = Exception.class)`.

In case specific exception handling is needed only for a specific exception, the specific exception class can be provided as the value for the value attribute of the annotation.

Internationalization

When we develop applications, we would want them to be usable in multiple locales. You would want the text that is shown to the user to be customized based on the location and language of the user. This is called **internationalization**. Internationalization, `i18n`, is also called **Localization**.

It can be implemented using two approaches:

- `SessionLocaleResolver`
- `CookieLocaleResolver`

In the case of `SessionLocaleResolver`, the locale chosen by the user is stored in the user session and, therefore, is valid for the user session only. However, in the case of a `CookieLocaleResolver`, the locale chosen is stored as a cookie.

Message bundle setup

First, let's set up a message bundler. The code snippet from the spring context is as follows:

```
<bean id="messageSource"  class=
  "org.springframework.context.support.
  ReloadableResourceBundleMessageSource">
  <property name="basename" value="classpath:messages" />
  <property name="defaultEncoding" value="UTF-8" />
</bean>
```

Important points to note are as follows:

- `class="org.springframework.context.support.ReloadableResourceBundleMessageSource"`: We are configuring a reloadable resource bundle. Support reloading properties through the cacheSeconds setting.
- `<property name="basename" value="classpath:messages" />`: Configure the loading of properties from the `messages.properties` and `messages_{locale}.properties file`. We will discuss the locale soon.

Let's configure a couple of property files and make them available in the `src/main/resources` folder:

```
message_en.properties
welcome.caption=Welcome in English
message_fr.properties
welcome.caption=Bienvenue - Welcome in French
```

We can display the message from the message bundle in a view using the `spring:message` tag:

```
<spring:message code="welcome.caption" />
```

Configuring a SessionLocaleResolver

There are two parts to configuring a `SessionLocaleResolver`. The first one is to configure a `localeResolver`. The second one is to configure an interceptor to handle the change in locale:

```
<bean id="springMVCLocaleResolver"
  class="org.springframework.web.servlet.i18n.
  SessionLocaleResolver">
  <property name="defaultLocale" value="en" />
</bean>
<mvc:interceptors>
```

```
    <bean id="springMVCLocaleChangeInterceptor"
    class="org.springframework.web.servlet.
    i18n.LocaleChangeInterceptor">
      <property name="paramName" value="language" />
    </bean>
</mvc:interceptors>
```

Important things to note are as follows:

- `<property name="defaultLocale" value="en" />`: By default, en locale is used.
- `<mvc:interceptors>`: LocaleChangeInterceptor is configured as a HandlerInterceptor. It would intercept all the handler requests and check for the locale.
- `<property name="paramName" value="language" />`: LocaleChangeInterceptor is configured to use a request param name called language to indicate the locale. So, any URL of the `http://server/uri?language={locale}` format would trigger a change in the locale.
- If you append `language=en` to any URL, you would be using en locale for the duration of the session. If you append `language=fr` to any URL, then you would be using a French locale.

Configuring a CookieLocaleResolver

We use a CookieLocaleResolver in the following example:

```
    <bean id="localeResolver"
     class="org.springframework.web.servlet.
     i18n.CookieLocaleResolver">
       <property name="defaultLocale" value="en" />
       <property name="cookieName" value="userLocaleCookie"/>
       <property name="cookieMaxAge" value="7200"/>
    </bean>
```

Important things to note are as follows:

- `<property name="cookieName" value="userLocaleCookie"/>`: The name of the cookie stored in the browser will be userLocaleCookie.
- `<property name="cookieMaxAge" value="7200"/>`: The lifetime of the cookie is 2 hours (7200 seconds).

- Since we are using `LocaleChangeInterceptor` from the previous example, if you append `language=en` to any URL, you would be using en locale for a duration of 2 hours (or until the locale is changed). If you append `language=fr` to any URL, then you would be using a French locale for 2 hours (or until locale is changed).

Integration testing Spring controllers

In the flows we discussed, we looked at using real unit tests--ones that only load up the specific controllers that are being tested.

Another possibility is to load up the entire Spring context. However, this would be more of an integration test as we would load up the entire context. The following code shows you how to do a complete launch of a Spring context, launching all controllers:

```
@RunWith(SpringRunner.class)
@WebAppConfiguration
@ContextConfiguration("file:src/main/webapp/
WEB-INF/user-web-context.xml")
public class BasicControllerSpringConfigurationIT {
  private MockMvc mockMvc;
  @Autowired
  private WebApplicationContext wac;
  @Before
  public void setup() {
    this.mockMvc =
    MockMvcBuilders.webAppContextSetup
    (this.wac).build();
  }
   @Test
   public void basicTest() throws Exception {
    this.mockMvc
    .perform(
       get("/welcome")
      .accept(MediaType.parseMediaType
      ("application/html;charset=UTF-8")))
      .andExpect(status().isOk())
      .andExpect(content().string
      ("Welcome to Spring MVC"));
   }
  }
```

A few things to note are as follows:

- `@RunWith(SpringRunner.class)`: `SpringRunner` helps us launch a Spring context.
- `@WebAppConfiguration`: Used to launch a web app context with Spring MVC
- `@ContextConfiguration("file:src/main/webapp/WEB-INF/user-web-context.xml")`: Specifies the location of the spring context XML.
- `this.mockMvc = MockMvcBuilders.webAppContextSetup(this.wac).build()`: In the earlier examples, we used a standalone setup. However, in this example, we want to launch the entire web app. So, we use `webAppContextSetup`.
- The execution of the test is very similar to how we did it in earlier tests.

Serving static resources

Most teams today have separate teams delivering frontend and backend content. The frontend is developed with modern JavaScript frameworks, such as AngularJs, Backbone, and so on. Backend is built through web applications or REST services based on frameworks such as Spring MVC.

With this evolution in frontend frameworks, it is very important to find the right solutions to version and deliver frontend static content.

The following are some of the important features provided by the Spring MVC framework:

- They expose static content from folders in the web application root
- They enable caching
- They enable GZip compression of static content

Exposing static content

Web applications typically have a lot of static content. Spring MVC provides options to expose static content from folders on the web application root as well locations on the classpath. The following snippet shows that content within the war can be exposed as static content:

```
<mvc:resources
mapping="/resources/**"
location="/static-resources/"/>
```

Things to note are as follows:

- `location="/static-resources/"`: The location specifies the folders inside the war or classpath that you would want to expose as static content. In this example, we want to expose all the content in the `static-resources` folder inside the root of war as static content. We can specify multiple comma-separated values to expose multiple folders under the same external facing URI.
- `mapping="/resources/**"`: The mapping specifies the external facing URI path. So, a CSS file named `app.css` inside the static-resources folder can be accessed using the `/resources/app.css` URI.

The complete Java configuration for the same configuration is shown here:

```
@Configuration
@EnableWebMvc
public class WebConfig extends WebMvcConfigurerAdapter {
  @Override
  public void addResourceHandlers
  (ResourceHandlerRegistry registry) {
    registry
    .addResourceHandler("/static-resources/**")
    .addResourceLocations("/static-resources/");
  }
}
```

Caching static content

Caching for static resources can be enabled for improved performance. The browser would cache the resources served for the specified time period. The `cache-period` attribute or the `setCachePeriod` method can be used to specify the caching interval (in seconds) based on the type of configuration used. The following snippets show the details:

This is the Java configuration:

```
registry
.addResourceHandler("/resources/**")
.addResourceLocations("/static-resources/")
.setCachePeriod(365 * 24 * 60 * 60);
```

This is the XML configuration:

```
<mvc:resources
 mapping="/resources/**"
 location="/static-resources/"
 cache-period="365 * 24 * 60 * 60"/>
```

The `Cache-Control: max-age={specified-max-age}` response header will be sent to the browser.

Enabling GZip compression of static content

Compressing a response is a simple way to make web applications faster. All modern browsers support GZip compression. Instead of sending the full static content file, a compressed file can be sent as a response. The browser will decompress and use the static content.

The browser can specify that it can accept the compressed content with a request header. If the server supports it, it can deliver the compressed content--again, marked with a response header.

Request Header sent from browser is as follows:

```
Accept-Encoding: gzip, deflate
```

Response Header sent from the web application is as follows:

```
Content-Encoding: gzip
```

The following snippet shows how to add a Gzip resolver to deliver compressed static content:

```
registry
  .addResourceHandler("/resources/**")
  .addResourceLocations("/static-resources/")
  .setCachePeriod(365 * 24 * 60 * 60)
  .resourceChain(true)
  .addResolver(new GzipResourceResolver())
  .addResolver(new PathResourceResolver());
```

Things to note are as follows:

- `resourceChain(true)`: We would want to enable Gzip compression, but would want to fall back to delivering the full file if full file was requested. So, we use resource chaining (chaining of resource resolvers).
- `addResolver(new PathResourceResolver())`: PathResourceResolver: This is the default resolver. It resolves based on the resource handlers and locations configured.
- `addResolver(new GzipResourceResolver())`: GzipResourceResolver: This enables Gzip compression when requested.

Integrating Spring MVC with Bootstrap

One of the approaches to using Bootstrap in a web application is to download the JavaScript and CSS files and make them available in their respective folders. However, this would mean that every time there is a new version of Bootstrap, we would need to download and make it available as part of the source code. The question is this--is there a way that we can introduce Bootstrap or any other static (js or css) libraries using dependency management such as Maven?

The answer is WebJars. WebJars are client-side js or css libraries packaged into JAR files. We can use Java build tools (Maven or Gradle) to download and make them available to the application. The biggest advantage is that WebJars are resolve transitive dependencies.

Now let's use Bootstrap WebJar and include it in our web application. The steps involved are as follows:

- Add Bootstrap WebJars as a Maven dependency
- Configure the Spring MVC resource handler to deliver static content from WebJar
- Use Bootstrap resources (css and js) in the JSP

Bootstrap WebJar as Maven dependency

Let's add this to the `pom.xml` file:

```
<dependency>
  <groupId>org.webjars</groupId>
  <artifactId>bootstrap</artifactId>
  <version>3.3.6</version>
</dependency>
```

Configure Spring MVC resource handler to deliver WebJar static content

This is very simple. We need to add the following mapping to the spring context:

```
<mvc:resources mapping="/webjars/**" location="/webjars/"/>
```

With this configuration, `ResourceHttpRequestHandler` makes the content from WebJars available as static content.

As discussed in the section on static content, we can specifically cache a period if we want to cache the content.

Using Bootstrap resources in JSP

We can add bootstrap resources just like other static resources in the JSP:

```
<script src=
 "webjars/bootstrap/3.3.6/js/bootstrap.min.js">
</script>
<link
 href="webjars/bootstrap/3.3.6/css/bootstrap.min.css"
 rel="stylesheet">
```

Spring Security

A critical part of web applications is authentication and authorization. Authentication is the process of establishing a user's identity, verifying that the user is who he/she claims to be. Authorization is checking whether the user has access to perform a specific action. Authorization specifies the access a user has. Can the user view a page? Can the user edit a page? Can the user delete a page?

A best practice is to enforce authentication and authorization on every page in the application. User credentials and authorization should be verified before executing any request to a web application.

Spring Security provides a comprehensive security solution for Java EE enterprise applications. While providing great support to Spring-based (and Spring MVC-based) applications, it can be integrated with other frameworks as well.

The following list highlights some of vast range of authentication mechanisms that Spring Security supports:

- **Form-based authentication**: Simple integration for basic applications
- **LDAP**: Typically used in most Enterprise applications
- **Java Authentication and Authorization Service (JAAS)**: Authentication and authorization standard; part of Java EE standard specification
- Container managed authentication
- Custom authentication systems

Let's consider a simple example to enable Spring Security on simple web application. We will use an in-memory configuration.

The steps involved are as follows:

1. Add Spring Security dependency.
2. Configure the interception of all requests.
3. Configure Spring Security.
4. Add the logout functionality.

Adding Spring Security dependency

We will start with adding the Spring Security dependencies to `pom.xml`:

```xml
<dependency>
  <groupId>org.springframework.security</groupId>
  <artifactId>spring-security-web</artifactId>
</dependency>
<dependency>
  <groupId>org.springframework.security</groupId>
  <artifactId>spring-security-config</artifactId>
</dependency>
```

The dependencies added in are `spring-security-web` and `spring-security-config`.

Configuring a filter to intercept all requests

The best practice when implementing security is to validate all incoming requests. We would want our security framework to look at the incoming request, authenticate the user and allow the action to be performed only if the user has access to perform the operation. We will make use of a filter to intercept and validate the request. The following example shows more details.

We would want to configure Spring Security to intercept all requests to a web application. We will use a filter, `DelegatingFilterProxy`, which delegates to a Spring-managed bean `FilterChainProxy`:

```xml
<filter>
  <filter-name>springSecurityFilterChain</filter-name>
  <filter-class>
    org.springframework.web.filter.DelegatingFilterProxy
  </filter-class>
</filter>
<filter-mapping>
  <filter-name>springSecurityFilterChain</filter-name>
```

```
    <url-pattern>/*</url-pattern>
  </filter-mapping>
```

Now, all requests to our web application will go through the filter. However, we have not configured anything related to security yet. Let's use a simple Java configuration example:

```
@Configuration
@EnableWebSecurity
public class SecurityConfiguration extends
WebSecurityConfigurerAdapter {
  @Autowired
  public void configureGlobalSecurity
  (AuthenticationManagerBuilder auth) throws Exception {
  auth
  .inMemoryAuthentication()
  .withUser("firstuser").password("password1")
  .roles("USER", "ADMIN");
  }
  @Override
  protected void configure(HttpSecurity http)
  throws Exception {
    http
  .authorizeRequests()
  .antMatchers("/login").permitAll()
  .antMatchers("/*secure*/**")
  .access("hasRole('USER')")
  .and().formLogin();
  }
}
```

Things to note are as follows:

- @EnableWebSecurity: This annotation enables any Configuration class to contain the definition of Spring Configuration. In this specific instance, we override a couple of methods to provide our specific Spring MVC configuration.
- WebSecurityConfigurerAdapter: This class provides a base class to create a Spring configuration (WebSecurityConfigurer).
- protected void configure(HttpSecurity http): This method provides the security needs for different URLs.
- antMatchers("/*secure*/**").access("hasRole('USER')"): You would need a role of USER to access any URL containing the sub-string secure.
- antMatchers("/login").permitAll(): Permits access to the login page to all users.

- `public void configureGlobalSecurity(AuthenticationManagerBuilder auth)`: In this example, we are using in-memory authentication. This can be used to connect to a database (`auth.jdbcAuthentication()`), or an LDAP(`auth.ldapAuthentication()`), or a custom authentication provider (created extending `AuthenticationProvider`).
- `withUser("firstuser").password("password1")`: Configures an in-memory valid user ID and password combination.
- `.roles("USER", "ADMIN")`: Assigns roles to the user.

When we try to access any secure URLs, we will be redirected to a login page. Spring Security provides ways of customizing the Logic page as well as the redirection. Only authenticated users with the right roles will be allowed to access the secured application pages.

Logout

Spring Security provides features to enable a user to log out and be redirected to a specified page. The URI of the `LogoutController` is typically mapped to the Logout link in the UI. The complete listing of `LogoutController` is as follows:

```
@Controller
public class LogoutController {
  @RequestMapping(value = "/secure/logout",
  method = RequestMethod.GET)
  public String logout(HttpServletRequest request,
  HttpServletResponse response) {
    Authentication auth =
    SecurityContextHolder.getContext()
    .getAuthentication();
    if (auth != null) {
        new SecurityContextLogoutHandler()
      .logout(request, response, auth);
        request.getSession().invalidate();
      }
    return "redirect:/secure/welcome";
  }
}
```

Things to note are as follows:

- `if (auth != null)`: If there is a valid authentication, then end the session
- `new SecurityContextLogoutHandler().logout(request, response, auth)`: `SecurityContextLogoutHandler` performs a logout by removing the authentication information from `SecurityContextHolder`
- `return "redirect:/secure/welcome"`: Redirects to the secure welcome page

Summary

In this chapter, we discussed the basics of developing web applications with Spring MVC. We also discussed implementing exception handling, internationalization and securing our applications with Spring Security.

Spring MVC can also be used to build REST services. We will discuss that and more related to REST services in the subsequent chapters.

In the next chapter, we will shift our attention toward microservices. We will try to understand why the world is looking keenly at microservices. We will also explore the importance of applications being Cloud-Native.

4
Evolution toward Microservices and Cloud-Native Applications

In the last decade, Spring Framework has evolved into the most popular framework to develop Java Enterprise applications. Spring Framework has made it easy to develop loosely coupled, testable applications. It has simplified the implementation of cross-cutting concerns.

The world today, however, is very different from a decade back. Over a period of time, applications grew into monoliths, which became difficult to manage. And because of this problems, new architectures started evolving. The buzzwords in the recent past have been RESTful services, microservices, and Cloud-Native applications.

In this chapter, we will start with reviewing the problems Spring Framework solved in the last decade. We will look at the problems with **monolithic applications** and get introduced to the world of smaller, independently deployable components.

We will explore why the world is moving toward microservices and Cloud-Native applications. We will end the chapter by looking at how Spring Framework and Spring projects are evolving to solve today's problems.

This chapter will cover the following topics:

- Architecture of a typical Spring-based application
- Problems solved by the Spring Framework in the last decade
- What are our goals when we develop applications?
- What are the challenges with monolithic applications?
- What are microservices?
- What are the advantages of microservices?

- What are the challenges with microservices?
- What are the good practices that help in deploying microservices to the Cloud?
- What are the Spring projects that help us in developing microservices and Cloud-Native applications?

Typical web application architecture with Spring

Spring has been the framework of choice to wire Java Enterprise applications during the last decade and half. Applications used a layered architecture with all cross-cutting concerns being managed using aspect-oriented programming. The following diagram shows a typical architecture for a web application developed with Spring:

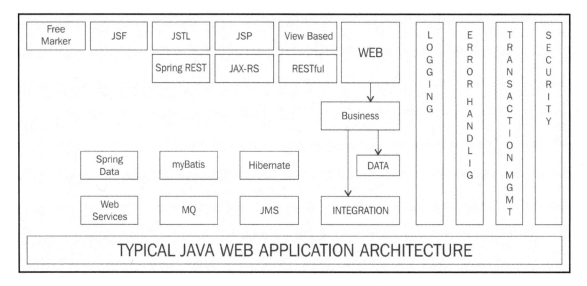

The typical layers in such an application are listed here. We will list cross-cutting concerns as a separate layer, though in reality, they are applicable across all layers:

- **Web layer**: This is typically responsible for controlling the web application flow (controller and/or Front Controller) and rendering the view.
- **Business layer**: This is where all your business logic is written. Most applications have transaction management starting from the business layer.
- **Data layer**: It is also responsible for talking to the database. This is responsible for persisting/retrieving data in Java objects to the tables in the database.

- **Integration layer**: Applications talk to other applications, either over queues or by invoking web services. The integration layer establishes such connections with other applications.
- **Cross-cutting concerns**: These are concerns across different layers--logging, security, transaction management, and so on. Since Spring IoC container manages the beans, it can weave these concerns around the beans through **Aspect-oriented programming (AOP)**.

Let's discuss each of the layers and the frameworks used in more detail.

Web layer

Web layer is dependent on how you would want to expose the business logic to the end user. Is it a web application? Or are you exposing RESTful web services?

Web application - rendering an HTML View

These web applications use a web MVC framework such as Spring MVC or Struts. The View can be rendered using JSP, JSF, or template-based frameworks such as Freemarker.

RESTful services

There are two typical approaches used to develop RESTful web services:

- **JAX-RS**: The Java API for REST services. This is a standard from the Java EE specification. Jersey is the reference implementation.
- **Spring MVC or Spring REST**: Restful services can also be developed with Spring MVC.

Spring MVC does not implement JAX-RS so, the choice is tricky. JAX-RS is a Java EE standard. But Spring MVC is more innovative and more likely to help you build new features faster.

Business layer

The business layer typically contains all the business logic in an application. Spring Framework is used in this layer to wire beans together.

This is also the layer where the boundary of transaction management begins. Transaction management can be implemented using Spring AOP or AspectJ. A decade back, **Enterprise Java Beans (EJB)** were the most popular approach to implement your business layer. With its lightweight nature, Spring is now the framework of choice for the business layer.

EJB3 is much simpler than EJB2. However, EJB3 is finding it difficult to recover the ground lost to Spring.

Data layer

Most applications talk to a database. The data layer is responsible for storing data from your Java objects to your database and vice versa. The following are the most popular approaches to building data layers:

- **JPA**: The **Java Persistence API** helps you to map Java objects (POJOs) to your database tables. Hibernate is the most popular implementation for JPA. JPA is typically preferred for all transactional applications. JPA is not the best choice for batch and reporting applications.
- **MyBatis**: MyBatis (previously, iBatis) is a simple data-mapping framework. As its website (http://www.mybatis.org/mybatis-3/) says, *MyBatis is a first class persistence framework with support for custom SQL, stored procedures and advanced mappings. MyBatis eliminates almost all of the JDBC code and manual setting of parameters and retrieval of results.* MyBatis can be considered for batch and reporting applications where SQLs and stored procedures are more typically used.
- **Spring JDBC**: JDBC and Spring JDBC are not that commonly used anymore.

We will discuss in detail the advantages and disadvantages of JDBC, Spring JDBC, MyBatis and JPA in Chapter 8, *Spring Data*.

Integration layer

The integration layer is typically where we talk to other applications. There might be other applications exposing SOAP or RESTful services over HTTP (the web) or MQ:

- Spring JMS is typically used to send or receive messages on queues or service buses.
- Spring MVC RestTemplate can be used to invoke RESTful services.
- Spring WS can be used to invoke SOAP-based web services.

- Spring Integration provides a higher level of abstraction for building enterprise integration solutions. It enables testability with a clear separation of concerns between the application and integration code. It supports all popular enterprise integration patterns. We will discuss more about Spring Integration in `Chapter 10`, *Spring Cloud Data Flow*.

Cross-cutting concerns

Cross-cutting concerns are concerns that are typically common to multiple layers of an application--logging, security, and transaction management, among others. Let's quickly discuss some of these:

- **Logging**: Audit logging at multiple layers can be implemented using Aspect-Oriented Programming (Spring AOP or AspectJ).
- **Security**: Security is typically implemented using the Spring Security framework. As discussed in the previous chapter, Spring Security makes the implementation of security very simple.
- **Transaction management**: Spring Framework provides a consistent abstraction for transaction management. More importantly, Spring Framework provides great support for declarative transaction management. The following are some of the transaction APIs that the Spring Framework supports:
    - The **Java Transaction API (JTA)** is a standard for transaction management. It is a part of Java EE's specifications.
    - JDBC.
    - JPA (including Hibernate).
- **Error handling**: Most abstractions provided by Spring use unchecked exceptions so unless required by business logic, it is sufficient to implement error handling in the layer that is exposed to the client (user or other application). Spring MVC provides Controller Advice to implement consistent error handling across the application.

The Spring Framework plays a major role in application architecture. Spring IoC is used to wire beans from different layers together. Spring AOP is used to weave cross-cutting concerns around the beans. Added to these is the fact that Spring provides great integration with frameworks in different layers.

In the next section, we will quickly review some of the important problems Spring has solved in the last decade or so.

Problems solved by Spring

Spring is the framework of choice to wire Enterprise Java applications. It has solved a number of problems that Enterprise Java applications have faced since the complexity associated with EJB2. A few of them are listed as follows:

- Loose coupling and testability
- Plumbing code
- Lightweight architecture
- Architectural flexibility
- Simplified implementation of cross-cutting concerns
- Best design patterns for free

Loose coupling and testability

Through dependency injection, Spring brings loose coupling between classes. While loose coupling is beneficial to application maintainability in the long run, the first benefits are realized with the testability that it brings in.

Testability was not a forte of Java EE (or J2EE, as it was called then) before Spring. The only way to test EJB2 applications was to run them in the container. Unit testing them was incredibly difficult.

That's exactly the problem Spring Framework set out to solve. As we saw in the earlier chapters, if objects are wired using Spring, writing unit tests becomes easier. We can easily stub or mock dependencies and wire them into objects.

Plumbing code

The developer of the late 1990s and early-to mid-2000s will be familiar with the amount of plumbing code that had to be written to execute a simple query through JDBC and populate the result into a Java object. You had to perform a **Java Naming and Directory Interface (JNDI)** lookup, get a connection, and populate the results. This resulted in duplicate code. Usually, problems were repeated with exception handling code in every method. And this problem is not limited to JDBC.

One of these problems Spring Framework solved was by eliminating all the plumbing code. With Spring JDBC, Spring JMS, and other abstractions, the developers could focus on writing business logic. Spring framework took care of the nitty-gritty.

Lightweight architecture

Using EJBs made the applications complex, and not all applications needed that complexity. Spring provided a simplified, lightweight way of developing applications. If distribution was needed, it could be added later.

Architecture flexibility

Spring Framework is used to wire objects across an application in different layers. In spite of its ever-looming presence, Spring Framework did not restrict the flexibility or choice of frameworks that application architects and developers had. A couple of examples are listed as follows:

- Spring Framework provided great flexibility in the web layer. If you wanted to use Struts or Struts 2 instead of Spring MVC, it was configurable. You had the choice of integrating with a wider range of view and template frameworks.
- Another good example is the data layer, where you had possibilities to connect with JPA, JDBC, and mapping frameworks, such as MyBatis.

Simplified implementation of cross-cutting concerns

When Spring Framework is used to manage beans, the Spring IoC container manages the life cycle--creation, use, auto-wiring, and destruction--of the beans. It makes it easier to weave an additional functionality--such as the cross-cutting concerns--around the beans.

Design patterns for free

Spring Framework encourages the use of a number of design patterns by default. A few examples are as follows:

- **Dependency Injection or Inversion of Controller**: This is the fundamental design pattern Spring Framework is built to enable. It enables loose coupling and testability.
- **Singleton**: All Spring beans are singletons by default.
- **Factory Pattern**: Using the bean factory to instantiate beans is a good example of the factory pattern.

- **Front Controller**: Spring MVC uses DispatcherServlet as the Front Controller. So we use the Front Controller pattern when we develop applications with Spring MVC.
- **Template Method**: Helps us avoid boilerplate code. Many Spring-based classes--JdbcTemplate and JmsTemplate--are implementations of this pattern.

Application development goals

Before we move on to the concepts of REST services, microservices, and Cloud-Native applications, let's take some time to understand the common goals we have when we develop applications. Understanding these goals will help us understand why applications are moving toward the microservices architecture.

First of all, we should remember that the software industry is still a relatively young industry. One thing that's been a constant in my decade and a half experience with developing, designing, and architecting software is that things change. The requirements of today are not the requirements of tomorrow. Technology today is not the technology we will use tomorrow. While we can try predicting what happens in the future, we are often wrong.

One of the things we did during the initial decades of software development was build software systems for the future. The design and architecture were made complex in preparation for future requirements.

During the last decade, with **agile** and **extreme programming**, the focus shifted to being **lean** and building good enough systems, adhering to basic principles of design. The focus shifted to evolutionary design. The thought process is this: *If a system has good design for today's needs, and is continuously evolving and has good tests, it can easily be refactored to meet tomorrow's needs.*

While we do not know where we are heading, we do know that a big chunk of our goals when developing applications have not changed.

The key goals of software development, for a large number of applications, can be described with the statement *speed and safety at scale*.

We will discuss each of these in elements in the next section.

Speed

The speed of delivering new requirements and innovations is increasingly becoming a key differentiator. It is not sufficient to develop (code and test) fast. It is important to deliver (to production) quickly. It is now common knowledge that the best software organizations in the world deliver software to production multiple times every day.

The technology and business landscape is in a constant flux, and is constantly evolving. The key question is "How fast can an application adapt to these changes?". Some of the important changes in the technology and business landscape are highlighted here:

- New programming languages
    - Go
    - Scala
    - Closure
- New programming paradigms
    - Functional programming
    - Reactive programming
- New frameworks
- New tools
    - Development
    - Code quality
    - Automation testing
    - Deployment
    - Containerizations
- New processes and practices
    - Agile
    - Test-driven development
    - Behavior-driven development
    - Continuous integration
    - Continuous delivery
    - DevOps
- New devices and opportunities
    - Mobile
    - Cloud

Safety

What is the use of speed without safety? Who would want to go in a car that can travel at 300 miles an hour but that has no proper safety features built in?

Let's consider a few characteristics of a safe application:

Reliability

Reliability is a measure of how accurately the system functions.

The key questions to ask are as follows:

- Is the system meeting its functional requirements?
- How many defects are leaked during different release phases?

Availability

Most external client-facing applications are expected to be available round the clock. Availability is a measure of how much percentage of time your application is available for your end user.

Security

The security of applications and data is critical to the success of organizations. There should be clear procedures for authentication (are you who you claim to be?), authorization (what access does a user have?), and data protection (is the data that is received or sent accurate? Is the data safe and not intercepted by unintended users?).

We will discuss more about implementing security using Spring Security in `Chapter 6,` *Extending Microservices*.

Performance

If a web application does not respond within a couple of seconds, there is a very high chance that the user of your application will be disappointed. Performance usually refers to the ability of a system to provide an agreed-upon response time for a defined number of users.

High resilience

As applications become distributed, the probability of failures increases. How does the application react in the case of localized failures or disruptions? Can it provide basic operations without completely crashing?

This behavior of an application to provide the bare minimum service levels in case of unexpected failures is called resilience.

As more and more applications move towards the Cloud, the resilience of applications becomes important.

We will discuss building highly resilient microservices using *Spring Cloud and Spring Data Flow* in `Chapter 9`, *Spring Cloud* and `Chapter 10`, *Spring Cloud Data Flow*.

Scalability

Scalability is a measure of how an application would react when the resources at its disposal are scaled up. If an application supports 10,000 users with a given infrastructure, can it support at least 20,000 users with double the infrastructure?

If a web application does not respond within a couple of seconds, there is a very high chance that the user of your application will be disappointed. Performance usually refers to the ability of a system to provide an agreed-upon response time for a defined number of users.

In the world of Cloud, the scalability of applications becomes even more important. It's difficult to guess how successful a startup might be. Twitter or Facebook might not have expected such success when they were incubated. Their success, for large measure, depends on how they were able to adapt to a multi-fold increase in their user base without affecting the performance.

We will discuss building highly scalable microservices using Spring Cloud and Spring Data Flow in `Chapter 9`, *Spring Cloud* and `Chapter 10`, *Spring Cloud Data Flow*.

Challenges with monolithic applications

Over the last few years, in parallel to working with several small applications, I had the opportunity to work on four different monolithic applications in varied domains-- insurance, banking, and health care. All these applications had very similar challenges. In this section, we will start with looking at the characteristics of monoliths and then look at the challenges they bring in.

First of all: What is a monolith? An application with a lot of code--may be greater than 100K lines of code? Yeah.

For me, monoliths are those applications for which getting a release out to production is a big challenge. Applications that fall into this category have a number of user requirements that are immediately needed, but these applications are able to do new feature releases once every few months. Some of these applications even do feature releases once a quarter or sometimes even as less as twice a year.

Typically, all monolithic applications have these characteristics:

- **Large size**: Most of these monolithic applications have more than 100K lines of code. Some have codebases with more than a million lines of code.
- **Large teams**: The team size could vary from 20 to 300.
- **Multiple ways of doing the same thing**: Since the team is huge, there is a communication gap. This results in multiple solutions for the same problem in different parts of the application.
- **Lack of automation testing**: Most of these applications have very few unit tests and a complete lack of integration tests. These applications have great dependence on manual testing.

Because of these characteristics, there are a number of challenges faced by these monolithic applications.

Long release cycles

Making a code change in one part of the monolith may impact some other part of the monolith. Most code changes will need a complete regression cycle. This results in long release cycles.

Because there is a lack of automation testing, these applications depend on manual testing to find defects. Taking the functionality live is a major challenge.

Difficult to scale

Typically, most monolithic applications are not Cloud-Native, which means that they are not easy to deploy on the Cloud. They depend on manual installation and manual configuration. There is typically a lot of work put in by the operations team before a new application instance is added to the cluster. This makes scaling up and down a big challenge.

The other important challenge is large databases. Typically, monolithic applications have databases running into **terabytes (TB)**. The database becomes the bottleneck when scaling up.

Adapting new technologies

Most monolithic applications use old technologies. Adding a new technology to the monolith only makes it more complex to maintain. Architects and developers are reluctant to bring in any new technologies.

Adapting new methodologies

New methodologies such as **agile** need small (four-seven team members), independent teams. The big questions with monolith are these: How do we prevent teams from stepping on each other's toes? How do we create islands that enable teams to work independently? This is a difficult challenge to solve.

Adapting modern development practices

Modern development practices such as **Test-Driven Development (TDD)**, **Behavior-Driven Development (BDD)** need loosely coupled, testable architecture. If the monolithic application has tightly coupled layers and frameworks, it is difficult to unit test. It makes adapting modern development practices challenging.

Understanding microservices

The challenges with monolithic applications lead to organizations searching for the silver bullet. How will we be able to make more features live more often?

Many organizations have tried different architectures and practices to find a solution.

In the last few years, a common pattern emerged among all the organizations that were successful at doing this. From this emerged an architectural style that was called **microservices architecture**.

> *As Sam Newman says in the book Building Microservices: Many organizations have found that by embracing fine-grained, microservice architectures, they can deliver software faster and embrace newer technologies.*

What is a microservice?

One of the principles I love in software is *keep it small*. This principle is applicable irrespective of what you are talking about--the scope of a variable, the size of a method, class, package, or a component. You would want all of these to be as small as they possibly could be.

Microservices is a simple extension of this principle. It's an architectural style focused on building small capability-based independently deployable services.

There is no single accepted definition of a microservice. We will look at some of the popular definitions:

> *"Microservices are small, autonomous services that work together"*

> *- Sam Newman, Thoughtworks*

> *"Loosely coupled service-oriented architecture with bounded contexts"*

> *- Adrian Cockcroft, Battery Ventures*

> *"A microservice is an independently deployable component of bounded scope that supports interoperability through message-based communication. Microservice architecture is a style of engineering highly automated, evolvable software systems made up of capability-aligned microservices" in the book Microservice Architecture*

> *- Irakli Nadareishvili, Ronnie Mitra, Matt McLarty*

While there is no accepted definition, there are a few characteristics that are commonly featured in all definitions of microservice. Before we look at the characteristics of microservices, we will try and understand the big picture--we will look at how architecture without microservices compares with architecture using microservices.

The microservice architecture

Monolithic applications--even those that are modularized--have a single deployable unit. The following figure shows an example of a monolithic application with three modules, module 1, 2, and 3. These modules can be a business capability that is part of the monolithic application. In a shopping application, one of the modules might be a product recommendation.

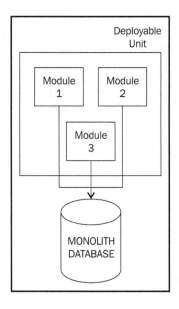

The following figure shows what the preceding monolith looks like when developed using microservice architecture:

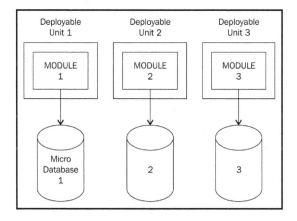

A few important things to note are as follows:

- Modules are identified based on business capabilities. What functionality is the module providing?
- Each module is independently deployable. In the following example, modules 1, 2, and 3 are separate deployable units. If there is a change in the business functionality of module 3, we can individually build and deploy module 3.

Microservice characteristics

In the previous section, we looked at an example of the microservice architecture. An evaluation of experiences at organizations successful at adapting the microservices architectural style reveals that there are a few characteristics that are shared by teams and architectures. Let's look at some of them:

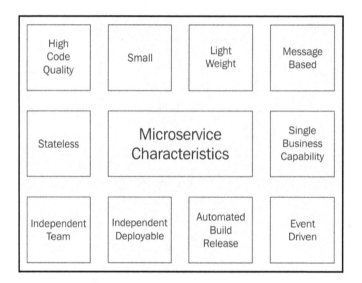

Small and lightweight microservices

A good microservice provides a business capability. Ideally, microservices should follow the **single responsibility principle**. Because of this, microservices are generally small in size. Typically, a rule of thumb I use is that it should be possible to build and deploy a microservice within 5 minutes. If the building and deployment takes any longer, it is likely that you are building a larger than recommended microservice.

Some examples of small and lightweight microservices are as follows:

- Product recommendation service
- Email notification service
- Shopping cart service

Interoperability with message-based communication

The key focus of microservices is on interoperability--communication between systems using diverse technologies. The best way to achieve interoperability is using message-based communication.

Capability-aligned microservices

It is essential that microservices have a clear boundary. Typically, every microservice has a single identified business capability that it delivers well. Teams have found success adapting the *Bounded Context* concept proposed in the book *Domain-Driven Design* by Eric J Evans.

Essentially, for large systems, it is very difficult to create one domain model. Evans talks about splitting the system into different bounded contexts. Identifying the right bounded contexts is the key to success with microservice architecture.

Independently deployable units

Each microservice can be individually built and deployed. In the example discussed earlier, modules 1, 2, and 3 can each be independently built and deployed.

Stateless

An ideal microservice does not have a state. It does not store any information between requests. All the information needed to create a response is present in the request.

Automated build and release process

Microservices have automated build and release processes. Take a look at the following figure. It shows a simple build and release process for a microservice:

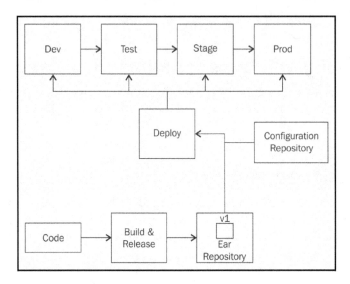

When a microservice is built and released, a version of the microservice is stored in the repository. The deploy tool has the capability of picking the right version of microservice from the repository, matching it with the configuration needed for the specific environment (from the configuration repository), and deploying the microservice to a specific environment.

Some teams take it a step further and combine the microservice package with the underlying infrastructure needed to run the microservice. The deploy tool will replicate this image and match it with an environment-specific configuration to create an environment.

Event-driven architecture

Microservices are typically built with event-driven architecture. Let's consider a simple example. Whenever a new customer is registered, there are three things that need to be performed:

- Store customer information to the database
- Mail a welcome kit
- Send an email notification

Let's look at two different approaches to design this.

Approach 1 - sequential approach

Let's consider three services--`CustomerInformationService`, `MailService`, and `EmailService`, which can provide the capabilities listed earlier. We can create `NewCustomerService` with the following steps:

1. Call `CustomerInformationService` to save customer information to the database.
2. Call `MailService` to mail the welcome kit.
3. Call `EmailService` to send the e-mail notification.

`NewCustomerService` becomes the central place for all business logic. Imagine if we have to do more things when a new customer is created. All that logic would start accumulating and bloating up `NewCustomerService`.

Approach 2 - event-driven approach

In this approach, we use a message broker. `NewCustomerService` will create a new event and post it to the message broker. The following figure shows a high-level representation:

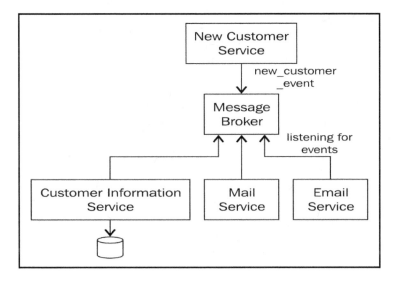

The three services--`CustomerInformationService`, `MailService`, and `EmailService`--will be listening on the message broker for new events. When they see the new customer event, they process it and execute the functionality of that specific service.

The key advantage of the event-driven approach is that there is no centralized magnet for all the business logic. Adding a new functionality is easier. We can create a new service to listen for the event on the message broker. Another important thing to note is that we don't need to make changes to any of the existing services.

Independent teams

The team developing a microservice is typically independent. It contains all the skills needed to develop, test, and deploy a microservice. It is also responsible for supporting the microservice in production.

Microservice advantages

Microservices have several advantages. They help in keeping up with technology and getting solutions to your customers faster.

Faster time to market

The faster time to market is one of the key factors in determining the success of an organization.

Microservices architecture involves creating small, independently deployable components. Microservice enhancements are easier and less brittle because each microservice focuses on a single business capability. All the steps in the process--building, releasing, deployment, testing, configuration management, and monitoring--are automated. Since the responsibility of a microservice is bounded, it is possible to write great automation unit and integration tests.

All these factors result in applications being able to react faster to customer needs.

Technology evolution

There are new languages, frameworks, practices, and automation possibilities emerging every day. It is important that the application architectures allow flexibility to adapt to emerging possibilities. The following figure shows how different services are developed in different technologies:

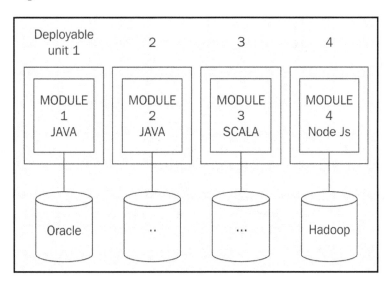

The microservice architecture involves creating small services. Within some boundaries, most organizations give the individual teams the of technology to make some of the technology decisions. This allows teams to experiment with new technologies and innovate faster. This helps applications adapt and stay in tune with the evolution of technology.

Availability and scaling

The load on different parts of the application is typically very different. For example, in the case of a flight booking application, a customer usually searches multiple times before making a decision on whether to book a flight. The load on the search module would typically be many times more than the load on the booking module. The microservices architecture provides the flexibility of setting up multiple instances of the search service with few instances of the booking service.

The following figure shows how we can scale up specific microservices based on the load:

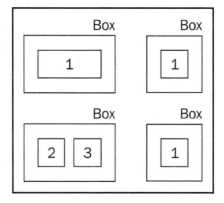

Microservices **2** and **3** share a single box (the deployment environment). Microservice **1**, which has more load, is deployed into multiple boxes.

Another example is the need for start-ups. When a start-up begins its operations, they are typically unaware of the extent to which they might grow. What happens if the demand for applications grows very fast? If they adapt the microservice architecture, it enables them to scale better when the need arises.

Team dynamics

Development methodologies such as agile advocate small, independent teams. Since microservices are small, it is possible to build small teams around them. Teams are cross-functional, with end-to-end ownership of specific microservices.

Microservice architecture fits in very well with agile and other modern development methodologies.

Microservice challenges

Microservice architecture has significant advantages. However, there are significant challenges too. Deciding the boundaries of microservices is a challenging but important decision. Since microservices are small, and there would be hundreds of microservices in a large enterprise, having great automation and visibility is critical.

Increased need for automation

With microservice architecture, you are splitting up a large application into multiple microservices, so the number of builds, releases, and deployments increases multifold. It would be very inefficient to have manual processes for these steps.

Test automation is critical to enable a faster time to market. Teams should be focused on identifying automation possibilities as they emerge.

Defining the boundaries of subsystems

Microservices should be intelligent. They are not weak CRUD services. They should model the business capability of the system. They own all the business logic in a bounded context. Having said this, microservices should not be large. Deciding the boundaries of microservices is a challenge. Finding the right boundaries might be difficult on the first go. It is important that as a team gains more knowledge about the business context, the knowledge flows into the architecture and new boundaries are determined. Generally, finding the right boundaries for microservices is an evolutionary process.

A couple of important points to note are as follows:

- Loose coupling and high cohesion are fundamental to any programming and architectural decisions. When a system is loosely coupled, changes in one part should not require a change in other parts.
- Bounded contexts represent autonomous business modules representing specific business capabilities.

As Sam Newman says in the book Building Microservices--"Specific responsibility enforced by explicit boundaries". Always think, "What capabilities are we providing to the rest of the domain?".

Visibility and monitoring

With microservices, one application is split into several microservices. To conquer the complexity associated with multiple microservices and asynchronous event-based collaboration, it is important to have great visibility.

Ensuring high availability means each microservice should be monitored. Automated health management of the microservices becomes important.

Debugging problems needs insights into what's happening behind multiple microservices. Centralized logging with aggregation of logs and metrics from different microservices is typically used. Mechanisms such as correlation IDs need to be used to isolate and debug issues.

Fault tolerance

Let's say we are building a shopping application. What happens if the recommendation microservice is down? How does the application react? Does it completely crash? Or will it let the customer shop? These kinds of situations happen more often as we adapt the microservices architecture.

As we make the services small, the chance that a service is down increases. How the application reacts to these situations becomes an important question. In the earlier example, a fault-tolerant application would show some default recommendations while letting the customer shop.

As we move into microservices architecture, applications should be more fault tolerant. Applications should be able to provide toned-down behavior when services are down.

Eventual consistency

It is important to have a degree of consistency between microservices in an organization. Consistency between microservices enables similar development, testing, release, deployment, and operational processes across the organization. This enables different developers and testers to be productive when they move across teams. It is important to be not very rigid and have a degree of flexibility within limits so as to not stifle innovation.

Shared capabilities (enterprise level)

Let's look at a few capabilities that have to be standardized at an enterprise level.

- **Hardware**: What hardware do we use? Do we use Cloud?
- **Code management**: What version control system do we use? What are our practices in branching and committing code?
- **Build and deployment**: How do we build? What tools do we use to automate deployment?
- **Data store**: What kind of data stores do we use?

- **Service orchestration**: How do we orchestrate services? What kind of message broker do we use?
- **Security and identity**: How do we authenticate and authorize users and services?
- **System visibility and monitoring**: How do we monitor our services? How do we provide fault isolation across the system?

Increased need for operations teams

As we move into a microservice world, there is a distinct shift in the responsibilities of operations team. The responsibilities shift to identifying opportunities for automation compared to manual operations such as executing releases and deployments.

With multiple microservices and an increase in communications across different parts of the system, the operations team becomes critical. It is important to involve operations as part of the team from the initial stages to enable them to identify solutions to make operations easier.

Cloud-Native applications

The Cloud is disrupting the world. A number of possibilities have emerged that were never possible before. Organizations are able to provision computing, network, and storage devices on demand. This has high potential to reduce costs in a number of industries.

Consider the retail industry, where there is high demand in pockets (Black Friday, holiday season, and so on). Why should they pay for hardware throughout the year when they could provision it on demand?

While we would like to be benefit from the possibilities of the Cloud, these possibilities are limited by architecture and the nature of applications.

How do we build applications that can be easily deployed on the Cloud? That's where Cloud-Native applications come into the picture.

Cloud-Native applications are those that can easily be deployed on the Cloud. These applications share a few common characteristics. We will begin by looking at the Twelve-Factor App--a combination of common patterns among Cloud-Native applications.

Twelve-Factor App

The Twelve-Factor App evolved from the experiences of engineers at Heroku. It is a list of patterns that are used in Cloud-Native application architectures.

It is important to note that an app here refers to a single deployable unit. Essentially, every microservice is an app (because each microservice is independently deployable).

Maintain one code base

Each app has one code base in revision control. There can be multiple environments where the app can be deployed. However, all these environments use code from a single codebase. An example antipattern is building a deployable from multiple codebases.

Dependencies

All dependencies must be explicitly declared and isolated. Typical Java applications use build management tools such as Maven and Gradle to isolate and track dependencies.

The following figure shows typical Java applications managing dependencies using Maven:

The following figure shows `pom.xml`, where the dependencies are managed for a Java application:

```
mastering-spring-chapter-3/pom.xml ⊠
42          </dependency>
43
44⊝|          <dependency>
45                  <groupId>org.springframework.security</groupId>
46                  <artifactId>spring-security-web</artifactId>
47                  <version>4.0.1.RELEASE</version>
48          </dependency>
49
50⊝          <dependency>
51                  <groupId>org.springframework.security</groupId>
52                  <artifactId>spring-security-config</artifactId>
53                  <version>4.0.1.RELEASE</version>
54          </dependency>
55
56⊝          <dependency>
57                  <groupId>org.hibernate</groupId>
58                  <artifactId>hibernate-validator</artifactId>
59                  <version>5.0.2.Final</version>
60          </dependency>
61
62⊝          <dependency>
63                  <groupId>org.webjars</groupId>
64                  <artifactId>bootstrap</artifactId>
65                  <version>3.3.6</version>
66          </dependency>
67
68⊝          <dependency>
69                  <groupId>org.webjars</groupId>
70                  <artifactId>jquery</artifactId>
71                  <version>1.9.1</version>
72          </dependency>
73
```

Config

All applications have configuration that varies from one environment to another. Configuration is found at multiple locations; application code, property files, databases, environment variables, JNDI, and system variables are a few examples.

A Twelve-Factor App

App should store configuration in the environment. While environment variables are recommended in order to manage configuration in a Twelve-Factor App, other alternatives, such as having a centralized repository for application configuration, should be considered for more complex systems.

Irrespective of the mechanism used, we recommend that you do the following:

Manage configuration outside the application code (independent of the application's deployable unit)
Use a standardized way of configuration

Backing services

Applications depend on other services being available--data stores and external services, among others. The Twelve-Factor App treats backing services as attached resources. A backing service is typically declared via an external configuration.

Loose coupling to a backing service has many advantages, including the ability to gracefully handle an outage of a backing service.

Build, release, run

The build, release, and run phases are described as follows. We should maintain a clear separation between all these three phases:

- **Build**: Creates an executable bundle (EAR, WAR, or JAR) from code, as well as dependencies that can be deployed to multiple environments
- **Release**: Combines the executable bundle with a specific environment configuration to deploy in an environment
- **Run**: Runs the app in an execution environment using a specific release

The build and release phases are highlighted in the following screenshot:

An antipattern is the building of separate executable bundles specific to each environment.

Stateless

A Twelve-Factor App does not have a state. All the data that it needs is stored in a persistent store.

An antipattern is a sticky session.

Port binding

A Twelve-Factor App exposes all services using port binding. While it is possible to have other mechanisms to expose services, these mechanisms are implementation-dependent. Port binding gives full control of receiving and handling messages irrespective of where an app is deployed.

Concurrency

A Twelve-Factor App is able to achieve more concurrency by scaling out horizontally. Scaling vertically has its limits. Scaling out horizontally provides opportunities to expand without limits.

Disposability

A Twelve-Factor App should promote elastic scaling. Hence, they should be disposable. They can be started and stopped when needed.

A Twelve-Factor App should do the following:

- Have minimum startup time. A long startup time means a long delay before an application can take requests.
- Shut down gracefully.
- Handle hardware failures gracefully.

Environment parity

All the environments--development, test, staging, and production--should be similar. They should use the same processes and tools. With continuous deployment, they should have very frequently have similar code. This makes finding and fixing problems easier.

Logs as event streams

Visibility is critical to a Twelve-Factor App. Since applications are deployed on the Cloud and are automatically scaled, it is important that you have a centralized view of what's happening across different instances of the applications.

Treating all logs as stream enables the routing of the log stream to different destinations for viewing and archival purposes. This stream can be used to debug issues, perform analytics, and create alerting systems based on error patterns.

No distinction of admin processes

Twelve-Factor Apps treat administrative tasks (migrations, scripts) similar to normal application processes.

Spring projects

As the world moves toward Cloud-Native applications and microservices, Spring projects are not far behind. There are a number of new Spring projects--Spring Boot, Spring Cloud, among others, that solve the problems of the emerging world.

Spring Boot

In the era of monoliths, we had the luxury of taking the time to set the frameworks up for an application. However, in the era of microservices, we want to create individual components faster. The Spring Boot project aims to solve this problem.

 As the official website highlights, Spring Boot makes it easy to create standalone, production-grade Spring-based applications that you can *just run*. We take an opinionated view of the Spring platform and third-party libraries so that you can get started with minimum fuss.

Spring Boot aims to take an opinionated view--basically making a lot of decisions for us--to developing Spring-based projects.

In the next couple of chapters, we will look at Spring Boot and the different features that enable us to create production-ready applications faster.

Spring Cloud

Spring Cloud aims to provide solutions to some commonly encountered patterns when building systems on the Cloud:

- **Configuration management**: As we discussed in the Twelve-Factor App section, managing configuration is an important part of developing Cloud-Native applications. Spring Cloud provides a centralized configuration management solution for microservices called Spring Cloud Config.
- **Service discovery**: Service discovery promotes loose coupling between services. Spring Cloud provides integration with popular service discovery options, such as Eureka, ZooKeeper, and Consul.
- **Circuit breakers**: Cloud-Native applications must be fault tolerant. They should be able to handle the failure of backing services gracefully. Circuit breakers play a key role in providing the default minimum service in case of failures. Spring Cloud provides integration with the Netflix Hystrix fault tolerance library.
- **API Gateway**: An API Gateway provides centralized aggregation, routing, and caching services. Spring Cloud provides integration with the API Gateway library Netflix Zuul.

Summary

In this chapter, we looked at how the world evolved toward microservices and Cloud-Native applications. We understood how Spring Framework and projects are evolving to meet the needs of today's world with projects such as Spring Boot, Spring Cloud, and Spring Data.

In the next chapter, we will start focusing on Spring Boot. We will look at how Spring Boot makes developing microservices easy.

5

Building Microservices with Spring Boot

As we discussed in the last chapter, we are moving toward architectures with smaller, independently deployable microservices. This would mean that there will be a huge number of smaller microservices developed.

An important consequence is that we would need to be able to quickly get off the ground and get running with new components.

Spring Boot aims to solve the problem of getting off fast with a new component. In this chapter, we will start with understanding the capabilities Spring Boot brings to the table. We will answer the following questions:

- Why Spring Boot?
- What are the features that Spring Boot provides?
- What is auto-configuration?
- What is Spring Boot not?
- What happens in the background when you use Spring Boot?
- How do you use Spring Initializr to create new Spring Boot projects?
- How do you create basic RESTful services with Spring Boot?

What is Spring Boot?

First of all, let's start with clearing out a few misconceptions about Spring Boot:

- Spring Boot is not a code generation framework. It does not generate any code.
- Spring Boot is neither an application server, nor is it a web server. It provides good integration with different ranges of applications and web servers.
- Spring Boot does not implement any specific frameworks or specifications.

These questions still remain:

- What is Spring Boot?
- Why has it become so popular in the last couple of years?

To answer these questions, let's build a quick example. Let's consider an example application that you want to quickly prototype.

Building a quick prototype for a microservice

Let's say we want to build a microservice with Spring MVC and use JPA (with Hibernate as the implementation) to connect to the database.

Let's consider the steps in setting up such an application:

1. Decide which versions of Spring MVC, JPA and Hibernate to use.
2. Set up a Spring context to wire all the different layers together.
3. Set up a web layer with Spring MVC (including Spring MVC configuration):
   - Configure beans for DispatcherServlet, handler, resolvers, view resolvers, and so on
4. Set up Hibernate in the data layer:
   - Configure beans for SessionFactory, data source, and so on
5. Decide and implement how to store your application configuration, which varies between different environments.
6. Decide how you would want to do your unit testing.
7. Decide and implement your transaction management strategy.
8. Decide and implement how to implement security.
9. Set up your logging framework.
10. Decide and implement how you want to monitor your application in production.

11. Decide and implement a metrics management system to provide statistics about the application.
12. Decide and implement how to deploy your application to a web or application server.

At least a few of the steps mentioned have to be completed before we can start with building our business logic. And this might take a few weeks at the least.

When we build microservices, we would want to make a quick start. All the preceding steps will not make it easy to develop a microservice. And that's the problem Spring Boot aims to solve.

The following quote is an extract from the Spring Boot website (`http://docs.spring.io/s pring-boot/docs/current-SNAPSHOT/reference/htmlsingle/#boot-documentation`):

> *Spring Boot makes it easy to create stand-alone, production-grade Spring based applications that you can "just run". We take an opinionated view of the Spring platform and third-party libraries so you can get started with minimum fuss. Most Spring Boot applications need very little Spring configuration.*

Spring Boot enables developers to focus on the business logic behind their microservice. It aims to take care of all the nitty-gritty technical details involved in developing microservices.

Primary goals

The primary goals of Spring Boot are as follows:

- Enable quickly getting off the ground with Spring-based projects.
- Be opinionated. Make default assumptions based on common usage. Provide configuration options to handle deviations from defaults.
- Provide a wide range of nonfunctional features out of the box.
- Do not use code generation and avoid using a lot of XML configuration.

Nonfunctional features

A few of the nonfunctional features provided by Spring Boot are as follows:

- Default handling of versioning and configuration of a wide range of frameworks, servers, and specifications

- Default options for application security
- Default application metrics with possibilities to extend
- Basic application monitoring using health checks
- Multiple options for externalized configuration

Spring Boot Hello World

We will start with building our first Spring Boot application in this chapter. We will use Maven to manage dependencies.

The following steps are involved in starting up with a Spring Boot application:

1. Configure spring-boot-starter-parent in your pom.xml file.
2. Configure the pom.xml file with the required starter projects.
3. Configure spring-boot-maven-plugin to be able to run the application.
4. Create your first Spring Boot launch class.

Let's start with step 1: configuring the starter projects.

Configure spring-boot-starter-parent

Let's start with a simple pom.xml file with spring-boot-starter-parent:

```
<project xmlns="http://maven.apache.org/POM/4.0.0"
  xmlns:xsi="http://www.w3.org/2001/XMLSchema-instance"
  xsi:schemaLocation="http://maven.apache.org/POM/4.0.0
  http://maven.apache.org/xsd/maven-4.0.0.xsd">
<modelVersion>4.0.0</modelVersion>
<groupId>com.mastering.spring</groupId>
<artifactId>springboot-example</artifactId>
<version>0.0.1-SNAPSHOT</version>
<name>First Spring Boot Example</name>
<packaging>war</packaging>
<parent>
  <groupId>org.springframework.boot</groupId>
  <artifactId>spring-boot-starter-parent</artifactId>
  <version>2.0.0.M1</version>
</parent>
<properties>
  <java.version>1.8</java.version>
</properties>
```

```xml
<repositories>
 <repository>
   <id>spring-milestones</id>
   <name>Spring Milestones</name>
   <url>https://repo.spring.io/milestone</url>
   <snapshots>
     <enabled>false</enabled>
   </snapshots>
 </repository>
</repositories>

<pluginRepositories>
 <pluginRepository>
   <id>spring-milestones</id>
   <name>Spring Milestones</name>
   <url>https://repo.spring.io/milestone</url>
     <snapshots>
       <enabled>false</enabled>
     </snapshots>
  </pluginRepository>
</pluginRepositories>

</project>
```

The first question is this: why do we need `spring-boot-starter-parent`?

A `spring-boot-starter-parent` dependency contains the default versions of Java to use, the default versions of dependencies that Spring Boot uses, and the default configuration of the Maven plugins.

> The `spring-boot-starter-parent` dependency is the parent POM providing dependency and plugin management for Spring Boot-based applications.

Let's look at some of the code inside `spring-boot-starter-parent` to get a deeper understanding about `spring-boot-starter-parent`.

spring-boot-starter-parent

The `spring-boot-starter-parent` dependency inherits from `spring-boot-dependencies`, which is defined at the top of the POM. The following code snippet shows an extract from `spring-boot-starter-parent`:

```
<parent>
  <groupId>org.springframework.boot</groupId>
  <artifactId>spring-boot-dependencies</artifactId>
  <version>2.0.0.M1</version>
  <relativePath>../../spring-boot-dependencies</relativePath>
</parent>
```

The `spring-boot-dependencies` provides default dependency management for all the dependencies that Spring Boot uses. The following code shows the different versions of various dependencies that are configured in `spring-boot-dependencies`:

```
<activemq.version>5.13.4</activemq.version>
<aspectj.version>1.8.9</aspectj.version>
<ehcache.version>2.10.2.2.21</ehcache.version>
<elasticsearch.version>2.3.4</elasticsearch.version>
<gson.version>2.7</gson.version>
<h2.version>1.4.192</h2.version>
<hazelcast.version>3.6.4</hazelcast.version>
<hibernate.version>5.0.9.Final</hibernate.version>
<hibernate-validator.version>5.2.4.Final</hibernate
  validator.version>
<hsqldb.version>2.3.3</hsqldb.version>
<htmlunit.version>2.21</htmlunit.version>
<jackson.version>2.8.1</jackson.version>
<jersey.version>2.23.1</jersey.version>
<jetty.version>9.3.11.v20160721</jetty.version>
<junit.version>4.12</junit.version>
<mockito.version>1.10.19</mockito.version>
<selenium.version>2.53.1</selenium.version>
<servlet-api.version>3.1.0</servlet-api.version>
<spring.version>4.3.2.RELEASE</spring.version>
<spring-amqp.version>1.6.1.RELEASE</spring-amqp.version>
<spring-batch.version>3.0.7.RELEASE</spring-batch.version>
<spring-data-releasetrain.version>Hopper-SR2</spring-
  data-releasetrain.version>
<spring-hateoas.version>0.20.0.RELEASE</spring-hateoas.version>
<spring-restdocs.version>1.1.1.RELEASE</spring-restdocs.version>
<spring-security.version>4.1.1.RELEASE</spring-security.version>
<spring-session.version>1.2.1.RELEASE</spring-session.version>
<spring-ws.version>2.3.0.RELEASE</spring-ws.version>
<thymeleaf.version>2.1.5.RELEASE</thymeleaf.version>
```

```
<tomcat.version>8.5.4</tomcat.version>
<xml-apis.version>1.4.01</xml-apis.version>
```

If we want to override a specific version of a dependency, we can do that by providing a property with the right name in the `pom.xml` file of our application. The following code snippet shows an example of configuring our application to use version 1.10.20 of Mockito:

```
<properties>
 <mockito.version>1.10.20</mockito.version>
</properties>
```

The following are some of the other things defined in `spring-boot-starter-parent`:

- The default Java version `<java.version>1.8</java.version>`
- The default configuration for Maven plugins:
    - `maven-failsafe-plugin`
    - `maven-surefire-plugin`
    - `git-commit-id-plugin`

Compatibility between different versions of frameworks is one of the major problems faced by developers. How do I find the latest Spring Session version that is compatible with a specific version of Spring? The usual answer would be to read the documentation. However, if we use Spring Boot, this is made simple by `spring-boot-starter-parent`. If we want to upgrade to a newer Spring version, all that we need to do is to find the `spring-boot-starter-parent` dependency for that Spring version. Once we upgrade our application to use that specific version of `spring-boot-starter-parent`, we would have all the other dependencies upgraded to the versions compatible with the new Spring version. One less problem for developers to handle. Always make me happy.

Configure pom.xml with the required starter projects

Whenever we want to build an application in Spring Boot, we would need to start looking for starter projects. Let's focus on understanding what a starter project is.

Understanding starter projects

Starters are simplified dependency descriptors customized for different purposes. For example, `spring-boot-starter-web` is the starter for building web apllication, including RESTful, using Spring MVC. It uses Tomcat as the default embedded container. If I want to develop a web application using Spring MVC, all we would need to do is include `spring-boot-starter-web` in our dependencies, and we get the following automatically pre-configured:

- Spring MVC
- Compatible versions of jackson-databind (for binding) and hibernate-validator (for form validation)
- `spring-boot-starter-tomcat` (starter project for Tomcat)

The following code snippet shows some of the dependencies configured in `spring-boot-starter-web`:

```xml
<dependencies>
    <dependency>
      <groupId>org.springframework.boot</groupId>
      <artifactId>spring-boot-starter</artifactId>
    </dependency>
    <dependency>
      <groupId>org.springframework.boot</groupId>
      <artifactId>spring-boot-starter-tomcat</artifactId>
    </dependency>
    <dependency>
      <groupId>org.hibernate</groupId>
      <artifactId>hibernate-validator</artifactId>
    </dependency>
    <dependency>
      <groupId>com.fasterxml.jackson.core</groupId>
      <artifactId>jackson-databind</artifactId>
    </dependency>
    <dependency>
      <groupId>org.springframework</groupId>
      <artifactId>spring-web</artifactId>
    </dependency>
    <dependency>
      <groupId>org.springframework</groupId>
      <artifactId>spring-webmvc</artifactId>
    </dependency>
</dependencies>
```

As we can see in the preceding snippet, when we use `spring-boot-starter-web`, we get a lot of frameworks auto-configured.

For the web application we would like to build, we would also want to do some good unit testing and deploy it on Tomcat. The following snippet shows the different starter dependencies that we would need. We would need to add this to our `pom.xml` file:

```xml
<dependencies>
  <dependency>
    <groupId>org.springframework.boot</groupId>
    <artifactId>spring-boot-starter-web</artifactId>
  </dependency>
  <dependency>
    <groupId>org.springframework.boot</groupId>
    <artifactId>spring-boot-starter-test</artifactId>
    <scope>test</scope>
  </dependency>
  <dependency>
    <groupId>org.springframework.boot</groupId>
    <artifactId>spring-boot-starter-tomcat</artifactId>
    <scope>provided</scope>
  </dependency>
</dependencies>
```

We add three starter projects:

- We've already discussed `spring-boot-starter-web`. It provides us with the frameworks needed to build a web application with Spring MVC.
- The `spring-boot-starter-test` dependency provides the following test frameworks needed for unit testing:
    - **JUnit**: Basic unit test framework
    - **Mockito**: For mocking
    - **Hamcrest, AssertJ**: For readable asserts
    - **Spring Test**: A unit testing framework for spring-context based applications
- The `spring-boot-starter-tomcat` dependency is the default for running web applications. We include it for clarity. `spring-boot-starter-tomcat` is the starter for using Tomcat as the embedded servlet container.

We now have our `pom.xml` file configured with the starter parent and the required starter projects. Let's add `spring-boot-maven-plugin` now, which would enable us to run Spring Boot applications.

Configuring spring-boot-maven-plugin

When we build applications using Spring Boot, there are a couple of situations that are possible:

- We would want to run the applications in place without building a JAR or a WAR
- We would want to build a JAR and a WAR for later deployment

The `spring-boot-maven-plugin` dependency provides capabilities for both of the preceding situations. The following snippet shows how we can configure `spring-boot-maven-plugin` in an application:

```
<build>
 <plugins>
  <plugin>
    <groupId>org.springframework.boot</groupId>
    <artifactId>spring-boot-maven-plugin</artifactId>
  </plugin>
 </plugins>
</build>
```

The `spring-boot-maven-plugin` dependency provides several goals for a Spring Boot application. The most popular goal is run (this can be executed as `mvn spring-boot:run` on the command prompt from the root folder of the project).

Creating your first Spring Boot launch class

The following class explains how to create a simple Spring Boot launch class. It uses the static run method from the `SpringApplication` class, as shown in the following code snippet:

```
package com.mastering.spring.springboot;
import org.springframework.boot.SpringApplication;
import org.springframework.boot.
autoconfigure.SpringBootApplication;
import org.springframework.context.ApplicationContext;
@SpringBootApplication public class Application {
```

```
public static void main(String[] args)
  {
   ApplicationContext ctx = SpringApplication.run
   (Application.class,args);
  }
}
```

The preceding code is a simple Java `main` method executing the static `run` method on the `SpringApplication` class.

SpringApplication class

The `SpringApplication` class can be used to Bootstrap and launch a Spring application from a Java `main` method.

The following are the steps that are typically performed when a Spring Boot application is bootstrapped:

1. Create an instance of Spring's `ApplicationContext`.
2. Enable the functionality to accept command-line arguments and expose them as Spring properties.
3. Load all the Spring beans as per the configuration.

The @SpringBootApplication annotation

The `@SpringBootApplication` annotation is a shortcut for three annotations:

- `@Configuration`: Indicates that this a Spring application context configuration file.
- `@EnableAutoConfiguration`: Enables auto-configuration, an important feature of Spring Boot. We will discuss auto-configuration later in a separate section.
- `@ComponentScan`: Enables scanning for Spring beans in the package of this class and all its subpackages.

Running our Hello World application

We can run the Hello World application in multiple ways. Let's start running it with the simplest option--running as a Java application. In your IDE, right-click on the application **class** and run it as **Java Application**. The following screenshot shows some of the log from running our Hello World application:

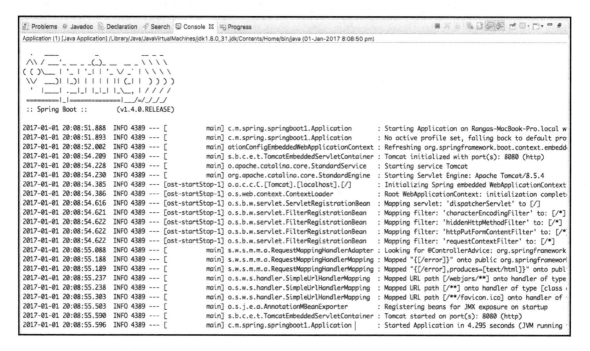

The following are the key things to note:

- Tomcat server is launched on port 8080--Tomcat started on port(s): 8080 (http).
- DispatcherServlet is configured. This means that Spring MVC Framework is ready to accept requests--Mapping servlet: 'dispatcherServlet' to [/].

- Four filters--`characterEncodingFilter`, `hiddenHttpMethodFilter`, `httpPutFormContentFilter` and `requestContextFilter`--are enabled by default
- The default error page is configured--`Mapped "{[/error]}" onto public org.springframework.http.ResponseEntity<java.util.Map<java.lang.String, java.lang.Object>> org.springframework.boot.autoconfigure.web.BasicErrorController.error(javax.servlet.http.HttpServletRequest)`
- WebJars are autoconfigured. As we discussed in `Chapter 3`, *Building a Web Application with Spring MVC*, WebJars enable dependency management for static dependencies such as Bootstrap and query--`Mapped URL path [/webjars/**] onto handler of type [class org.springframework.web.servlet.resource.ResourceHttpRequestHandler]`

The following screenshot shows the application layout as of now. We have just two files, `pom.xml` and `Application.java`:

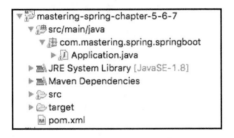

With a simple `pom.xml` file and one Java class, we were able to get to launch the Spring MVC application, with all the preceding functionality described. The most important thing about Spring Boot is to understand what happens in the background. Understanding the preceding start up log is the first. Let's look at the Maven dependencies to get a deeper picture.

The following screenshot shows some of the dependencies that are configured with the basic configuration in the `pom.xml` file that we created:

```
▶ 🏷 spring-boot-starter-web-1.4.0.RELEASE.jar - /Users/rangaraokaranam/.m2/repository/org/springframework/boot/spring-boot-starter-web/1.4.0.RELEASE
▶ 🏷 spring-boot-starter-1.4.0.RELEASE.jar - /Users/rangaraokaranam/.m2/repository/org/springframework/boot/spring-boot-starter/1.4.0.RELEASE
▶ 🏷 spring-boot-1.4.0.RELEASE.jar - /Users/rangaraokaranam/.m2/repository/org/springframework/boot/spring-boot/1.4.0.RELEASE
▶ 🏷 spring-boot-autoconfigure-1.4.0.RELEASE.jar - /Users/rangaraokaranam/.m2/repository/org/springframework/boot/spring-boot-autoconfigure/1.4.0.RELEASE
▶ 🏷 spring-boot-starter-logging-1.4.0.RELEASE.jar - /Users/rangaraokaranam/.m2/repository/org/springframework/boot/spring-boot-starter-logging/1.4.0.RELEASE
▶ 🏷 logback-classic-1.1.7.jar - /Users/rangaraokaranam/.m2/repository/ch/qos/logback/logback-classic/1.1.7
▶ 🏷 logback-core-1.1.7.jar - /Users/rangaraokaranam/.m2/repository/ch/qos/logback/logback-core/1.1.7
▶ 🏷 jcl-over-slf4j-1.7.21.jar - /Users/rangaraokaranam/.m2/repository/org/slf4j/jcl-over-slf4j/1.7.21
▶ 🏷 jul-to-slf4j-1.7.21.jar - /Users/rangaraokaranam/.m2/repository/org/slf4j/jul-to-slf4j/1.7.21
▶ 🏷 log4j-over-slf4j-1.7.21.jar - /Users/rangaraokaranam/.m2/repository/org/slf4j/log4j-over-slf4j/1.7.21
▶ 🏷 snakeyaml-1.17.jar - /Users/rangaraokaranam/.m2/repository/org/yaml/snakeyaml/1.17
▶ 🏷 hibernate-validator-5.2.4.Final.jar - /Users/rangaraokaranam/.m2/repository/org/hibernate/hibernate-validator/5.2.4.Final
▶ 🏷 validation-api-1.1.0.Final.jar - /Users/rangaraokaranam/.m2/repository/javax/validation/validation-api/1.1.0.Final
▶ 🏷 jboss-logging-3.3.0.Final.jar - /Users/rangaraokaranam/.m2/repository/org/jboss/logging/jboss-logging/3.3.0.Final
▶ 🏷 classmate-1.3.1.jar - /Users/rangaraokaranam/.m2/repository/com/fasterxml/classmate/1.3.1
▶ 🏷 jackson-databind-2.8.1.jar - /Users/rangaraokaranam/.m2/repository/com/fasterxml/jackson/core/jackson-databind/2.8.1
▶ 🏷 jackson-annotations-2.8.1.jar - /Users/rangaraokaranam/.m2/repository/com/fasterxml/jackson/core/jackson-annotations/2.8.1
▶ 🏷 jackson-core-2.8.1.jar - /Users/rangaraokaranam/.m2/repository/com/fasterxml/jackson/core/jackson-core/2.8.1
▶ 🏷 spring-web-4.3.2.RELEASE.jar - /Users/rangaraokaranam/.m2/repository/org/springframework/spring-web/4.3.2.RELEASE
▶ 🏷 spring-aop-4.3.2.RELEASE.jar - /Users/rangaraokaranam/.m2/repository/org/springframework/spring-aop/4.3.2.RELEASE
▶ 🏷 spring-beans-4.3.2.RELEASE.jar - /Users/rangaraokaranam/.m2/repository/org/springframework/spring-beans/4.3.2.RELEASE
▶ 🏷 spring-context-4.3.2.RELEASE.jar - /Users/rangaraokaranam/.m2/repository/org/springframework/spring-context/4.3.2.RELEASE
▶ 🏷 spring-webmvc-4.3.2.RELEASE.jar - /Users/rangaraokaranam/.m2/repository/org/springframework/spring-webmvc/4.3.2.RELEASE
▶ 🏷 spring-expression-4.3.2.RELEASE.jar - /Users/rangaraokaranam/.m2/repository/org/springframework/spring-expression/4.3.2.RELEASE
▶ 🏷 spring-boot-starter-test-1.4.0.RELEASE.jar - /Users/rangaraokaranam/.m2/repository/org/springframework/boot/spring-boot-starter-test/1.4.0.RELEASE
▶ 🏷 spring-boot-test-1.4.0.RELEASE.jar - /Users/rangaraokaranam/.m2/repository/org/springframework/boot/spring-boot-test/1.4.0.RELEASE
▶ 🏷 spring-boot-test-autoconfigure-1.4.0.RELEASE.jar - /Users/rangaraokaranam/.m2/repository/org/springframework/boot/spring-boot-test-autoconfigure/1.4.0.RELEASE
▶ 🏷 json-path-2.2.0.jar - /Users/rangaraokaranam/.m2/repository/com/jayway/jsonpath/json-path/2.2.0
▶ 🏷 json-smart-2.2.1.jar - /Users/rangaraokaranam/.m2/repository/net/minidev/json-smart/2.2.1
▶ 🏷 accessors-smart-1.1.jar - /Users/rangaraokaranam/.m2/repository/net/minidev/accessors-smart/1.1
▶ 🏷 asm-5.0.3.jar - /Users/rangaraokaranam/.m2/repository/org/ow2/asm/asm/5.0.3
▶ 🏷 slf4j-api-1.7.21.jar - /Users/rangaraokaranam/.m2/repository/org/slf4j/slf4j-api/1.7.21
▶ 🏷 junit-4.12.jar - /Users/rangaraokaranam/.m2/repository/junit/junit/4.12
▶ 🏷 assertj-core-2.5.0.jar - /Users/rangaraokaranam/.m2/repository/org/assertj/assertj-core/2.5.0
▶ 🏷 mockito-core-1.10.19.jar - /Users/rangaraokaranam/.m2/repository/org/mockito/mockito-core/1.10.19
```

Spring Boot does a lot of magic. Once you have the application configured and running, I recommend that you play around with it to gain a deeper understanding that will be useful when you are debugging problems.

As Spiderman says, *with great power, comes great responsibility*. This is absolutely true in the case of Spring Boot. In the time to come, the best developers with Spring Boot would be the ones who understand what happens in the background--dependencies and auto-configuration.

Auto-configuration

To enable us to understand auto-configuration further, let's expand our application class to include a few more lines of code:

```
ApplicationContext ctx = SpringApplication.run(Application.class,
  args);
String[] beanNames = ctx.getBeanDefinitionNames();
```

```
    Arrays.sort(beanNames);

  for (String beanName : beanNames) {
    System.out.println(beanName);
  }
```

We get all the beans that are defined in the Spring application context and print their names. When `Application.java` is run as a Java program, it prints the list of beans, as shown in the following output :

```
application
basicErrorController
beanNameHandlerMapping
beanNameViewResolver
characterEncodingFilter
conventionErrorViewResolver
defaultServletHandlerMapping
defaultViewResolver
dispatcherServlet
dispatcherServletRegistration
duplicateServerPropertiesDetector
embeddedServletContainerCustomizerBeanPostProcessor
error
errorAttributes
errorPageCustomizer
errorPageRegistrarBeanPostProcessor
faviconHandlerMapping
faviconRequestHandler
handlerExceptionResolver
hiddenHttpMethodFilter
httpPutFormContentFilter
httpRequestHandlerAdapter
jacksonObjectMapper
jacksonObjectMapperBuilder
jsonComponentModule
localeCharsetMappingsCustomizer
mappingJackson2HttpMessageConverter
mbeanExporter
mbeanServer
messageConverters
multipartConfigElement
multipartResolver
mvcContentNegotiationManager
mvcConversionService
mvcPathMatcher
mvcResourceUrlProvider
mvcUriComponentsContributor
mvcUrlPathHelper
```

```
mvcValidator
mvcViewResolver
objectNamingStrategy
autoconfigure.AutoConfigurationPackages
autoconfigure.PropertyPlaceholderAutoConfiguration
autoconfigure.condition.BeanTypeRegistry
autoconfigure.context.ConfigurationPropertiesAutoConfiguration
autoconfigure.info.ProjectInfoAutoConfiguration
autoconfigure.internalCachingMetadataReaderFactory
autoconfigure.jackson.JacksonAutoConfiguration
autoconfigure.jackson.JacksonAutoConfiguration$Jackson2ObjectMapperBuilderC
ustomizerConfiguration
autoconfigure.jackson.JacksonAutoConfiguration$JacksonObjectMapperBuilderCo
nfiguration
autoconfigure.jackson.JacksonAutoConfiguration$JacksonObjectMapperConfigura
tion
autoconfigure.jmx.JmxAutoConfiguration
autoconfigure.web.DispatcherServletAutoConfiguration
autoconfigure.web.DispatcherServletAutoConfiguration$DispatcherServletConfi
guration
autoconfigure.web.DispatcherServletAutoConfiguration$DispatcherServletRegis
trationConfiguration
autoconfigure.web.EmbeddedServletContainerAutoConfiguration
autoconfigure.web.EmbeddedServletContainerAutoConfiguration$EmbeddedTomcat
autoconfigure.web.ErrorMvcAutoConfiguration
autoconfigure.web.ErrorMvcAutoConfiguration$WhitelabelErrorViewConfiguratio
n
autoconfigure.web.HttpEncodingAutoConfiguration
autoconfigure.web.HttpMessageConvertersAutoConfiguration
autoconfigure.web.HttpMessageConvertersAutoConfiguration$StringHttpMessageC
onverterConfiguration
autoconfigure.web.JacksonHttpMessageConvertersConfiguration
autoconfigure.web.JacksonHttpMessageConvertersConfiguration$MappingJackson2
HttpMessageConverterConfiguration
autoconfigure.web.MultipartAutoConfiguration
autoconfigure.web.ServerPropertiesAutoConfiguration
autoconfigure.web.WebClientAutoConfiguration
autoconfigure.web.WebClientAutoConfiguration$RestTemplateConfiguration
autoconfigure.web.WebMvcAutoConfiguration
autoconfigure.web.WebMvcAutoConfiguration$EnableWebMvcConfiguration
autoconfigure.web.WebMvcAutoConfiguration$WebMvcAutoConfigurationAdapter
autoconfigure.web.WebMvcAutoConfiguration$WebMvcAutoConfigurationAdapter$Fa
viconConfiguration
autoconfigure.websocket.WebSocketAutoConfiguration
autoconfigure.websocket.WebSocketAutoConfiguration$TomcatWebSocketConfigura
tion
context.properties.ConfigurationPropertiesBindingPostProcessor
context.properties.ConfigurationPropertiesBindingPostProcessor.store
```

```
annotation.ConfigurationClassPostProcessor.enhancedConfigurationProcessor
annotation.ConfigurationClassPostProcessor.importAwareProcessor
annotation.internalAutowiredAnnotationProcessor
annotation.internalCommonAnnotationProcessor
annotation.internalConfigurationAnnotationProcessor
annotation.internalRequiredAnnotationProcessor
event.internalEventListenerFactory
event.internalEventListenerProcessor
preserveErrorControllerTargetClassPostProcessor
propertySourcesPlaceholderConfigurer
requestContextFilter
requestMappingHandlerAdapter
requestMappingHandlerMapping
resourceHandlerMapping
restTemplateBuilder
serverProperties
simpleControllerHandlerAdapter
spring.http.encoding-autoconfigure.web.HttpEncodingProperties
spring.http.multipart-autoconfigure.web.MultipartProperties
spring.info-autoconfigure.info.ProjectInfoProperties
spring.jackson-autoconfigure.jackson.JacksonProperties
spring.mvc-autoconfigure.web.WebMvcProperties
spring.resources-autoconfigure.web.ResourceProperties
standardJacksonObjectMapperBuilderCustomizer
stringHttpMessageConverter
tomcatEmbeddedServletContainerFactory
viewControllerHandlerMapping
viewResolver
websocketContainerCustomizer
```

Important things to think about are as follows:

- Where are these beans defined?
- How are these beans created?

That's the magic of Spring auto-configuration.

Whenever we add a new dependency to a Spring Boot project, Spring Boot auto-configuration automatically tries to configure the beans based on the dependency.

For example, when we add a dependency in `spring-boot-starter-web`, the following beans are auto-configured:

- `basicErrorController`, `handlerExceptionResolver`: Basic exception handling. Shows a default error page when an exception occurs.
- `beanNameHandlerMapping`: Used to resolve paths to a handler (controller).

- `characterEncodingFilter`: Provides default character encoding UTF-8.
- `dispatcherServlet`: DispatcherServlet is the Front Controller in Spring MVC applications.
- `jacksonObjectMapper`: Translates objects to JSON and JSON to objects in REST services.
- `messageConverters`: The default message converters to convert from objects into XML or JSON and vice versa.
- `multipartResolver`: Provides support to upload files in web applications.
- `mvcValidator`: Supports validation of HTTP requests.
- `viewResolver`: Resolves a logical view name to a physical view.
- `propertySourcesPlaceholderConfigurer`: Supports the externalization of application configuration.
- `requestContextFilter`: Defaults the filter for requests.
- `restTemplateBuilder`: Used to make calls to REST services.
- `tomcatEmbeddedServletContainerFactory`: Tomcat is the default embedded servlet container for Spring Boot-based web applications.

In the next section, let's look at some of the starter projects and the auto-configuration they provide.

Starter projects

The following table shows some of the important starter projects provided by Spring Boot:

Starter	Description
`spring-boot-starter-web-services`	This is a starter project to develop XML-based web services.
`spring-boot-starter-web`	This is a starter project to build Spring MVC-based web applications or RESTful applications. It uses Tomcat as the default embedded servlet container.
`spring-boot-starter-activemq`	This supports message-based communication using JMS on ActiveMQ.
`spring-boot-starter-integration`	This supports the Spring Integration Framework that provides implementations for Enterprise Integration Patterns.

`spring-boot-starter-test`	This provides support for various unit testing frameworks, such as JUnit, Mockito, and Hamcrest matchers.
`spring-boot-starter-jdbc`	This provides support for using Spring JDBC. It configures a Tomcat JDBC connection pool by default.
`spring-boot-starter-validation`	This provides support for the Java Bean Validation API. Its default implementation is hibernate-validator.
`spring-boot-starter-hateoas`	HATEOAS stands for Hypermedia as the Engine of Application State. RESTful services that use HATEOAS return links to additional resources that are related to the current context in addition to data.
`spring-boot-starter-jersey`	JAX-RS is the Java EE standard to develop REST APIs. Jersey is the default implementation. This starter project provides support to build JAX-RS-based REST APIs.
`spring-boot-starter-websocket`	HTTP is stateless. WebSockets allow you to maintain a connection between the server and the browser. This starter project provides support for Spring WebSockets.
`spring-boot-starter-aop`	This provides support for Aspect Oriented Programming. It also provides support for AspectJ for advanced aspect-oriented programming.
`spring-boot-starter-amqp`	With RabbitMQ as the default, this starter project provides message passing with AMQP.
`spring-boot-starter-security`	This starter project enables auto-configuration for Spring Security.
`spring-boot-starter-data-jpa`	This provides support for Spring Data JPA. Its default implementation is Hibernate.
`spring-boot-starter`	This is a base starter for Spring Boot applications. It provides support for auto-configuration and logging.
`spring-boot-starter-batch`	This provides support to develop batch applications using Spring Batch.

`spring-boot-starter-cache`	This is the basic support for caching using Spring Framework.
`spring-boot-starter-data-rest`	This is the support to expose REST services using Spring Data REST.

Until now, we have set up a basic web application and understood some of the important concepts related to Spring Boot:

- Auto-configuration
- Starter projects
- `spring-boot-maven-plugin`
- `spring-boot-starter-parent`
- Annotation `@SpringBootApplication`

Now let's shift our focus to understanding what REST is and building a REST Service.

What is REST?

Representational State Transfer (**REST**) is basically an architectural style for the web. REST specifies a set of constraints. These constraints ensure that clients (service consumers and browsers) can interact with servers in flexible ways.

Let's first understand some common terminologies:

- **Server**: Service provider. Exposes services which can be consumed by clients.
- **Client**: Service consumer. Could be a browser or another system.
- **Resource**: Any information can be a resource: a person, an image, a video, or a product you want to sell.
- **Representation**: A specific way a resource can be represented. For example, the product resource can be represented using JSON, XML, or HTML. Different clients might request different representations of the resource.

Some of the important REST constraints are listed as follows:

- **Client-Server**: There should be a server (service provider) and a client (service consumer). This enables loose coupling and independent evolution of the server and client as new technologies emerge.

- **Stateless**: Each service should be stateless. Subsequent requests should not depend on some data from a previous request being temporarily stored. Messages should be self-descriptive.
- **Uniform interface**: Each resource has a resource identifier. In the case of web services, we use this URI example: `/users/Jack/todos/1`. In this, URI Jack is the name of the user. `1` is the ID of the todo we would want to retrieve.
- **Cacheable**: The service response should be cacheable. Each response should indicate whether it is cacheable.
- **Layered system**: The consumer of the service should not assume a direct connection to the service provider. Since requests can be cached, the client might be getting the cached response from a middle layer.
- **Manipulation of resources through representations**: A resource can have multiple representations. It should be possible to modify the resource through a message with any of these representations.
- **Hypermedia as the engine of application state** (**HATEOAS**): The consumer of a RESTful application should know about only one fixed service URL. All subsequent resources should be discoverable from the links included in the resource representations.

An example response with the HATEOAS link is shown here. This is the response to a request to retrieve all todos:

```
{
"_embedded":{
"todos":[
        {
            "user":"Jill",
            "desc":"Learn Hibernate",
            "done":false,
            "_links":{
              "self":{
                    "href":"http://localhost:8080/todos/1"
                },
                "todo":{
                    "href":"http://localhost:8080/todos/1"
                }
            }
        }
    ]
},
"_links":{
    "self":{
        "href":"http://localhost:8080/todos"
    },
```

```
        "profile":{
            "href":"http://localhost:8080/profile/todos"
        },
        "search":{
            "href":"http://localhost:8080/todos/search"
        }
    }
}
```

The preceding response includes links to the following:

- Specific todos (`http://localhost:8080/todos/1`)
- Search resource (`http://localhost:8080/todos/search`)

If the service consumer wants to do a search, it has the option of taking the search URL from the response and sending the search request to it. This would reduce coupling between the service provider and the service consumer.

The initial services we develop will not be adhering to all these constraints. As we move on to the next chapters, we will introduce you to the details of these constraints and add them to the services to make them more RESTful.

First REST service

Let's start with creating a simple REST service returning a welcome message. We will create a simple POJO `WelcomeBean` class with a member field called message and one argument constructor, as shown in the following code snippet:

```
package com.mastering.spring.springboot.bean;

public class WelcomeBean {
  private String message;

    public WelcomeBean(String message) {
      super();
      this.message = message;
    }

    public String getMessage() {
      return message;
    }
  }
```

Simple method returning string

Let's start with creating a simple REST Controller method returning a string:

```
@RestController
public class BasicController {
  @GetMapping("/welcome")
  public String welcome() {
    return "Hello World";
  }
}
```

A few important things to note are as follows:

- @RestController: The @RestController annotation provides a combination of @ResponseBody and @Controller annotations. This is typically used to create REST Controllers.
- @GetMapping("welcome"): @GetMapping is a shortcut for @RequestMapping(method = RequestMethod.GET). This annotation is a readable alternative. The method with this annotation would handle a Get request to the welcome URI.

If we run Application.java as a Java application, it would start up the embedded Tomcat container. We can launch up the URL in the browser, as shown in the following screenshot:

Unit testing

Let's quickly write a unit test to test the preceding controller method:

```
@RunWith(SpringRunner.class)
@WebMvcTest(BasicController.class)
public class BasicControllerTest {

  @Autowired
  private MockMvc mvc;
```

```
@Test
public void welcome() throws Exception {
  mvc.perform(
  MockMvcRequestBuilders.get("/welcome")
  .accept(MediaType.APPLICATION_JSON))
  .andExpect(status().isOk())
  .andExpect(content().string(
  equalTo("Hello World")));
  }
}
```

In the preceding unit test, we will launch up a Mock MVC instance with
`BasicController`. A few quick things to note are as follows:

- `@RunWith(SpringRunner.class)`: SpringRunner is a shortcut to the
  `SpringJUnit4ClassRunner` annotation. This launches up a simple Spring
  context for unit testing.
- `@WebMvcTest(BasicController.class)`: This annotation can be used along
  with SpringRunner to write simple tests for Spring MVC controllers. This will
  load only the beans annotated with Spring-MVC-related annotations. In this
  example, we are launching a Web MVC Test context with the class under test
  being BasicController.
- `@Autowired private MockMvc mvc`: Autowires the MockMvc bean that can be
  used to make requests.
- `mvc.perform(MockMvcRequestBuilders.get("/welcome").accept(Media
  Type.APPLICATION_JSON))`: Performs a request to `/welcome` with the `Accept`
  header value `application/json`.
- `andExpect(status().isOk())`: Expects that the status of the response is 200
  (success).
- `andExpect(content().string(equalTo("Hello World")))`: Expects that
  the content of the response is equal to `"Hello World"`.

Integration testing

When we do integration testing, we would want to launch the embedded server with all the
controllers and beans that are configured. This code snippet shows how we can create a
simple integration test:

```
@RunWith(SpringRunner.class)
@SpringBootTest(classes = Application.class,
webEnvironment = SpringBootTest.WebEnvironment.RANDOM_PORT)
public class BasicControllerIT {
```

```
private static final String LOCAL_HOST =
"http://localhost:";

@LocalServerPort
private int port;

private TestRestTemplate template = new TestRestTemplate();

@Test
public void welcome() throws Exception {
  ResponseEntity<String> response = template
  .getForEntity(createURL("/welcome"), String.class);
  assertThat(response.getBody(), equalTo("Hello World"));
  }

private String createURL(String uri) {
  return LOCAL_HOST + port + uri;
  }
}
```

A few important things to note are as follows:

- `@SpringBootTest(classes = Application.class, webEnvironment = SpringBootTest.WebEnvironment.RANDOM_PORT)`: Provides additional functionality on top of the Spring TestContext. Provides support to configure the port for fully running the container and TestRestTemplate (to execute requests).
- `@LocalServerPort private int port`: `SpringBootTest` would ensure that the port on which the container is running is autowired into the port variable.
- `private String createURL(String uri)`: The method to append the local host URL and port to the URI to create a full URL.
- `private TestRestTemplate template = new TestRestTemplate()`: `TestRestTemplate` is typically used in integration tests. It provides additional functionality on top of RestTemplate, which is especially useful in the integration test context. It does not follow redirects so that we can assert response location.
- `template.getForEntity(createURL("/welcome"), String.class)`: Executes a get request for the given URI.
- `assertThat(response.getBody(), equalTo("Hello World"))`: Asserts that the response body content is `"Hello World"`.

Simple REST method returning an object

In the previous method, we returned a string. Let's create a method that returns a proper JSON response. Take a look at the following method:

```
@GetMapping("/welcome-with-object")
public WelcomeBean welcomeWithObject() {
  return new WelcomeBean("Hello World");
}
```

This preceding method returns a simple `WelcomeBean` initialized with a message: `"Hello World"`.

Executing a request

Let's send a test request and see what response we get. The following screenshot shows the output:

The response for the `http://localhost:8080/welcome-with-object` URL is shown as follows:

```
{"message":"Hello World"}
```

The question that needs to be answered is this: how does the `WelcomeBean` object that we returned get converted into JSON?

Again, it's the magic of Spring Boot auto-configuration. If Jackson is on the classpath of an application, instances of the default object to JSON (and vice versa) converters are auto-configured by Spring Boot.

Unit testing

Let's quickly write a unit test checking for the JSON response. Let's add the test to `BasicControllerTest`:

```
@Test
public void welcomeWithObject() throws Exception {
  mvc.perform(
    MockMvcRequestBuilders.get("/welcome-with-object")
   .accept(MediaType.APPLICATION_JSON))
   .andExpect(status().isOk())
   .andExpect(content().string(containsString("Hello World")));
}
```

This test is very similar to the earlier unit test except that we are using `containsString` to check whether the content contains a substring `"Hello World"`. We will learn how to write proper JSON tests a little later.

Integration testing

Let's shift our focus to writing an integration test. Let's add a method to `BasicControllerIT`, as shown in the following code snippet:

```
@Test
public void welcomeWithObject() throws Exception {
  ResponseEntity<String> response =
  template.getForEntity(createURL("/welcome-with-object"),
  String.class);
  assertThat(response.getBody(),
  containsString("Hello World"));
}
```

This method is similar to the earlier integration test except that we are asserting for a substring using the `String` method.

Get method with path variables

Let's shift our attention to path variables. Path variables are used to bind values from the URI to a variable on the controller method. In the following example, we want to parameterize the name so that we can customize the welcome message with a name:

```
private static final String helloWorldTemplate = "Hello World,
%s!";
```

```
@GetMapping("/welcome-with-parameter/name/{name}")
public WelcomeBean welcomeWithParameter(@PathVariable String name)
{
    return new WelcomeBean(String.format(helloWorldTemplate, name));
}
```

A few important things to note are as follows:

- `@GetMapping("/welcome-with-parameter/name/{name}")`: `{name}` indicates that this value will be the variable. We can have multiple variable templates in a URI.
- `welcomeWithParameter(@PathVariable String name)`: `@PathVariable` ensures that the variable value from the URI is bound to the variable name.
- `String.format(helloWorldTemplate, name)`: A simple string format to replace `%s` in the template with the name.

Executing a request

Let's send a test request and see what response we get. The following screenshot shows the response:

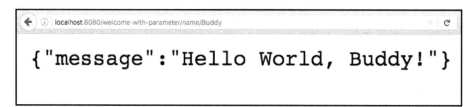

The response for the `http://localhost:8080/welcome-with-parameter/name/Buddy` URL is as follows:

```
{"message":"Hello World, Buddy!"}
```

As expected, the name in the URI is used to form the message in the response.

Unit testing

Let's quickly write a unit test for the preceding method. We would want to pass a name as part of the URI and check whether the response contains the name. The following code shows how we can do that:

```
@Test
public void welcomeWithParameter() throws Exception {
  mvc.perform(
  MockMvcRequestBuilders.get("/welcome-with-parameter/name/Buddy")
  .accept(MediaType.APPLICATION_JSON))
  .andExpect(status().isOk())
  .andExpect(
  content().string(containsString("Hello World, Buddy")));
}
```

A few important things to note are as follows:

- `MockMvcRequestBuilders.get("/welcome-with-parameter/name/Buddy")`: This matches against the variable template in the URI. We pass in the name `Buddy`.
- `.andExpect(content().string(containsString("Hello World, Buddy")))`: We expect the response to contain the message with the name.

Integration testing

The integration test for the preceding method is very simple. Take a look at the following test method:

```
@Test
public void welcomeWithParameter() throws Exception {
  ResponseEntity<String> response =
  template.getForEntity(
  createURL("/welcome-with-parameter/name/Buddy"), String.class);
  assertThat(response.getBody(),
  containsString("Hello World, Buddy"));
}
```

A few important things to note are as follows:

- `createURL("/welcome-with-parameter/name/Buddy")`: This matches against the variable template in the URI. We are passing in the name, Buddy.
- `assertThat(response.getBody(), containsString("Hello World, Buddy"))`: We expect the response to contain the message with the name.

In this section, we looked at the basics of creating a simple REST service with Spring Boot. We also ensured that we have good unit tests and integration tests. While these are really basic, they lay the foundation for more complex REST services we will build in the next section.

The unit tests and integration tests we implemented can have better asserts using a JSON comparison instead of a simple substring comparison. We will focus on it in the tests we write for the REST services we will create in the next sections.

Creating a todo resource

We will focus on creating REST services for a basic todo management system. We will create services for the following:

- Retrieving a list of todos for a given user
- Retrieving details for a specific todo
- Creating a todo for a user

Request methods, operations, and URIs

One of the best practices of REST services is to use the appropriate HTTP request method based on the action we perform. In the services we exposed until now, we used the `GET` method, as we focused on services that read data.

The following table shows the appropriate HTTP Request method based on the operation that we perform:

HTTP Request Method	Operation
GET	Read--Retrieve details for a resource
POST	Create--Create a new item or resource
PUT	Update/replace
PATCH	Update/modify a part of the resource
DELETE	Delete

Let's quickly map the services that we want to create to the appropriate request methods:

- **Retrieving a list of todos for a given user**: This is READ. We will use GET. We will use a URI: /users/{name}/todos. One more good practice is to use plurals for static things in the URI: users, todo, and so on. This results in more readable URIs.
- **Retrieving details for a specific todo**: Again, we will use GET. We will use a URI /users/{name}/todos/{id}. You can see that this is consistent with the earlier URI that we decided for the list of todos.
- **Creating a todo for a user**: For the create operation, the suggested HTTP Request method is POST. To create a new todo, we will post to URI /users/{name}/todos.

Beans and services

To be able to retrieve and store details of a todo, we need a Todo bean and a service to retrieve and store the details.

Let's create a Todo Bean:

```
public class Todo {
  private int id;
  private String user;

  private String desc;

  private Date targetDate;
  private boolean isDone;

  public Todo() {}
```

```
      public Todo(int id, String user, String desc,
      Date targetDate, boolean isDone) {
         super();
         this.id = id;
         this.user = user;
         this.desc = desc;
         this.targetDate = targetDate;
         this.isDone = isDone;
      }

      //ALL Getters
   }
```

We have a created a simple Todo bean with the ID, the name of user, the description of the todo, the todo target date, and an indicator for the completion status. We added a constructor and getters for all fields.

Let's add `TodoService` now:

```
@Service
public class TodoService {
   private static List<Todo> todos = new ArrayList<Todo>();
   private static int todoCount = 3;

   static {
      todos.add(new Todo(1, "Jack", "Learn Spring MVC",
      new Date(), false));
      todos.add(new Todo(2, "Jack", "Learn Struts", new Date(),
      false));
      todos.add(new Todo(3, "Jill", "Learn Hibernate", new Date(),
      false));
   }

   public List<Todo> retrieveTodos(String user) {
      List<Todo> filteredTodos = new ArrayList<Todo>();
      for (Todo todo : todos) {
         if (todo.getUser().equals(user))
         filteredTodos.add(todo);
      }
      return filteredTodos;
   }

   public Todo addTodo(String name, String desc,
   Date targetDate, boolean isDone) {
      Todo todo = new Todo(++todoCount, name, desc, targetDate,
      isDone);
      todos.add(todo);
      return todo;
```

```
    }

    public Todo retrieveTodo(int id) {
      for (Todo todo : todos) {
      if (todo.getId() == id)
        return todo;
      }
      return null;
    }
  }
```

Quick things to note are as follows:

- To keep things simple, this service does not talk to the database. It maintains an in-memory array list of todos. This list is initialized using a static initializer.
- We are exposing a couple of simple retrieve methods and a method to add a to-do.

Now that we have the service and bean ready, we can create our first service to retrieve a list of to-do's for a user.

Retrieving a Todo list

We will create a new `RestController` annotation called `TodoController`. The code for the retrieve todos method is shown as follows:

```
@RestController
public class TodoController {
 @Autowired
 private TodoService todoService;

 @GetMapping("/users/{name}/todos")
 public List<Todo> retrieveTodos(@PathVariable String name) {
    return todoService.retrieveTodos(name);
 }
}
```

A couple of things to note are as follows:

- We are autowiring the todo service using the `@Autowired` annotation
- We use the `@GetMapping` annotation to map the Get request for the `"/users/{name}/todos"` URI to the `retrieveTodos` method

Executing the service

Let's send a test request and see what response we get. The following screenshot shows the output:

The response for the `http://localhost:8080/users/Jack/todos` URL is as follows:

```
[
 {"id":1,"user":"Jack","desc":"Learn Spring
  MVC","targetDate":1481607268779,"done":false},
 {"id":2,"user":"Jack","desc":"Learn
 Struts","targetDate":1481607268779, "done":false}
]
```

Unit testing

The code to unit test the `TodoController` class is shown in the following screenshot:

```
@RunWith(SpringRunner.class)
@WebMvcTest(TodoController.class)
public class TodoControllerTest {

  @Autowired
  private MockMvc mvc;

  @MockBean
  private TodoService service;

  @Test
  public void retrieveTodos() throws Exception {
   List<Todo> mockList = Arrays.asList(new Todo(1, "Jack",
   "Learn Spring MVC", new Date(), false), new Todo(2, "Jack",
   "Learn Struts", new Date(), false));

   when(service.retrieveTodos(anyString())).thenReturn(mockList);
   MvcResult result = mvc
   .perform(MockMvcRequestBuilders.get("/users
   /Jack/todos").accept(MediaType.APPLICATION_JSON))
   .andExpect(status().isOk()).andReturn();
```

```
String expected = "["
  + "{id:1,user:Jack,desc:\"Learn Spring MVC\",done:false}" +","
  + "{id:2,user:Jack,desc:\"Learn Struts\",done:false}" + "]";

JSONAssert.assertEquals(expected, result.getResponse()
  .getContentAsString(), false);
  }
}
```

A few important things to note are as follows:

- We are writing a unit test. So, we want to test only the logic present in the `TodoController` class. So, we initialize a Mock MVC framework with only the `TodoController` class using `@WebMvcTest(TodoController.class)`.
- `@MockBean private TodoService service`: We are mocking out the TodoService using the `@MockBean` annotation. In test classes that are run with SpringRunner, the beans defined with `@MockBean` will be replaced by a mock, created using the Mockito framework.
- `when(service.retrieveTodos(anyString())).thenReturn(mockList)`: We are mocking the retrieveTodos service method to return the mock list.
- `MvcResult result = ..`: We are accepting the result of the request into an MvcResult variable to enable us to perform assertions on the response.
- `JSONAssert.assertEquals(expected, result.getResponse().getContentAsString(), false)`: JSONAssert is a very useful framework to perform asserts on JSON. It compares the response text with the expected value. JSONAssert is intelligent enough to ignore values that are not specified. Another advantage is a clear failure message in case of assertion failures. The last parameter, false, indicates using non-strict mode. If it is changed to true, then the expected should exactly match the result.

Integration testing

The code to perform integration testing on the `TodoController` class is shown in the following code snippet. It launches up the entire Spring context with all the controllers and beans defined:

```
@RunWith(SpringJUnit4ClassRunner.class)
@SpringBootTest(classes = Application.class, webEnvironment =
SpringBootTest.WebEnvironment.RANDOM_PORT)
public class TodoControllerIT {

@LocalServerPort
```

```
        private int port;

        private TestRestTemplate template = new TestRestTemplate();

        @Test
        public void retrieveTodos() throws Exception {
         String expected = "["
         + "{id:1,user:Jack,desc:\"Learn Spring MVC\",done:false}" + ","
         + "{id:2,user:Jack,desc:\"Learn Struts\",done:false}" + "]";

         String uri = "/users/Jack/todos";

         ResponseEntity<String> response =
         template.getForEntity(createUrl(uri), String.class);

         JSONAssert.assertEquals(expected, response.getBody(), false);
        }

         private String createUrl(String uri) {
         return "http://localhost:" + port + uri;
         }
    }
```

This test is very similar to the integration test for `BasicController`, except that we are using `JSONAssert` to assert the response.

Retrieving details for a specific Todo

We will now add the method to retrieve details for a specific Todo:

```
        @GetMapping(path = "/users/{name}/todos/{id}")
        public Todo retrieveTodo(@PathVariable String name, @PathVariable
        int id) {
           return todoService.retrieveTodo(id);
        }
```

A couple of things to note are as follows:

- The URI mapped is `/users/{name}/todos/{id}`
- We have two path variables defined for `name` and `id`

Executing the service

Let's send a test request and see what response we will get, as shown in the following screenshot:

```
localhost:8080/users/Jack/todos/1

{"id":1,"user":"Jack","desc":"Learn Spring
MVC","targetDate":1481607268779,"done":false}
```

The response for the `http://localhost:8080/users/Jack/todos/1` URL is shown as follows:

```
{"id":1,"user":"Jack","desc":"Learn Spring MVC",
"targetDate":1481607268779,"done":false}
```

Unit testing

The code to unit test `retrieveTodo` is as follows:

```java
@Test
public void retrieveTodo() throws Exception {
  Todo mockTodo = new Todo(1, "Jack", "Learn Spring MVC",
  new Date(), false);

  when(service.retrieveTodo(anyInt())).thenReturn(mockTodo);

  MvcResult result = mvc.perform(
  MockMvcRequestBuilders.get("/users/Jack/todos/1")
  .accept(MediaType.APPLICATION_JSON))
  .andExpect(status().isOk()).andReturn();

  String expected = "{id:1,user:Jack,desc:\"Learn Spring
  MVC\",done:false}";

  JSONAssert.assertEquals(expected,
    result.getResponse().getContentAsString(), false);

}
```

A few important things to note are as follows:

- `when(service.retrieveTodo(anyInt())).thenReturn(mockTodo)`: We are mocking the retrieveTodo service method to return the mock todo.
- `MvcResult result = ..`: We are accepting the result of the request into an MvcResult variable to enable us to perform assertions on the response.
- `JSONAssert.assertEquals(expected, result.getResponse().getContentAsString(), false)`: Asserts whether the result is as expected.

Integration testing

The code to perform integration testing on `retrieveTodos` in `TodoController` is shown in the following code snippet. This would be added to the `TodoControllerIT` class:

```
@Test
public void retrieveTodo() throws Exception {
    String expected = "{id:1,user:Jack,desc:\"Learn Spring
    MVC\",done:false}";
    ResponseEntity<String> response = template.getForEntity(
    createUrl("/users/Jack/todos/1"), String.class);
    JSONAssert.assertEquals(expected, response.getBody(), false);
}
```

Adding a Todo

We will now add the method to create a new Todo. The HTTP method to be used for creation is `Post`. We will post to a `"/users/{name}/todos"` URI:

```
@PostMapping("/users/{name}/todos")
ResponseEntity<?> add(@PathVariable String name,
@RequestBody Todo todo) {
    Todo createdTodo = todoService.addTodo(name, todo.getDesc(),
    todo.getTargetDate(), todo.isDone());
    if (createdTodo == null) {
        return ResponseEntity.noContent().build();
    }

    URI location = ServletUriComponentsBuilder.fromCurrentRequest()

    .path("/{id}").buildAndExpand(createdTodo.getId()).toUri();
    return ResponseEntity.created(location).build();
}
```

A few things to note are as follows:

- `@PostMapping("/users/{name}/todos")`: `@PostMapping` annotations map the `add()` method to the HTTP Request with a `POST` method.
- `ResponseEntity<?> add(@PathVariable String name, @RequestBody Todo todo)`: An HTTP post request should ideally return the URI to the created resources. We use `ResourceEntity` to do this. `@RequestBody` binds the body of the request directly to the bean.
- `ResponseEntity.noContent().build()`: Used to return that the creation of the resource failed.
- `ServletUriComponentsBuilder.fromCurrentRequest().path("/{id}").buildAndExpand(createdTodo.getId()).toUri()`: Forms the URI for the created resource that can be returned in the response.
- `ResponseEntity.created(location).build()`: Returns a status of `201(CREATED)` with a link to the resource created.

Postman

If you are on Mac, you might want to try the Paw application as well.

Let's send a test request and see what response we get. The following screenshot shows the response:

We will use Postman app to interact with the REST Services. You can install it from the website, `https://www.getpostman.com/`. It is available on Windows and Mac. A Google Chrome plugin is also available.

Executing the POST service

To create a new Todo using `POST`, we would need to include the JSON for the Todo in the body of the request. The following screenshot shows how we can use the Postman app to create the request and the response after executing the request:

A few important things to note are as follows:

- We are sending a POST request. So, we choose the **POST** from the top-left dropdown.
- To send the Todo JSON as part of the body of the request, we select the **raw** option in the **Body** tab (highlighted with a blue dot). We choose the content type as JSON (`application/json`).

- Once the request is successfully executed, you can see the status of the request in the bar in the middle of the screen: **Status: 201 Created**.
- The location is `http://localhost:8080/users/Jack/todos/5`. This is the URI of the newly created todo that is received in the response.

Complete details of the request to `http://localhost:8080/users/Jack/todos` are shown in the block, as follows:

```
Header
Content-Type:application/json

Body
{
   "user": "Jack",
   "desc": "Learn Spring Boot",
    "done": false
  }
```

Unit testing

The code to unit test the created Todo is shown as follows:

```
@Test
public void createTodo() throws Exception {
  Todo mockTodo = new Todo(CREATED_TODO_ID, "Jack",
  "Learn Spring MVC", new Date(), false);
  String todo = "{"user":"Jack","desc":"Learn Spring MVC",
  "done":false}";

  when(service.addTodo(anyString(), anyString(),
  isNull(),anyBoolean()))
  .thenReturn(mockTodo);

mvc
  .perform(MockMvcRequestBuilders.post("/users/Jack/todos")
  .content(todo)
  .contentType(MediaType.APPLICATION_JSON)
  )
  .andExpect(status().isCreated())
  .andExpect(
    header().string("location",containsString("/users/Jack/todos/"
  + CREATED_TODO_ID)));
}
```

A few important things to note are as follows:

- `String todo = "{"user":"Jack","desc":"Learn Spring MVC","done":false}"`: The Todo content to post to the create todo service.
- `when(service.addTodo(anyString(), anyString(), isNull(), anyBoolean())).thenReturn(mockTodo)`: Mocks the service to return a dummy todo.
- `MockMvcRequestBuilders.post("/users/Jack/todos").content(todo).contentType(MediaType.APPLICATION_JSON))`: Creates a POST to a given URI with the given content type.
- `andExpect(status().isCreated())`: Expects that the status is created.
- `andExpect(header().string("location",containsString("/users/Jack/todos/" + CREATED_TODO_ID)))`: Expects that the header contains `location` with the URI of created resource.

Integration testing

The code to perform integration testing on the created todo in `TodoController` is shown as follows. This would be added to the `TodoControllerIT` class, as follows:

```
@Test
public void addTodo() throws Exception {
  Todo todo = new Todo(-1, "Jill", "Learn Hibernate", new Date(),
  false);
  URI location = template
  .postForLocation(createUrl("/users/Jill/todos"),todo);
  assertThat(location.getPath(),
  containsString("/users/Jill/todos/4"));
}
```

A few important things to note are as follows:

- `URI location = template.postForLocation(createUrl("/users/Jill/todos"), todo)`: `postForLocation` is a utility method especially useful in tests to create new resources. We are posting the todo to the given URI and getting the location from the header.
- `assertThat(location.getPath(), containsString("/users/Jill/todos/4"))`: Asserts that the location contains the path to the newly created resource.

Spring Initializr

Do you want to auto-generate Spring Boot projects? Do you want to quickly get started with developing your application? Spring Initializr is the answer.

Spring Initializr is hosted at `http://start.spring.io`. The following screenshot shows how the website looks:

Spring Initializr provides a lot of flexibility in creating projects. You have options to do the following:

- Choose your build tool: Maven or Gradle.
- Choose the Spring Boot version you want to use.
- Configure a **Group ID** and **Artifact ID** for your component.
- Choose the starters (dependencies) that you would want for your project. You can click on the link at the bottom of the screen, **Switch to the full version**, to see all the starter projects you can choose from.
- Choose how to package your component: JAR or WAR.
- Choose the Java version you want to use.
- Choose the JVM language you want to use.

The following screenshot shows some of the options Spring Initializr provides when you expand (click on the link) to the full version:

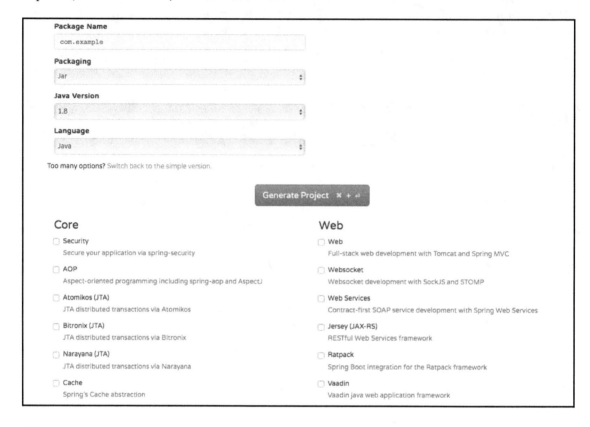

Creating your first Spring Initializr project

We will use the full version and enter the values, as follows:

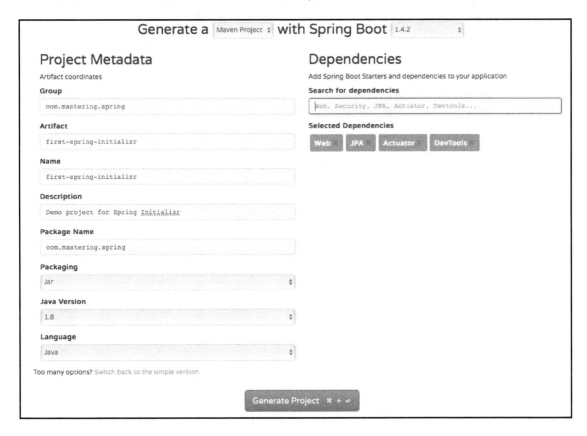

Things to note are as follows:

- **Build tool**: Maven
- **Spring Boot version**: Choose the latest available
- **Group**: com.mastering.spring
- **Artifact**: first-spring-initializr
- **Selected dependencies**: Choose Web, JPA, Actuator and Dev Tools. Type in each one of these in the textbox and press *Enter* to choose them. We will learn more about Actuator and Dev Tools in the next section
- **Java version**: 1.8

Go ahead and click on the **Generate Project** button. This will create a `.zip` file and you can download it to your computer.

The following screenshot shows the structure of the project created:

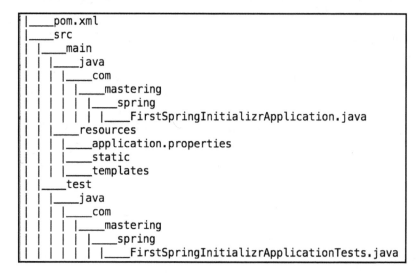

```
|____pom.xml
|____src
| |____main
| | |____java
| | | |____com
| | | | |____mastering
| | | | | |____spring
| | | | | | |____FirstSpringInitializrApplication.java
| | |____resources
| | | |____application.properties
| | | |____static
| | | |____templates
| |____test
| | |____java
| | | |____com
| | | | |____mastering
| | | | | |____spring
| | | | | | |____FirstSpringInitializrApplicationTests.java
```

We will now import this project into your IDE. In Eclipse, you can perform the following steps:

1. Launch Eclipse.
2. Navigate to **File | Import**.
3. Choose the existing Maven projects.
4. Browse and select the folder that is the root of the Maven project (the one containing the `pom.xml` file).
5. Proceed with the defaults and click on **Finish.**

This will import the project into Eclipse. The following screenshot shows the structure of the project in Eclipse:

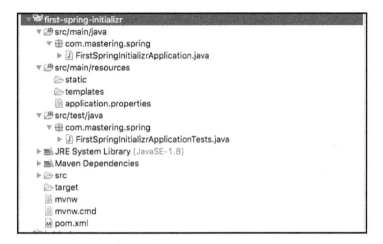

Let's look at some of the important files from the generated project.

pom.xml

The following snippet shows the dependencies that are declared:

```
<dependencies> <dependency> <groupId>org.springframework.boot</groupId>
<artifactId>spring-boot-starter-web</artifactId> </dependency> <dependency>
<groupId>org.springframework.boot</groupId> <artifactId>spring-boot-
starter-data-jpa</artifactId> </dependency> <dependency>
<groupId>org.springframework.boot</groupId> <artifactId>spring-boot-
starter-actuator</artifactId> </dependency> <dependency>
<groupId>org.springframework.boot</groupId> <artifactId>spring-boot-
devtools</artifactId> <scope>runtime</scope> </dependency> <dependency>
<groupId>org.springframework.boot</groupId> <artifactId>spring-boot-
starter-test</artifactId> <scope>test</scope> </dependency> </dependencies>
```

A few other important observations are as follows:

- The packaging for this component is `.jar`
- `org.springframework.boot:spring-boot-starter-parent` is declared as the parent POM
- `<java.version>1.8</java.version>`: The Java version is 1.8
- Spring Boot Maven Plugin (`org.springframework.boot:spring-boot-maven-plugin`) is configured as a plugin

FirstSpringInitializrApplication.java class

`FirstSpringInitializrApplication.java` is the launcher for Spring Boot:

```
package com.mastering.spring;
import org.springframework.boot.SpringApplication;
import org.springframework.boot.autoconfigure
.SpringBootApplication;

@SpringBootApplication
public class FirstSpringInitializrApplication {
    public static void main(String[] args) {
      SpringApplication.run(FirstSpringInitializrApplication.class,
      args);
    }
}
```

FirstSpringInitializrApplicationTests class

`FirstSpringInitializrApplicationTests` contains the basic context that can be used to start writing the tests as we start developing the application:

```
package com.mastering.spring;
import org.junit.Test;
import org.junit.runner.RunWith;
import org.springframework.boot.test.context.SpringBootTest;
import org.springframework.test.context.junit4.SpringRunner;

@RunWith(SpringRunner.class)
@SpringBootTest
public class FirstSpringInitializrApplicationTests {

  @Test
  public void contextLoads() {
  }
}
```

A quick peek into auto-configuration

Auto-configuration is one of the most important features of Spring Boot. In this section, we will take a quick peek behind the scenes to understand how Spring Boot auto-configuration works.

Most of the Spring Boot auto-configuration magic comes from `spring-boot-autoconfigure-{version}.jar`. When we start any Spring Boot applications, a number of beans get auto-configured. How does this happen?

The following screenshot shows an extract from `spring.factories` from `spring-boot-autoconfigure-{version}.jar`. We have filtered out some of the configuration in the interest of space:

```
spring.factories ⊠
31 org.springframework.boot.autoconfigure.data.jpa.JpaRepositoriesAutoConfiguration,\
32 org.springframework.boot.autoconfigure.data.mongo.MongoDataAutoConfiguration,\
33 org.springframework.boot.autoconfigure.data.mongo.MongoRepositoriesAutoConfiguration,\
34 org.springframework.boot.autoconfigure.data.neo4j.Neo4jDataAutoConfiguration,\
35 org.springframework.boot.autoconfigure.data.neo4j.Neo4jRepositoriesAutoConfiguration,\
36 org.springframework.boot.autoconfigure.data.solr.SolrRepositoriesAutoConfiguration,\
37 org.springframework.boot.autoconfigure.data.redis.RedisAutoConfiguration,\
38 org.springframework.boot.autoconfigure.data.redis.RedisRepositoriesAutoConfiguration,\
39 org.springframework.boot.autoconfigure.data.rest.RepositoryRestMvcAutoConfiguration,\
40 org.springframework.boot.autoconfigure.data.web.SpringDataWebAutoConfiguration,\
41 org.springframework.boot.autoconfigure.elasticsearch.jest.JestAutoConfiguration,\
42 org.springframework.boot.autoconfigure.freemarker.FreeMarkerAutoConfiguration,\
43 org.springframework.boot.autoconfigure.gson.GsonAutoConfiguration,\
44 org.springframework.boot.autoconfigure.h2.H2ConsoleAutoConfiguration,\
45 org.springframework.boot.autoconfigure.hateoas.HypermediaAutoConfiguration,\
46 org.springframework.boot.autoconfigure.hazelcast.HazelcastAutoConfiguration,\
47 org.springframework.boot.autoconfigure.hazelcast.HazelcastJpaDependencyAutoConfiguration,\
48 org.springframework.boot.autoconfigure.info.ProjectInfoAutoConfiguration,\
49 org.springframework.boot.autoconfigure.integration.IntegrationAutoConfiguration,\
50 org.springframework.boot.autoconfigure.jackson.JacksonAutoConfiguration,\
51 org.springframework.boot.autoconfigure.jdbc.DataSourceAutoConfiguration,\
52 org.springframework.boot.autoconfigure.jdbc.JdbcTemplateAutoConfiguration,\
53 org.springframework.boot.autoconfigure.jdbc.JndiDataSourceAutoConfiguration,\
54 org.springframework.boot.autoconfigure.jdbc.XADataSourceAutoConfiguration,\
55 org.springframework.boot.autoconfigure.jdbc.DataSourceTransactionManagerAutoConfiguration,\
56 org.springframework.boot.autoconfigure.jms.JmsAutoConfiguration,\
57 org.springframework.boot.autoconfigure.jmx.JmxAutoConfiguration,\
58 org.springframework.boot.autoconfigure.jms.JndiConnectionFactoryAutoConfiguration,\
59 org.springframework.boot.autoconfigure.jms.activemq.ActiveMQAutoConfiguration,\
60 org.springframework.boot.autoconfigure.jms.artemis.ArtemisAutoConfiguration,\
61 org.springframework.boot.autoconfigure.jms.hornetq.HornetQAutoConfiguration,\
62 org.springframework.boot.autoconfigure.flyway.FlywayAutoConfiguration,\
```

The preceding list of auto-configuration classes is run whenever a Spring Boot application is launched. Let's take a quick look at one of them:

`org.springframework.boot.autoconfigure.web.WebMvcAutoConfiguration`.

Here's a small snippet:

```
@Configuration
@ConditionalOnWebApplication
@ConditionalOnClass({ Servlet.class, DispatcherServlet.class,
WebMvcConfigurerAdapter.class })
@ConditionalOnMissingBean(WebMvcConfigurationSupport.class)
@AutoConfigureOrder(Ordered.HIGHEST_PRECEDENCE + 10)
@AutoConfigureAfter(DispatcherServletAutoConfiguration.class)
public class WebMvcAutoConfiguration {
```

Some of the important points to note are as follows:

- `@ConditionalOnClass({ Servlet.class, DispatcherServlet.class, WebMvcConfigurerAdapter.class })` : This auto-configuration is enabled if any of the mentioned classes are in the classpath. When we add a web starter project, we bring in dependencies with all these classes. Hence, this auto-configuration will be enabled.
- `@ConditionalOnMissingBean(WebMvcConfigurationSupport.class)`: This auto-configuration is enabled only if the application does not explicitly declare a bean of the `WebMvcConfigurationSupport.class` class.
- `@AutoConfigureOrder(Ordered.HIGHEST_PRECEDENCE + 10)`: This specifies the precedence of this specific auto-configuration.

Let's look at another small snippet showing one of the methods from the same class:

```
@Bean
@ConditionalOnBean(ViewResolver.class)
@ConditionalOnMissingBean(name = "viewResolver",
value = ContentNegotiatingViewResolver.class)
public ContentNegotiatingViewResolver
viewResolver(BeanFactory beanFactory) {
  ContentNegotiatingViewResolver resolver = new
  ContentNegotiatingViewResolver();
  resolver.setContentNegotiationManager
  (beanFactory.getBean(ContentNegotiationManager.class));
  resolver.setOrder(Ordered.HIGHEST_PRECEDENCE);
  return resolver;
  }
```

View resolvers are one of the beans configured by `WebMvcAutoConfiguration` class. The preceding snippet ensures that if a view resolver is not provided by the application, then Spring Boot auto-configures a default view resolver. Here are a few important points to note:

- `@ConditionalOnBean(ViewResolver.class)`: Create this bean if `ViewResolver.class` is on the classpath
- `@ConditionalOnMissingBean(name = "viewResolver", value = ContentNegotiatingViewResolver.class)`: Create this bean if there are no explicitly declared beans of the name `viewResolver` and of type `ContentNegotiatingViewResolver.class`
- The rest of the method is configured in the view resolver

To summarize, all the auto-configuration logic is executed at the start of a Spring Boot application. If a specific class (from a specific dependency or starter project) is available on the classpath, then the auto configuration classes are executed. These auto-configuration classes look at what beans are already configured. Based on the existing beans, they enable the creation of the default beans.

Summary

Spring Boot makes the development of Spring-based applications easy. It enables us to create production-ready applications from day one of a project.

In this chapter, we covered the basics of Spring Boot and REST services. We discussed the different features of Spring Boot and created a few REST services with great tests. We understood what happens in the background with an in-depth look at auto-configuration.

In the next chapter, we will shift our attention toward adding more features to the REST services.

6
Extending Microservices

We built a basic component offering a few services in `Chapter 5`, *Building Microservices with Spring Boot*. In this chapter, we will focus on adding more features to make our microservice production ready.

We will discuss how to add these features to our microservice:

- Exception handling
- HATEOAS
- Caching
- Internationalisation

We will also discuss how to document our microservice using Swagger. We will look at the basics of securing the microservice with Spring Security.

Exception handling

Exception handling is one of the important parts of developing web services. When something goes wrong, we would want to return a good description of what went wrong to the service consumer. You would not want the service to crash without returning anything useful to the service consumer.

Spring Boot provides good default exception handling. We will start with looking at the default exception handling features provided by Spring Boot before moving on to customizing them.

Spring Boot default exception handling

To understand the default exception handling provided by Spring Boot, let's start with firing a request to a nonexistent URL.

Nonexistent resource

Let's send a GET request to http://localhost:8080/non-existing-resource using a header (**Content-Type:application/json**).

The following screenshot shows the response when we execute the request:

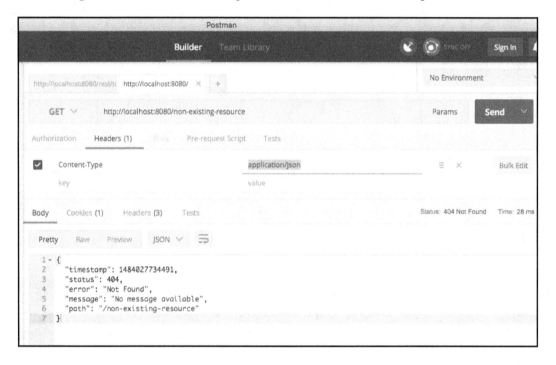

The response is as shown in the following code snippet:

```
{
    "timestamp": 1484027734491,
    "status": 404,
    "error": "Not Found",
    "message": "No message available",
    "path": "/non-existing-resource"
}
```

Some important things to note are as follows:

- The response header has an HTTP status of `404 - Resource Not Found`
- Spring Boot returns a valid JSON message as a response with the message stating that the resource is not found

Resource throwing an exception

Let's create a resource that throws an exception, and send a `GET` request to it in order to understand how the application reacts to runtime exceptions.

Let's create a dummy service that throws an exception. The following code snippet shows a simple service:

```
@GetMapping(path = "/users/dummy-service")
public Todo errorService() {
    throw new RuntimeException("Some Exception Occured");
}
```

Some important things to note are as follows:

- We are creating a `GET` service with the URI `/users/dummy-service`.
- The service throws `RuntimeException`. We chose `RuntimeException` to be able to create the exception easily. We can easily replace it with a custom exception if needed.

Let's fire a `GET` request to the preceding service at `http://localhost:8080/users/dummy-service` using Postman. The response is as shown in the following code:

```
{
    "timestamp": 1484028119553,
    "status": 500,
    "error": "Internal Server Error",
    "exception": "java.lang.RuntimeException",
    "message": "Some Exception Occured",
    "path": "/users/dummy-service"
}
```

Some important things to note are as follows:

- The response header has an HTTP status of `500; Internal server error`
- Spring Boot also returns the message with which the exception is thrown

As we can see in the preceding two examples, Spring Boot provides good default exception handling. In the next section, we will focus on understanding how the application reacts to custom exceptions.

Throwing a custom exception

Let's create a custom exception and throw it from a service. Take a look at the following code:

```
public class TodoNotFoundException extends RuntimeException {
  public TodoNotFoundException(String msg) {
    super(msg);
  }
}
```

It's a very simple piece of code that defines TodoNotFoundException.

Now let's enhance our TodoController class to throw TodoNotFoundException when a todo with a given ID is not found:

```
@GetMapping(path = "/users/{name}/todos/{id}")
public Todo retrieveTodo(@PathVariable String name,
@PathVariable int id) {
  Todo todo = todoService.retrieveTodo(id);
  if (todo == null) {
    throw new TodoNotFoundException("Todo Not Found");
  }

 return todo;
}
```

If todoService returns a null todo, we throw TodoNotFoundException.

When we execute the service with a GET request to a nonexistent todo (http://localhost:8080/users/Jack/todos/222), we get the response shown in the following code snippet:

```
{
  "timestamp": 1484029048788,
  "status": 500,
  "error": "Internal Server Error",
  "exception":
  "com.mastering.spring.springboot.bean.TodoNotFoundException",
  "message": "Todo Not Found",
  "path": "/users/Jack/todos/222"
}
```

As we can see, a clear exception response is sent back to the service consumer. However, there is one thing that can be improved further--the response status. When a resource is not found, it is recommended that you return a `404 - Resource Not Found` status. We will look at how to customize the response status in the next example.

Customizing the exception message

Let's look at how to customize the preceding exception and return the proper response status with a customized message.

Let's create a bean to define the structure of our custom exception message:

```
public class ExceptionResponse {
  private Date timestamp = new Date();
  private String message;
  private String details;

  public ExceptionResponse(String message, String details) {
    super();
    this.message = message;
    this.details = details;
  }

  public Date getTimestamp() {
    return timestamp;
  }

  public String getMessage() {
    return message;
  }

  public String getDetails() {
    return details;
  }
}
```

We have created a simple exception response bean with an auto-populated timestamp with a few additional properties namely messages and details.

When `TodoNotFoundException` is thrown, we would want to return a response using the `ExceptionResponse` bean. The following code shows how we can create a global exception handling for `TodoNotFoundException.class`:

```
@ControllerAdvice
@RestController
public class RestResponseEntityExceptionHandler
    extends  ResponseEntityExceptionHandler
    {
      @ExceptionHandler(TodoNotFoundException.class)
      public final ResponseEntity<ExceptionResponse>
      todoNotFound(TodoNotFoundException ex) {
        ExceptionResponse exceptionResponse =
        new ExceptionResponse(  ex.getMessage(),
        "Any details you would want to add");
        return new ResponseEntity<ExceptionResponse>
        (exceptionResponse, new HttpHeaders(),
        HttpStatus.NOT_FOUND);
      }
    }
```

Some important things to note are as follows:

- `RestResponseEntityExceptionHandler extends ResponseEntityExceptionHandler`: We are extending `ResponseEntityExceptionHandler`, which is the base class provided by Spring MVC for centralised exception handling `ControllerAdvice` classes.
- `@ExceptionHandler(TodoNotFoundException.class)`: This defines that the method to follow will handle the specific exception `TodoNotFoundException.class`. Any other exceptions for which custom exception handling is not defined will follow the default exception handling provided by Spring Boot.
- `ExceptionResponse exceptionResponse = new ExceptionResponse(ex.getMessage(), "Any details you would want to add")`: This creates a custom exception response.
- `new ResponseEntity<ExceptionResponse>(exceptionResponse,new HttpHeaders(), HttpStatus.NOT_FOUND)`: This is the definition to return a `404 Resource Not Found` response with the custom exception defined earlier.

When we execute the service with a `GET` request to a nonexistent `todo` (`http://localhost:8080/users/Jack/todos/222`), we get the following response:

```
{
    "timestamp": 1484030343311,
    "message": "Todo Not Found",
    "details": "Any details you would want to add"
}
```

If you want to create a generic exception message for all exceptions, we can add a method to `RestResponseEntityExceptionHandler` with the `@ExceptionHandler(Exception.class)` annotation.

The following code snippet shows how we can do this:

```
@ExceptionHandler(Exception.class)
public final ResponseEntity<ExceptionResponse> todoNotFound(
Exception ex) {
    //Customize and return the response
}
```

Any exception for which a custom exception handler is not defined will be handled by the preceding method.

Response status

One of the important things to focus on with REST services is the response status of an error response. The following table shows the scenarios and the error response status to use:

Situation	Response Status
The request body does not meet the API specification. It does not contain enough details or contains validation errors.	400 BAD REQUEST
Authentication or authorization failure.	401 UNAUTHORIZED
The user cannot perform the operation due to various factor, such as exceeding limits.	403 FORBIDDEN
The resource does not exist.	404 NOT FOUND
Unsupported operation, for example, trying POST on a resource where only GET is allowed.	405 METHOD NOT ALLOWED

Error on a server. Ideally, this should not happen. The consumer would not be able to fix this.	500 INTERNAL SERVER ERROR

In this section, we looked at the default exception handling provided by Spring Boot and how we can customize it further to suit our needs.

HATEOAS

HATEOAS (Hypermedia as the Engine of Application State) is one of the constraints of the REST application architecture.

Let's consider a situation where a service consumer is consuming numerous services from a service provider. The easiest way to develop this kind of system is to have the service consumer store the individual resource URIs of every resource they need from the service provider. However, this would create tight coupling between the service provider and the service consumer. Whenever any of the resource URIs change on the service provider, the service consumer needs to be updated.

Consider a typical web application. Let's say I navigate to my bank account details page. Almost all banking websites would show links to all the transactions that are possible on my bank account on the screen so that I can easily navigate using the link.

What if we can bring a similar concept to RESTful services so that a service returns not only the data about the requested resource, but also provides details of other related resources?

HATEOAS brings this concept of displaying related links for a given resource to RESTful services. When we return the details of a specific resource, we also return links to operations that can be performed on the resource, as well as links to related resources. If a service consumer can use the links from the response to perform transactions, then it would not need to hardcode all links.

An extract of constraints related to HATEOAS presented by Roy Fielding (`http://roy.gbi v.com/untangled/2008/rest-apis-must-be-hypertext-driven`) is as follows:

A REST API must not define fixed resource names or hierarchies (an obvious coupling of client and server). Servers must have the freedom to control their own namespace. Instead, allow servers to instruct clients on how to construct appropriate URIs, such as is done in HTML forms and URI templates, by defining those instructions within media types and link relations. A REST API should be entered with no prior knowledge beyond the initial URI (bookmark) and set of standardized media types that are appropriate for the intended audience (i.e., expected to be understood by any client that might use the API). From that point on, all application state transitions must be driven by client selection of server-provided choices that are present in the received representations or implied by the user's manipulation of those representations. The transitions may be determined (or limited by) the client's knowledge of media types and resource communication mechanisms, both of which may be improved on-the-fly (e.g., code-on-demand).

An example response with HATEOAS link is shown here. This is the response to the `/todos` request in order to retrieve all todos:

```
{
  "_embedded" : {
    "todos" : [ {
      "user" : "Jill",
      "desc" : "Learn Hibernate",
      "done" : false,
     "_links" : {
      "self" : {
            "href" : "http://localhost:8080/todos/1"
            },
      "todo" : {
            "href" : "http://localhost:8080/todos/1"
             }
         }
    } ]
  },
  "_links" : {
  "self" : {
            "href" : "http://localhost:8080/todos"
            },
  "profile" : {
            "href" : "http://localhost:8080/profile/todos"
            },
  "search" : {
            "href" : "http://localhost:8080/todos/search"
            }
     },
  }
```

The preceding response includes links to the following:

- Specific `todos` (`http://localhost:8080/todos/1`)
- Search resource (`http://localhost:8080/todos/search`)

If the service consumer wants to do a search, it has the option of taking the search URL from the response and sending the search request to it. This would reduce coupling between the service provider and the service consumer.

Sending HATEOAS links in response

Now that we understand what HATEOAS is, let's look at how we can send links related to a resource in the response.

Spring Boot starter HATEOAS

Spring Boot has a specific starter for HATEOAS called `spring-boot-starter-hateoas`. We need to add it to the `pom.xml` file.

The following code snippet shows the dependency block:

```
<dependency>
  <groupId>org.springframework.boot</groupId>
  <artifactId>spring-boot-starter-hateoas</artifactId>
</dependency>
```

One of the important dependencies of `spring-boot-starter-hateoas` is `spring-hateoas`, which provides the HATEOAS features:

```
<dependency>
  <groupId>org.springframework.hateoas</groupId>
  <artifactId>spring-hateoas</artifactId>
</dependency>
```

Let's enhance the `retrieveTodo` resource (`/users/{name}/todos/{id}`) to return a link to retrieve all `todos` (`/users/{name}/todos`) in the response:

```
@GetMapping(path = "/users/{name}/todos/{id}")
public Resource<Todo> retrieveTodo(
@PathVariable String name, @PathVariable int id) {
Todo todo = todoService.retrieveTodo(id);
  if (todo == null) {
      throw new TodoNotFoundException("Todo Not Found");
```

```
    }

    Resource<Todo> todoResource = new Resource<Todo>(todo);
    ControllerLinkBuilder linkTo =
    linkTo(methodOn(this.getClass()).retrieveTodos(name));
    todoResource.add(linkTo.withRel("parent"));

    return todoResource;
    }
```

Some important points to note are as follows:

- `ControllerLinkBuilder linkTo = linkTo(methodOn(this.getClass()).retrieveTodos(name))`: We want to get a link to the `retrieveTodos` method on the current class
- `linkTo.withRel("parent")`: Relationship with the current resource is parent

The following snippet shows the response when a `GET` request is sent to `http://localhost:8080/users/Jack/todos/1`:

```
{
    "id": 1,
    "user": "Jack",
    "desc": "Learn Spring MVC",
    "targetDate": 1484038262110,
    "done": false,
    "_links": {
            "parent": {
            "href": "http://localhost:8080/users/Jack/todos"
            }
        }
}
```

The `_links` section will contain all the links. Currently, we have one link with the relation parent and `href` as `http://localhost:8080/users/Jack/todos`.

If you have problems executing the preceding request, try executing using an Accept header--`application/json`.

HATEOAS is not something that is commonly used in most of the resources today. However, it has the potential to be really useful in reducing the coupling between the service provider and the consumer.

Validation

A good service always validates data before processing it. In this section, we will look at the Bean Validation API and use its reference implementation to implement validation in our services.

The Bean Validation API provides a number of annotations that can be used to validate beans. The *JSR 349* specification defines Bean Validation API 1.1. Hibernate-validator is the reference implementation. Both are already defined as dependencies in the spring-boot-web-starter project:

- hibernate-validator-5.2.4.Final.jar
- validation-api-1.1.0.Final.jar

We will create a simple validation for the createTodo service method.

Creating validations involves two steps:

1. Enabling validation on the controller method.
2. Adding validations on the bean.

Enabling validation on the controller method

It's very simple to enable validation on the controller method. The following snippet shows an example:

```
@RequestMapping(method = RequestMethod.POST,
path = "/users/{name}/todos")
ResponseEntity<?> add(@PathVariable String name
@Valid @RequestBody Todo todo) {
```

The @Valid(package javax.validation) annotation is used to mark a parameter for validation. Any validation that is defined in the Todo bean is executed before the add method is executed.

Defining validations on the bean

Let's define a few validations on the Todo bean:

```
public class Todo {
    private int id;

    @NotNull
    private String user;

    @Size(min = 9, message = "Enter atleast 10 Characters.")
    private String desc;
```

Some important points to note are as follows:

- @NotNull: Validates that the user field is not empty
- @Size(min = 9, message = "Enter atleast 10 Characters."): Checks whether the desc field has at least nine characters

There are a number of other annotations that can be used to validate beans. The following are some of the Bean Validation annotations:

- @AssertFalse, @AssertTrue: For Boolean elements. Checks the annotated element.
- @AssertFalse: Checks for false. @Assert checks for true.
- @Future: The annotated element must be a date in the future.
- @Past: The annotated element must be a date in the past.
- @Max: The annotated element must be a number whose value must be lower or equal to the specified maximum.
- @Min: The annotated element must be a number whose value must be higher or equal to the specified minimum.
- @NotNull: The annotated element cannot be null.
- @Pattern: The annotated {@code CharSequence} element must match the specified regular expression. The regular expression follows the Java regular expression conventions.
- @Size: The annotated element size must be within the specified boundaries.

Unit testing validations

The following example shows how we can unit test the validations we added in:

```
@Test
public void createTodo_withValidationError() throws Exception {
    Todo mockTodo = new Todo(CREATED_TODO_ID, "Jack",
    "Learn Spring MVC", new Date(), false);

    String todo = "{"user":"Jack","desc":"Learn","done":false}";

    when( service.addTodo(
      anyString(), anyString(), isNull(), anyBoolean()))
     .thenReturn(mockTodo);

      MvcResult result = mvc.perform(
      MockMvcRequestBuilders.post("/users/Jack/todos")
     .content(todo)
     .contentType(MediaType.APPLICATION_JSON))
     .andExpect(
        status().is4xxClientError()).andReturn();
}
```

Some important points to note are as follows:

- `"desc":"Learn"`: We are using a desc value of length 5. This would cause a validation failure for the `@Size(min = 9, message = "Enter atleast 10 Characters.")` check.
- `.andExpect(status().is4xxClientError())`: Checks for validation error status.

Documenting REST services

Before a service provider can consume a service, they need a service contract. A service contract defines all the details about a service:

- How can I call a service? What is the URI of the service?
- What should be the request format?
- What kind of response should I expect?

There are multiple options to define a service contract for RESTful services. The most popular one in the last couple of years is **Swagger**. Swagger is gaining a lot of ground, with support from major vendors in the last couple of years. In this section, we will generate Swagger documentation for our services.

The following quote from the Swagger website (`http://swagger.io`) defines the purpose of the Swagger specification:

> *Swagger specification creates the RESTful contract for your API, detailing all of its resources and operations in a human and machine readable format for easy development, discovery, and integration.*

Generating a Swagger specification

One of the interesting developments in the last few years of RESTful services development is the evolution of tools to generate service documentation (specification) from the code. This ensures that the code and documentation are always in sync.

Springfox Swagger can be used to generate Swagger documentation from the RESTful services code. What's more, there is a wonderful tool called **Swagger UI**, which, when integrated into the application, provides human-readable documentation.

The following code snippet shows how we can add both these tools to the pom.xml file:

```
<dependency>
  <groupId>io.springfox</groupId>
  <artifactId>springfox-swagger2</artifactId>
  <version>2.4.0</version>
</dependency>

<dependency>
  <groupId>io.springfox</groupId>
  <artifactId>springfox-swagger-ui</artifactId>
  <version>2.4.0</version>
</dependency>
```

The next step is to add the configuration class to enable and generate Swagger documentation. The following snippet shows how to do it:

```
@Configuration
@EnableSwagger2
public class SwaggerConfig {
  @Bean
  public Docket api() {
    return new Docket(DocumentationType.SWAGGER_2)
    .select()
    .apis(RequestHandlerSelectors.any())
    .paths(PathSelectors.any()).build();
  }
}
```

Some important points to note are as follows:

- `@Configuration`: Defines a Spring configuration file
- `@EnableSwagger2`: The annotation to enable Swagger support
- `Docket` : A simple builder class to configure the generation of Swagger documentation using the Swagger Spring MVC framework
- `new Docket(DocumentationType.SWAGGER_2)` : Configures Swagger 2 as the Swagger version to be used
- `.apis(RequestHandlerSelectors.any()).paths(PathSelectors.any())` : Includes all APIs and paths in the documentation

When we bring the server up, we can launch the API Docs URL (`http://localhost:8080/v2/api-docs`). The following screenshot shows some of the generated documentation:

Let's look at some of the generated documentation. Listed here is the documentation to retrieve the `todos` service:

```
"/users/{name}/todos": {
  "get": {
  "tags": [
        "todo-controller"
        ],
  "summary": "retrieveTodos",
```

```
"operationId": "retrieveTodosUsingGET",
"consumes": [
        "application/json"
        ],
"produces": [
        "*/*"
        ],
"parameters": [
        {
          "name": "name",
          "in": "path",
          "description": "name",
          "required": true,
          "type": "string"
        }
      ],
 "responses": {
 "200": {
        "description": "OK",
        "schema": {
                "type": "array",
                items": {
                    "$ref": "#/definitions/Todo"
                }
             }
          },
 "401": {
        "description": "Unauthorized"
        },
 "403": {
        "description": "Forbidden"
        },
 "404": {
        "description": "Not Found"
        }
    }
}
```

The service definition clearly defines the request and response of the service. Also defined are the different response statuses that the service can return in different situations.

The following code snippet shows the definition of the `Todo` bean:

```
"Resource«Todo»": {
  "type": "object",
  "properties": {
  "desc": {
          "type": "string"
        },
  "done": {
          "type": "boolean"
        },
  "id": {
          "type": "integer",
          "format": "int32"
      },
  "links": {
          "type": "array",
          "items": {
                  "$ref": "#/definitions/Link"
              }
        },
  "targetDate": {
              "type": "string",
              "format": "date-time"
          },
  "user": {
          "type": "string"
      }
    }
  }
```

It defines all the elements in the `Todo` bean, along with their formats.

Swagger UI

Swagger UI (`http://localhost:8080/swagger-ui.html`) can also be used to look at the documentation. Swagger UI is enabled by the dependency (`io.springfox:springfox-swagger-ui`) that was added in our `pom.xml`, in the previous step.

Swagger UI (`http://petstore.swagger.io`) is also available online. We can visualise any Swagger documentation (swagger JSON) using Swagger UI.

The following screenshot shows the list of controller-exposing services. When we click on any controller, it expands to show the list of request methods and URIs each controller supports:

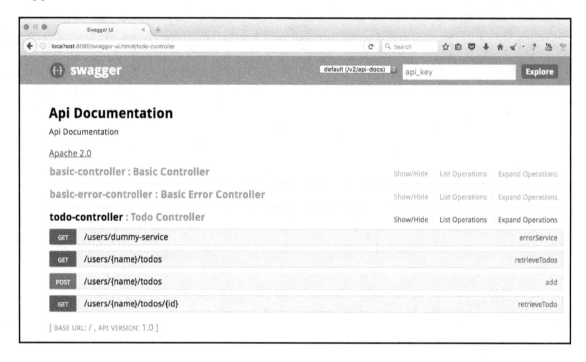

The following screenshot shows the details for the POST service to create a `todo` for the user in Swagger UI:

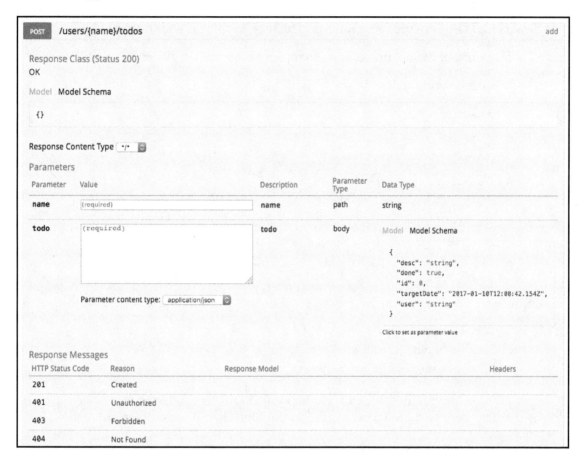

Some important things to note are as follows:

- **Parameters** show all the important parameters including the request body
- The **Parameter Type** body (for the `todo` parameter) shows the expected structure for the body of the request
- The **Response Messages** sections show different HTTP status codes returned by the service

The Swagger UI provides an excellent way to expose service definitions for your API without a lot of additional effort.

Customizing Swagger documentation using annotations

The Swagger UI also provides annotations to further customize your documentation.

Listed here is some of the documentation to retrieve the `todos` service:

```
"/users/{name}/todos": {
  "get": {
  "tags": [
        "todo-controller"
        ],
  "summary": "retrieveTodos",
  "operationId": "retrieveTodosUsingGET",
  "consumes": [
          "application/json"
          ],
  "produces": [
            "*/*"
            ],
```

As you can see, the documentation generated is very raw. There are a number of things we can improve in the documentation to describe the services better. Here are a couple of examples:

- Provide a better summary
- Add application/JSON to produces

Swagger provides annotations we can add to our RESTful services in order to customize the documentation. Let's add a few annotations to the controller in order to improve the documentation:

```
@ApiOperation(
  value = "Retrieve all todos for a user by passing in his name",
  notes = "A list of matching todos is returned. Current pagination
  is not supported.",
  response = Todo.class,
  responseContainer = "List",
  produces = "application/json")
  @GetMapping("/users/{name}/todos")
  public List<Todo> retrieveTodos(@PathVariable String name) {
    return todoService.retrieveTodos(name);
  }
```

A few important points to note are as follows:

- `@ApiOperation(value = "Retrieve all todos for a user by passing in his name")`: Produced in the documentation as a summary of the service
- `notes = "A list of matching todos is returned. Current pagination is not supported."`: Produced in the documentation as a description of the service
- `produces = "application/json"`: Customizes the `produces` section of the service documentation

Here is an extract of the documentation after the update:

```
get": {
     "tags": [
                "todo-controller"
            ],
     "summary": "Retrieve all todos for a user by passing in his
       name",
     "description": "A list of matching todos is returned. Current
       pagination is not supported.",
     "operationId": "retrieveTodosUsingGET",
     "consumes": [
                "application/json"
            ],
     "produces": [
                "application/json",
                "*/*"
            ],
```

Swagger provides a lot of other annotations to customize the documentation. Listed here are some of the important annotations:

- `@Api`: Marks a class as a Swagger resource
- `@ApiModel`: Provides additional information about Swagger models
- `@ApiModelProperty`: Adds and manipulates the data of a model property
- `@ApiOperation`: Describes an operation or an HTTP method against a specific path
- `@ApiParam`: Adds additional metadata for operation parameters
- `@ApiResponse`: Describes an example response of an operation
- `@ApiResponses`: A wrapper to allow a list of multiple `ApiResponse` objects.
- `@Authorization`: Declares an authorization scheme to be used on a resource or an operation

- @AuthorizationScope: Describes an OAuth 2 authorization scope
- @ResponseHeader: Represents a header that can be provided as part of the response

Swagger provides a few Swagger definition annotations that can be used to customize high-level information about a group of services--contacts, licensing, and other general information. Listed here are some of the important ones:

- @SwaggerDefinition: Definition-level properties to be added to the generated Swagger definition
- @Info: General metadata for a Swagger definition
- @Contact: Properties to describe the person to be contacted for a Swagger definition
- @License: Properties to describe the license for a Swagger definition

Securing REST services with Spring Security

All the services we have created up until now are unsecured. A consumer does not need to provide any credentials to access these services. However, all services in the real world are usually secured.

In this section, we will discuss two ways of authenticating REST services:

- Basic authentication
- OAuth 2.0 authentication

We will implement these two types of authentication with Spring Security.

Spring Boot provides a starter for Spring Security using `spring-boot-starter-security`. We will start with adding Spring Security starter to our `pom.xml` file.

Adding Spring Security starter

Add the following dependency to your file `pom.xml`:

```
<dependency>
  <groupId>org.springframework.boot</groupId>
  <artifactId>spring-boot-starter-security</artifactId>
</dependency>
```

The `Spring-boot-starter-security` dependency brings in three important Spring Security dependencies:

- `spring-security-config`
- `spring-security-core`
- `spring-security-web`

Basic authentication

The `Spring-boot-starter-security` dependency also auto-configures basic authentication for all services by default.

If we try to access any of the services now, we would get `"Access Denied"`.

The response when we send a request to `http://localhost:8080/users/Jack/todos` is shown as an example in the following code snippet:

```
{
  "timestamp": 1484120815039,
  "status": 401,
  "error": "Unauthorized",
  "message": "Full authentication is required to access this
   resource",
   "path": "/users/Jack/todos"
}
```

The response status is `401 - Unauthorized`.

When a resource is secured with basic authentication, we would need to send a user ID and password to authenticate our request. Since we did not configure a user ID and password, Spring Boot auto-configures a default user ID and password. The default user ID is `user`. The default password is usually printed in the log.

An example is shown in the following code snippet:

```
2017-01-11 13:11:58.696 INFO 3888 --- [ restartedMain]
b.a.s.AuthenticationManagerConfiguration :

Using default security password: 3fb5564a-ce53-4138-9911-8ade17b2f478

2017-01-11 13:11:58.771 INFO 3888 --- [ restartedMain]
o.s.s.web.DefaultSecurityFilterChain : Creating filter chain: Ant
[pattern='/css/**'], []
```

Underlined in the preceding code snippet is the default security password printed in the log.

We can use Postman to fire a request with basic authentication. The following screenshot shows how basic authentication details can be sent along with a request:

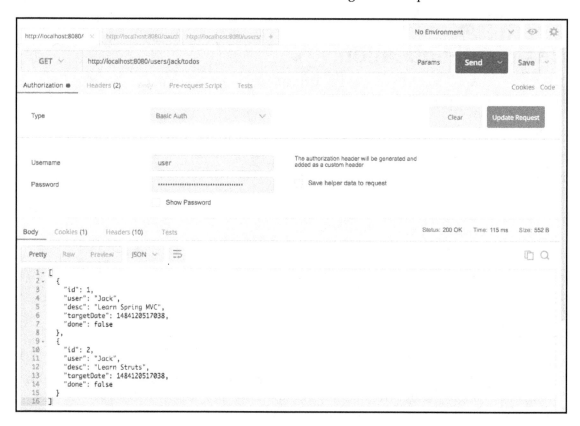

As you can see, authentication succeeds and we get a proper response back.

We can configure the user ID and password of our choice in `application.properties`, as shown here:

```
security.user.name=user-name
security.user.password=user-password
```

Spring Security also provides options to authenticate with LDAP or JDBC or any other data source with user credentials.

Integration testing

The integration test we wrote for the service earlier will start failing because of invalid credentials. We will now update the integration test to supply basic authentication credentials:

```
private TestRestTemplate template = new TestRestTemplate();
HttpHeaders headers = createHeaders("user-name", "user-password");

HttpHeaders createHeaders(String username, String password) {
  return new HttpHeaders() {
    {
      String auth = username + ":" + password;
      byte[] encodedAuth = Base64.getEncoder().encode
      (auth.getBytes(Charset.forName("US-ASCII")));
      String authHeader = "Basic " + new String(encodedAuth);
      set("Authorization", authHeader);
    }
  };
}

@Test
public void retrieveTodos() throws Exception {
  String expected = "["
  + "{id:1,user:Jack,desc:\"Learn Spring MVC\",done:false}" + ","
  + "{id:2,user:Jack,desc:\"Learn Struts\",done:false}" + "]";
  ResponseEntity<String> response = template.exchange(
  createUrl("/users/Jack/todos"), HttpMethod.GET,
  new HttpEntity<String>(null, headers),
  String.class);
  JSONAssert.assertEquals(expected, response.getBody(), false);
}
```

Some important things to note are as follows:

- `createHeaders("user-name", "user-password")`: This method creates `Base64. getEncoder().encode` basic authentication headers

- `ResponseEntity<String> response = template.exchange(createUrl("/users/Jack/todos"), HttpMethod.GET,new HttpEntity<String>(null, headers), String.class)`: The key change is the use of `HttpEntity` to supply the headers that we created earlier to the REST template

Unit testing

We would not want to use security for our unit tests. The following code snippet shows how we can disable security for the unit test:

```
@RunWith(SpringRunner.class)
@WebMvcTest(value = TodoController.class, secure = false)
public class TodoControllerTest {
```

The key part is the `secure = false` parameter on the `WebMvcTest` annotation. This will disable Spring Security for the unit test.

OAuth 2 authentication

OAuth is a protocol that provides flows in order to exchange authorization and authentication information between a range of web-enabled applications and services. It enables third-party applications to get restricted access to user information from a service, for example, Facebook, Twitter, or GitHub.

Before we get into the details, it would be useful to review the terminology typically used with respect to OAuth 2 authentication.

Let's consider an example. Let's say we want to expose the Todo API to third-party applications on the internet.

The following are the important players in a typical OAuth 2 exchange:

- **Resource owner**: This is the user of the third-party application that wants to use our Todo API. It decides how much of the information available with our API can be made available to the third-party application.
- **Resource server**: This hosts the Todo API, the resource we want to secure.
- **Client**: This is the third-party application that wants to consume our API.
- **Authorization server**: This is the server that provides the OAuth service.

High-level flow

The following steps show a high-level flow of a typical OAuth authentication:

1. The application requests that the user authorizes access to API resources.
2. When the user provides access, the application receives an authorization grant.
3. The application provides user authorization grant and its own client credentials to the authorization server.
4. If the authentication is successful, the authorization server responds with an access token.
5. The application calls the API (the resource server) that provides the access token for authentication.
6. If the access token is valid, the resource server returns the details of the resource.

Implementing OAuth 2 authentication for our service

OAuth 2 for Spring Security (`spring-security-oauth2`) is the module to provide OAuth 2 support to Spring Security. We will add it as a dependency in our `pom.xml` file:

```
<dependency>
  <groupId>org.springframework.security.oauth</groupId>
  <artifactId>spring-security-oauth2</artifactId>
</dependency>
```

Setting up authorization and resource servers

spring-security-oauth2 has not yet been (June 2017) been updated with the changes for Spring Framework 5.x and Spring Boot 2.x. We will use Spring Boot 1.5.x for examples related to OAuth 2 authentication. Code examples are here in the GitHub repository `https://github.com/PacktPublishing /Mastering-Spring-5.0`.

Typically, an authorization server would be a different server from the application where the API is exposed. To keep things simple, we will make our current API server act both as the resource server and as the authorization server.

The following code snippet shows how we can enable our application to act as the resource and authorization server:

```
@EnableResourceServer
@EnableAuthorizationServer
@SpringBootApplication
public class Application {
```

Here are a couple of important things to note:

- `@EnableResourceServer`: A convenient annotation for OAuth 2 resource servers, enabling a Spring Security filter that authenticates requests via an incoming OAuth 2 token
- `@EnableAuthorizationServer`: A convenience annotation to enable an authorization server with `AuthorizationEndpoint` and `TokenEndpoint` in the current application context, which must be a `DispatcherServlet` context

Now we can configure the access details in `application.properties`, as shown in the following code snippet:

```
security.user.name=user-name
security.user.password=user-password
security.oauth2.client.clientId: clientId
security.oauth2.client.clientSecret: clientSecret
security.oauth2.client.authorized-grant-types:
authorization_code,refresh_token,password
security.oauth2.client.scope: openid
```

A few important details are as follows:

- `security.user.name` and `security.user.password` are the authentication details of the resource owner that is an end user of a third-party application
- `security.oauth2.client.clientId` and `security.oauth2.client.clientSecret` are the authentication details of the client that is the third-party application (the service consumer)

Executing OAuth requests

We need a two-step process to access the APIs:

1. Obtain an access token.
2. Execute the request using the access token.

Obtaining an access token

To get an access token, we call the authorization server
(`http://localhost:8080/oauth/token`), providing the client authentication details in
the basic authentication mode and the user credentials as part of the form data. The
following screenshot shows how we can configure the client authentication details in basic
authentication:

The following screenshot shows how to configure the user authentication details as part of
the **POST** parameters:

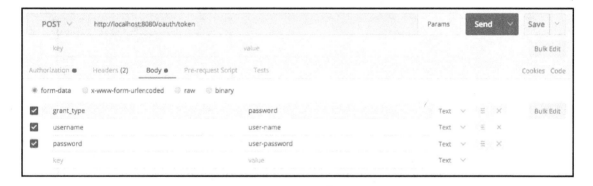

We are using `grant_type` as the password, indicating that we are sending the user authentication details to get the access token. When we execute the request, we get a response similar to the one shown in the following code snippet:

```
{
    "access_token": "a633dd55-102f-4f53-bcbd-a857df54b821",
    "token_type": "bearer",
    "refresh_token": "d68d89ec-0a13-4224-a29b-e9056768c7f0",
    "expires_in": 43199,
    "scope": "openid"
}
```

Here are a couple of important details:

- `access_token`: Client application can use the access token to authenticate further API calls. However, the access token will expire, typically in a very short time period.
- `refresh_token`: Client application can submit a new request to the authentication server with the `refresh_token` to get a new `access_token`.

Executing the request using the access token

Once we have `access_token`, we can execute the request using `access_token`, as shown in the following screenshot:

As you can see in the preceding screenshot, we provide the access token in the request header called **Authorization**. We use the value of the format `"Bearer {access_token}"`. Authentication succeeds and we get the expected resource details.

Integration test

We will now update our integration test to provide the OAuth 2 credentials. The following test highlights the important details:

```
@Test
public void retrieveTodos() throws Exception {
  String expected = "["
  + "{id:1,user:Jack,desc:\"Learn Spring MVC\",done:false}" + ","
  +"{id:2,user:Jack,desc:\"Learn Struts\",done:false}" + "]";
  String uri = "/users/Jack/todos";
  ResourceOwnerPasswordResourceDetails resource =
  new ResourceOwnerPasswordResourceDetails();
  resource.setUsername("user-name");
  resource.setPassword("user-password");
  resource.setAccessTokenUri(createUrl("/oauth/token"));
  resource.setClientId("clientId");
  resource.setClientSecret("clientSecret");
  resource.setGrantType("password");
  OAuth2RestTemplate oauthTemplate = new
  OAuth2RestTemplate(resource,new
  DefaultOAuth2ClientContext());
  ResponseEntity<String> response =
  oauthTemplate.getForEntity(createUrl(uri), String.class);
 JSONAssert.assertEquals(expected, response.getBody(), false);
}
```

Some important things to note are as follows:

- `ResourceOwnerPasswordResourceDetails resource = new ResourceOwnerPasswordResourceDetails()`: We set up `ResourceOwnerPasswordResourceDetails` with the user credentials and the client credentials
- `resource.setAccessTokenUri(createUrl("/oauth/token"))`: Configures the URL of the authentication server
- `OAuth2RestTemplate oauthTemplate = new OAuth2RestTemplate(resource,new DefaultOAuth2ClientContext())`: `OAuth2RestTemplate` is an extension of `RestTemplate`, which supports the OAuth 2 protocol

In this section, we looked at how to enable OAuth 2 authentication in our resources.

Internationalization

Internationalization (i18n) is the process of developing applications and services so that they can be customized for different languages and cultures across the world. It is also called **localization**. The goal of internationalization or localization is to build applications that can offer content in multiple languages and formats.

Spring Boot has built-in support for internationalization.

Let's build a simple service to understand how we can build internationalization in our APIs.

We would need to add a `LocaleResolver` and a message source to our Spring Boot application. The following code snippet should be included in `Application.java`:

```
@Bean
public LocaleResolver localeResolver() {
  SessionLocaleResolver sessionLocaleResolver =
  new SessionLocaleResolver();
  sessionLocaleResolver.setDefaultLocale(Locale.US);
  return sessionLocaleResolver;
}

@Bean
public ResourceBundleMessageSource messageSource() {
  ResourceBundleMessageSource messageSource =
  new ResourceBundleMessageSource();
  messageSource.setBasenames("messages");
  messageSource.setUseCodeAsDefaultMessage(true);
  return messageSource;
}
```

Some important things to note are as follows:

- `sessionLocaleResolver.setDefaultLocale(Locale.US)`: We are a setting a default locale of `Locale.US`.
- `messageSource.setBasenames("messages")`: We're setting the base name of the message source as `messages`. If we are in fr locale (France), we would use messages from `message_fr.properties`. If a message is not available in `message_fr.properties`, it would be searched for in the default `message.properties`.

- `messageSource.setUseCodeAsDefaultMessage(true)`: If a message is not found, then the code is returned as the default message.

Let's configure the messages in the respective files. Let's start with the `messages` properties. The messages in this file would act as the defaults:

```
welcome.message=Welcome in English
```

Let's also configure `messages_fr.properties`. The messages in this file would be used for the locale. If a message is not present here, then the defaults from `messages.properties` will be used:

```
welcome.message=Welcome in French
```

Let's create a service that returns a specific message using the locale specified in the "`Accept-Language`" header:

```
@GetMapping("/welcome-internationalized")
public String msg(@RequestHeader(value = "Accept-Language",
required = false) Locale locale) {
  return messageSource.getMessage("welcome.message", null,
  locale);
}
```

Here are a couple of things to note:

- `@RequestHeader(value = "Accept-Language", required = false) Locale locale`: The locale is picked up from the request header `Accept-Language`. It is not required. If a locale is not specified, the default locale is used.
- `messageSource.getMessage("welcome.message", null, locale)`: `messageSource` is autowired into the controller. We get the welcome message based on the given locale.

The following screenshot shows the response when the preceding service is called without specifying a default `Accept-Language`:

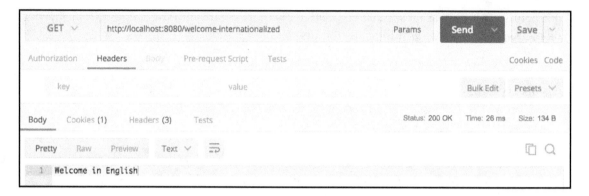

The default message from `messages.properties` is returned.

The following screenshot shows the response when the preceding service is called with `Accept-Language fr`:

The localized message from `messages_fr.properties` is returned.

In the preceding example, we customized the service to return localized messages based on the locale in the request. A similar approach can be used to internationalize all services in a component.

Caching

Caching data from services plays a crucial role in improving the performance and scalability of applications. In this section, we will look at the implementation options that Spring Boot provides.

Spring provides a caching abstraction based on annotations. We will start with using Spring caching annotations. Later, we will introduce *JSR-107* caching annotations and compare them with Spring abstractions.

Spring-boot-starter-cache

Spring Boot provides a starter project for caching `spring-boot-starter-cache`. Adding this to an application brings in all the dependencies to enable *JSR-107* and Spring caching annotations. The following code snippet shows the dependency details for `spring-boot-starter-cache`. Let's add this to our file `pom.xml`:

```
<dependency>
  <groupId>org.springframework.boot</groupId>
  <artifactId>spring-boot-starter-cache</artifactId>
</dependency>
```

Enabling caching

Before we can start using caching, we need to enable caching on the application. The following code snippet shows how we can enable caching:

```
@EnableCaching
@SpringBootApplication
public class Application {
```

`@EnableCaching` would enable caching in a Spring Boot application.

Spring Boot automatically configures a suitable CacheManager framework to serve as a provider for the relevant cache. We will look at the details of how Spring Boot decides the CacheManager a little later.

Caching data

Now that we have enabled caching, we can add the `@Cacheable` annotation to the methods where we want to cache the data. The following code snippet shows how to enable caching on `retrieveTodos`:

```
@Cacheable("todos")
public List<Todo> retrieveTodos(String user) {
```

In the preceding example, the `todos` for a specific user are cached. On the first call to the method for a specific user, the `todos` will be retrieved from the service. On subsequent calls for the same user, the data will be returned from the cache.

Spring also provides conditional caching. In the following snippet, caching is enabled only if the specified condition is satisfied:

```
@Cacheable(cacheNames="todos", condition="#user.length < 10")
public List<Todo> retrieveTodos(String user) {
```

Spring also provides additional annotations to evict data from the cache and add some custom data to cache. A few important ones are listed as follows:

- `@CachePut`: Used to explicitly add data to the cache
- `@CacheEvict`: Used to remove stale data from the cache
- `@Caching`: Allows multiple nested `@Cacheable`, `@CachePut` , and `@CacheEvict` annotations to be used on the same method

JSR-107 caching annotations

JSR-107 aims to standardize caching annotations. Listed here are some of the important *JSR-107* annotations:

- `@CacheResult`: Similar to `@Cacheable`
- `@CacheRemove`: Similar to `@CacheEvict`; `@CacheRemove` supports conditional eviction if an exception occurs
- `@CacheRemoveAll`: Similar to `@CacheEvict(allEntries=true)`; used to remove all entries from the cache

JSR-107 and Spring's caching annotations are fairly similar in terms of the features they offer. Either of them is a good choice. We lean slightly toward *JSR-107* because it's a standard. However, make sure you are not using both in the same project.

Auto-detection order

When caching is enabled, Spring Boot auto-configuration starts looking for a caching provider. The following list shows the order in which Spring Boot searches for caching providers. The list is in order of decreasing preference:

- JCache (*JSR-107*) (EhCache 3, Hazelcast, Infinispan, and so on)
- EhCache 2.x
- Hazelcast
- Infinispan
- Couchbase
- Redis
- Caffeine
- Guava
- Simple

Summary

Spring Boot makes developing Spring-based applications easy. It enables us to create production-ready applications very quickly.

In this chapter, we covered how to add features such as exception handling, caching, and internationalization to our application. We discussed the best practices of documenting REST services using Swagger. We looked at the basics of securing our microservice with Spring Security.

In the next chapter, we will shift our attention toward advanced features in Spring Boot. We will look at how to provide monitoring on top of our REST services, learn how to deploy the microservice to the Cloud, and understand how to become more productive when developing applications with Spring Boot.

7
Advanced Spring Boot Features

In the previous chapter, we extended our microservice with exception handling, HATEOAS, caching, and internationalization. In this chapter, let's turn our attention to deploying our services to production. To be able to deploy the services to production, we need to be able to set up and create functionality to configure, deploy, and monitor services.

The following are some of the questions we will answer during this chapter:

- How to externalize application configuration?
- How to use profiles to configure environment-specific values?
- How to deploy our application to the Cloud?
- What is an embedded server? How can you use Tomcat, Jetty, and Undertow?
- What monitoring features does Spring Boot Actuator provide?
- How can you be a more productive developer with Spring Boot?

Externalised configuration

Applications are typically built once (in JAR or WAR) and then deployed into multiple environments. The following figure shows some of the different environments an application can be deployed to:

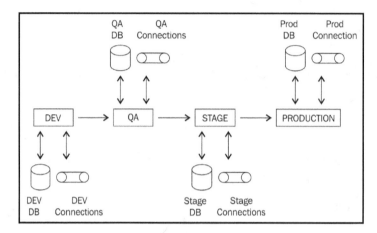

In each of the preceding environments, an application typically has the following:

- Connections to databases
- Connections to multiple services
- Specific environment configurations

It is a good practice to externalize configurations that change between different environments into a configuration file or database.

Spring Boot provides a flexible, standardized approach for externalized configuration.

In this section, we will look at the following:

- How can properties from `application.properties` be used inside our services?
- How do type-safe Configuration Properties make application configuration a cakewalk?
- What kind of support does Spring Boot provide for **Spring Profiles**?
- How can you configure properties in `application.properties`?

In Spring Boot, `application.properties` is the default file from which configuration values are picked up. Spring Boot can pick the `application.properties` file from anywhere on the classpath. Typically, `application.properties` is located at `src\main\resources`, as shown in the following screenshot:

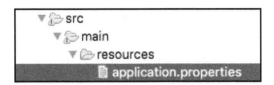

In `Chapter 6`, *Extending Microservices*, we looked at examples of customizing Spring Security using configuration in `application.properties`:

```
security.basic.enabled=false
management.security.enabled=false
security.user.name=user-name
security.user.password=user-password
security.oauth2.client.clientId: clientId
security.oauth2.client.clientSecret: clientSecret
security.oauth2.client.authorized-grant-types:
authorization_code,refresh_token,password
security.oauth2.client.scope: openid
```

Similar to these, all other Spring Boot starters, modules, and frameworks can be customized through configuration in `application.properties`. In the next section, let's look at some of the configuration options Spring Boot provides for these frameworks.

Customizing frameworks through application.properties

In this section, we will discuss some of the important things that can be configured through `application.properties`.

For the complete list, refer to `https://docs.spring.io/spring-boot/doc s/current-SNAPSHOT/reference/htmlsingle/#common-application-pr operties`.

Logging

Some of the things that can be configured are as follows:

- The location of the logging configuration file
- the location of the log file
- Logging level

The following snippet shows a few examples:

```
# Location of the logging configuration file.
  logging.config=
# Log file name.
  logging.file=
# Configure Logging level.
# Example `logging.level.org.springframework=TRACE`
  logging.level.*=
```

Embedded server configuration

An embedded server is one of the most important features of Spring Boot. Some of the embedded server features that can be configured through application properties include:

- Server ports
- SSL support and configuration
- Access log configuration

The following snippet shows some of the embedded server features that can be configured through application properties:

```
# Path of the error controller.
server.error.path=/error
# Server HTTP port.
server.port=8080
# Enable SSL support.
server.ssl.enabled=
# Path to key store with SSL certificate
server.ssl.key-store=
# Key Store Password
server.ssl.key-store-password=
# Key Store Provider
server.ssl.key-store-provider=
# Key Store Type
server.ssl.key-store-type=
# Should we enable access log of Tomcat?
```

```
server.tomcat.accesslog.enabled=false
# Maximum number of connections that server can accept
server.tomcat.max-connections=
```

Spring MVC

Spring MVC can be extensively configured through `application.properties`. Listed here are some of the important configurations:.

```
# Date format to use. For instance `dd/MM/yyyy`.
 spring.mvc.date-format=
# Locale to use.
 spring.mvc.locale=
# Define how the locale should be resolved.
 spring.mvc.locale-resolver=accept-header
# Should "NoHandlerFoundException" be thrown if no Handler is found?
 spring.mvc.throw-exception-if-no-handler-found=false
# Spring MVC view prefix. Used by view resolver.
 spring.mvc.view.prefix=
# Spring MVC view suffix. Used by view resolver.
 spring.mvc.view.suffix=
```

Spring starter security

Spring Security can be extensively configured through `application.properties`. The following examples show some of the important configuration options related to Spring Security:

```
# Set true to Enable basic authentication
 security.basic.enabled=true
# Provide a Comma-separated list of uris you would want to secure
 security.basic.path=/**
# Provide a Comma-separated list of paths you don't want to secure
 security.ignored=
# Name of the default user configured by spring security
 security.user.name=user
# Password of the default user configured by spring security.
 security.user.password=
# Roles granted to default user
 security.user.role=USER
```

Data Sources, JDBC and JPA

Data Sources, JDBC, and can also be extensively configured through `application.properties`. Listed here are some of the important options:

```
# Fully qualified name of the JDBC driver.
 spring.datasource.driver-class-name=
# Populate the database using 'data.sql'.
 spring.datasource.initialize=true
# JNDI location of the datasource.
 spring.datasource.jndi-name=
# Name of the datasource.
 spring.datasource.name=testdb
# Login password of the database.
 spring.datasource.password=
# Schema (DDL) script resource references.
 spring.datasource.schema=
# Db User to use to execute DDL scripts
 spring.datasource.schema-username=
# Db password to execute DDL scripts
 spring.datasource.schema-password=
# JDBC url of the database.
 spring.datasource.url=
# JPA - Initialize the schema on startup.
 spring.jpa.generate-ddl=false
# Use Hibernate's newer IdentifierGenerator for AUTO, TABLE and SEQUENCE.
 spring.jpa.hibernate.use-new-id-generator-mappings=
# Enable logging of SQL statements.
 spring.jpa.show-sql=false
```

Other configuration options

Some other things that can be configured through `application.properties` are as follows:

- Profiles
- HTTP message converters (Jackson/JSON)
- Transaction management
- Internationalization

The following examples show some of the configuration options:

```
# Comma-separated list (or list if using YAML) of active profiles.
spring.profiles.active=
# HTTP message conversion. jackson or gson
spring.http.converters.preferred-json-mapper=jackson
# JACKSON Date format string. Example `yyyy-MM-dd HH:mm:ss`.
spring.jackson.date-format=
# Default transaction timeout in seconds.
spring.transaction.default-timeout=
# Perform the rollback on commit failures.
spring.transaction.rollback-on-commit-failure=
# Internationalisation : Comma-separated list of basenames
spring.messages.basename=messages
# Cache expiration for resource bundles, in sec. -1 will cache for ever
spring.messages.cache-seconds=-1
```

Custom properties in application.properties

Until now, we have looked at using prebuilt properties provided by Spring Boot for various frameworks. In this section, we will look at creating our application-specific configuration that can also be configured in application.properties.

Let's consider an example. We want to be able to interact with an external service. We want to be able to externalize the configuration of the URL of this service.

The following example shows how we would want to configure the external service in application.properties:

```
somedataservice.url=http://abc.service.com/something
```

We want to use the value of the somedataservice.url property in our data service. The following snippet shows how we can do that in an example data service.

```
@Component
public class SomeDataService {
  @Value("${somedataservice.url}")
  private String url;
  public String retrieveSomeData() {
    // Logic using the url and getting the data
    return "data from service";
  }
}
```

A couple of important things to note are as follows:

- `@Component public class SomeDataService`: The data service bean is managed by Spring because of the `@Component` annotation.
- `@Value("${somedataservice.url}")`: The value of `somedataservice.url` will be autowired into the `url` variable. The `url` value can be used in the methods of the bean.

Configuration properties - type-safe Configuration Management

While the `@Value` annotation provides dynamic configuration, it also has several drawbacks:

- If we want to use three property values in a service, we would need to autowire them using `@Value` three times.
- The `@Value` annotations and the keys of the messages would be spread across the application. If we want to find the list of the configurable values in an application, we have to search through the application for `@Value` annotations.

Spring Boot provides a better approach to application configuration through the strongly typed `ConfigurationProperties` feature. This allows us to do the following:

- Have all the properties in a predefined bean structure
- This bean would act as the centralized store for all application properties
- The configuration bean can be autowired wherever application configuration is needed

An example configuration bean is shown as follows:

```
@Component
@ConfigurationProperties("application")
public class ApplicationConfiguration {
  private boolean enableSwitchForService1;
  private String service1Url;
  private int service1Timeout;
  public boolean isEnableSwitchForService1() {
    return enableSwitchForService1;
  }
 public void setEnableSwitchForService1
 (boolean enableSwitchForService1) {
    this.enableSwitchForService1 = enableSwitchForService1;
```

```
    }
  public String getService1Url() {
     return service1Url;
  }
  public void setService1Url(String service1Url) {
     this.service1Url = service1Url;
  }
  public int getService1Timeout() {
     return service1Timeout;
  }
  public void setService1Timeout(int service1Timeout) {
     this.service1Timeout = service1Timeout;
  }
 }
}
```

A couple of important things to note are as follows:

- @ConfigurationProperties("application") is the annotation for an externalized configuration. We can add this annotation to any class to bind to external properties. The value in the double quotes--application--is used as a prefix while binding external configuration to this bean.
- We are defining multiple configurable values in the bean.
- Getters and setters are needed since binding happens through Java beans property descriptors.

The following snippet shows how the values for these properties can be defined in application.properties:

```
application.enableSwitchForService1=true
application.service1Url=http://abc-dev.service.com/somethingelse
application.service1Timeout=250
```

A couple of important things to note are as follows:

- application: The prefix is defined as part of @ConfigurationProperties("application") while defining the configuration bean
- Values are defined by appending the prefix to the name of the property

We can use configuration properties in other beans by autowiring `ApplicationConfiguration` into the bean:

```
@Component
public class SomeOtherDataService {
  @Autowired
  private ApplicationConfiguration configuration;
  public String retrieveSomeData() {
    // Logic using the url and getting the data
    System.out.println(configuration.getService1Timeout());
    System.out.println(configuration.getService1Url());
    System.out.println(configuration.isEnableSwitchForService1());
    return "data from service";
  }
}
```

A couple of important things to note are as follows:

- `@Autowired private ApplicationConfiguration configuration`: `ApplicationConfiguration` is autowired into `SomeOtherDataService`
- `configuration.getService1Timeout()`, `configuration.getService1Url()`, `configuration.isEnableSwitchForService1()`: Values can be accessed in bean methods using the getter methods on the configuration bean

By default, any failure in binding externally configured values to configuration properties bean would result in the failure of the server start up. This prevents problems that arise because of misconfigured applications running in production.

Let's use the misconfigure service timeout to see what happens:

```
application.service1Timeout=SOME_MISCONFIGURATION
```

The application will fail to start up with an error.

```
***************************
APPLICATION FAILED TO START
***************************
Description:
Binding to target
com.mastering.spring.springboot.configuration.ApplicationConfiguration@79d3
473e failed:

Property: application.service1Timeout
Value: SOME_MISCONFIGURATION
Reason: Failed to convert property value of type 'java.lang.String' to
```

```
required type 'int' for property 'service1Timeout'; nested exception is
org.springframework.core.convert.ConverterNotFoundException: No converter
found capable of converting from type [java.lang.String] to type [int]

Action:
Update your application's configuration
```

Profiles

Until now, we looked at how to externalize application configuration to a property file, `application.properties`. What we want to be able to do is have different values for the same property in different environments.

Profiles provide a way to provide different configurations in different environments.

The following snippet shows how to configure an active profile in `application.properties`:

```
spring.profiles.active=dev
```

Once you have an active profile configured, you can define properties specific to that profile in `application-{profile-name}.properties`. For `dev` profile, the name of the properties file would be `application-dev.properties`. The following example shows the configuration in `application-dev.properties`:

```
application.enableSwitchForService1=true
application.service1Url=http://abc-dev.service.com/somethingelse
application.service1Timeout=250
```

The values in `application-dev.properties` will override the default configuration in `application.properties` if the active profile is `dev`.

We can have configurations for multiple environments, as shown here:

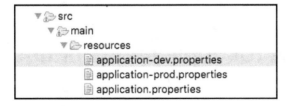

Profiles-based Bean configuration

Profiles can also be used to define different beans or different bean configurations in different environments. All classes marked with `@Component` or `@Configuration` can also be marked with an additional `@Profile` annotation to specify the profile in which the bean or configuration is enabled.

Let's consider an example. An application needs different caches enabled in different environments. In the `dev` environment, it uses a very simple cache. In production, we would want to use a distributed cache. This can be implemented using profiles.

The following bean shows the configuration enabled in a `dev` environment:

```
@Profile("dev")
@Configuration
public class DevSpecificConfiguration {
  @Bean
  public String cache() {
    return "Dev Cache Configuration";
  }
}
```

The following bean shows the configuration enabled in a production environment:

```
@Profile("prod")
@Configuration
public class ProdSpecificConfiguration {
  @Bean
  public String cache() {
    return "Production Cache Configuration - Distributed Cache";
  }
}
```

Based on the active profile configured, the respective configuration is picked up. Note that we are not really configuring a distributed cache in this example. We are returning a simple string to illustrate that profiles can be used to implement these kinds of variations.

Other options for application configuration values

Until now, the approaches we took to configure application properties was using the key value pairs from either `application.properties` or `application-{profile-name}.properties`.

Spring Boot provides a number of other ways to configure application properties.

Listed here are some of the important ways of providing application configuration:

- Command-line arguments
- Creating a system property with the name `SPRING_APPLICATION_JSON` and including the JSON configuration
- ServletConfig init parameters
- ServletContext init parameters
- Java System properties (`System.getProperties()`)
- Operating system environment variables
- Profile-specific application properties outside of `.jar`, somewhere in the classpath of the application (`application-{profile}.properties`)
- Profile-specific application properties packaged inside your `.jar` (`application-{profile}.properties` and YAML variants)
- Application properties outside the `.jar`
- Application properties packaged inside the `.jar`

More information can be found in the Spring Boot documentation at `http://docs.spring.io/spring-boot/docs/current-SNAPSHOT/reference/htmlsingle/#boot-features-external-config`.

The approaches at the top of this list have higher priority than those at the bottom of the list. For example, if a command-line argument with the name `spring.profiles.active` is provided when launching the application, it would override any configuration provided through `application.properties` because command-line arguments have higher preference.

This provides great flexibility in determining how you would want to configure your application in different environments.

YAML configuration

Spring Boot also supports **YAML** to configure your properties.

YAML is an abbreviation for "YAML Ain't Markup Language". It is a human readable structured format. YAML is commonly used for configuration files.

To understand basic syntax of YAML, look at the example below (`application.yaml`). This shows how our application configuration can be specified in YAML.

```
spring:
   profiles:
      active: prod
security:
   basic:
      enabled: false
   user:
      name=user-name
      password=user-password
oauth2:
   client:
      clientId: clientId
      clientSecret: clientSecret
      authorized-grant-types: authorization_code, refresh_token, password
      scope: openid
application:
   enableSwitchForService1: true
   service1Url: http://abc-dev.service.com/somethingelse
   service1Timeout: 250
```

As you can see, the YAML configuration is much more readable than `application.properties`, as it allows better grouping of properties.

Another advantage of YAML is that it allows you to specify the configuration for multiple profiles in a single configuration file. The following snippet shows an example:

```
application:
   service1Url: http://service.default.com
---
spring:
   profiles: dev
   application:
      service1Url: http://service.dev.com
---
spring:
   profiles: prod
   application:
      service1Url: http://service.prod.com
```

In this example, `http://service.dev.com` will be used in the `dev` profile, and `http://service.prod.com` is used in the `prod` profile. In all other profiles, `http://service.default.com` will be used as the service URL.

Embedded servers

One of the important concepts Spring Boot brings in is embedded servers.

Let's first understand the difference between traditional Java web application deployment and this new concept called embedded server.

Traditionally, with Java web applications, we build **Web Application Archive (WAR)** or **Enterprise Application Archive (EAR)** and deploy them into servers. Before we can deploy a WAR on the server, we need a web server or an application server installed on the server. The application server would be on top of the Java instance installed on the server. So, we need Java and an application (or web server) installed on the machine before we can deploy our application. The following figure shows an example installation in Linux:

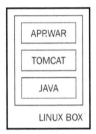

Spring Boot brings in the concept of embedded servers, where the web server is part of the application deployable--JAR. To deploy applications using embedded servers, it is sufficient if Java is installed on the server. The following figure shows an example installation:

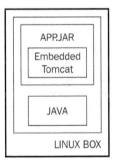

When we build any application with Spring Boot, the default is to build a JAR. With `spring-boot-starter-web`, the default embedded server is Tomcat.

When we use `spring-boot-starter-web`, a few Tomcat-related dependencies can be seen in the Maven dependencies section. These dependencies will be included as part of the application deployment package:

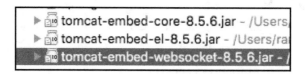

To deploy the application, we need to build a JAR. We can build a JAR using the command below:

```
mvn clean install
```

The following screenshot shows the structure of the JAR created.

`BOOT-INF\classes` contains all application-related class files (from `src\main\java`) as well as the application properties from `src\main\resources`:

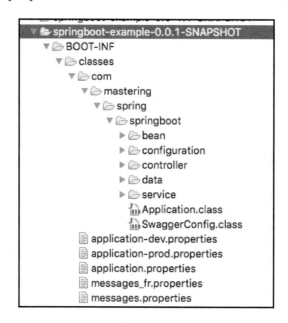

Some of the libraries in BOOT-INF\lib are shown in the following screenshot:

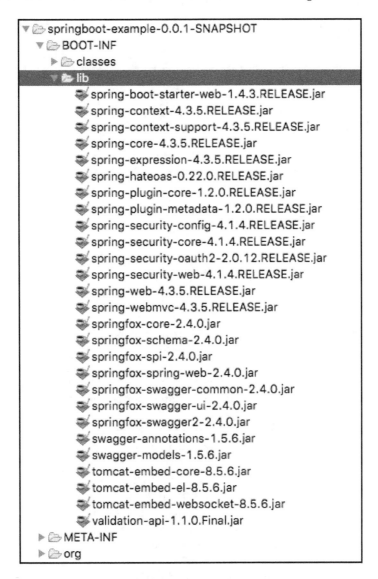

BOOT-INF\lib contains all the JAR dependencies of the application. There are three Tomcat-specific JARs among these. These three JARs enable the launch of an embedded Tomcat service when the application is run as a Java application. Because of this, a Java installation is sufficient to deploy this application on a server.

Switching to Jetty and Undertow

The following screenshot shows the changes needed in order to switch to using Jetty embedded server:

```xml
<dependency>
    <groupId>org.springframework.boot</groupId>
    <artifactId>spring-boot-starter-web</artifactId>
    <exclusions>
        <exclusion>
            <groupId>org.springframework.boot</groupId>
            <artifactId>spring-boot-starter-tomcat</artifactId>
        </exclusion>
    </exclusions>
</dependency>

<dependency>
    <groupId>org.springframework.boot</groupId>
    <artifactId>spring-boot-starter-jetty</artifactId>
</dependency>
```

All that we need to do is exclude the Tomcat starter dependency in `spring-boot-starter-web` and include a dependency in `spring-boot-starter-jetty`.

You can now see a number of Jetty dependencies in the Maven dependencies section. The following screenshot shows a few of the Jetty-related dependencies:

```
▶ jetty-servlets-9.3.14.v20161028.jar - /Us
▶ jetty-continuation-9.3.14.v20161028.jar
▶ jetty-http-9.3.14.v20161028.jar - /Users/
▶ jetty-util-9.3.14.v20161028.jar - /Users/r
▶ jetty-io-9.3.14.v20161028.jar - /Users/ra
▶ jetty-webapp-9.3.14.v20161028.jar - /Us
▶ jetty-xml-9.3.14.v20161028.jar - /Users/
▶ jetty-servlet-9.3.14.v20161028.jar - /Use
▶ jetty-security-9.3.14.v20161028.jar - /Us
▶ jetty-server-9.3.14.v20161028.jar - /Use
```

Switching to Undertow is equally easy. Use `spring-boot-starter-undertow` instead of `spring-boot-starter-jetty`:

```
<dependency>
   <groupId>org.springframework.boot</groupId>
   <artifactId>spring-boot-starter-undertow</artifactId>
</dependency>
```

Building a WAR file

Spring Boot also provides the option of building a traditional WAR file instead of using a JAR.

First, we need to change our packaging in `pom.xml` to `WAR`:

```
<packaging>war</packaging>
```

We would want to prevent tomcat server to be embedded as a dependency in the WAR file. We can do this by modifying the dependency on the embedded server (Tomcat in the following example) to have a scope of provided. The following snippet shows the exact details:

```
<dependency>
   <groupId>org.springframework.boot</groupId>
   <artifactId>spring-boot-starter-tomcat</artifactId>
   <scope>provided</scope>
</dependency>
```

When you build the WAR file, Tomcat dependencies are not included. We can use this WAR to deploy on an application server, such as WebSphere or Weblogic, or a web server, such as Tomcat.

Developer tools

Spring Boot provides tools that can improve the experience of developing Spring Boot applications. One of these is Spring Boot developer tools.

To use Spring Boot developer tools, we need to include a dependency:

```
<dependencies>
  <dependency>
    <groupId>org.springframework.boot</groupId>
    <artifactId>spring-boot-devtools</artifactId>
    <optional>true</optional>
  </dependency>
</dependencies>
```

Spring Boot developer tools, by default, disables the caching of view templates and static files. This enables a developer to see the changes as soon as they make them.

Another important feature is the automatic restart when any file in the classpath changes. So, the application automatically restarts in the following scenarios:

- When we make a change to a controller or a service class
- When we make a change to the property file

The advantages of Spring Boot developer tools are as follows:

- The developer does not need to stop and start the application each time. The application is automatically restarted as soon as there is a change.
- The restart feature in Spring Boot developer tools is intelligent. It only reloads the actively developed classes. It does not reload the third-party JARs (using two different class-loaders). Thereby, the restart when something in the application changes is much faster compared to cold-starting an application.

Live reload

Another useful Spring Boot developer tools feature is **live reload**. You can download a specific plugin for your browser from `http://livereload.com/extensions/`.

You can enable live reload by clicking on the button in the browser. The button in the Safari browser is shown in the following screenshot. It's in the top-left corner beside the address bar.

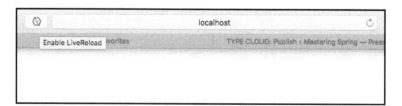

If there are code changes made on the pages or services that are shown in the browser, they are auto-refreshed with new content. There is no need to hit that refresh button anymore!

Spring Boot Actuator

When an application is deployed into production:

- We want to know immediately if some service goes down or is very slow
- We want to know immediately if any of the servers does not have sufficient free space or memory

This is called **application monitoring**.

Spring Boot Actuator provides a number of production-ready monitoring features.

We will add Spring Boot Actuator by adding a simple dependency:

```
<dependencies>
  <dependency>
    <groupId>org.springframework.boot</groupId>
    <artifactId>spring-boot-starter-actuator</artifactId>
  </dependency>
</dependencies>
```

As soon as the actuator is added to an application, it enables a number of endpoints. When we start the application, we see a number of added new mappings. The following screenshot shows an extract of these new mappings from the start up log:

```
Mapped "{[/application/mappings || /application/mappings.json],methods=[GET],produces=[application/vnd.spring-boot.actuator.v2+json || application/json]}" o
Mapped "{[/application/health || /application/health.json],methods=[GET],produces=[application/vnd.spring-boot.actuator.v2+json || application/json]}" onto
Mapped "{[/application/trace || /application/trace.json],methods=[GET],produces=[application/vnd.spring-boot.actuator.v2+json || application/json]}" onto pu
Mapped "{[/application/loggers/{name:.*}],methods=[GET],produces=[application/vnd.spring-boot.actuator.v2+json || application/json]}" onto public java.lang.
Mapped "{[/application/loggers/{name:.*}],methods=[POST],consumes=[application/vnd.spring-boot.actuator.v2+json || application/json],produces=[application/v
Mapped "{[/application/loggers || /application/loggers.json],methods=[GET],produces=[application/vnd.spring-boot.actuator.v2+json || application/json]}" ont
Mapped "{[/application/metrics/{name:.*}],methods=[GET],produces=[application/vnd.spring-boot.actuator.v2+json || application/json]}" onto public java.lang.
Mapped "{[/application/metrics || /application/metrics.json],methods=[GET],produces=[application/vnd.spring-boot.actuator.v2+json || application/json]}" ont
Mapped "{[/application || /application.json],produces=[text/html]}" onto public java.lang.String org.springframework.boot.actuate.endpoint.mvc.HalBrowserMvc
Mapped "{[/application || /application.json],methods=[GET],produces=[application/vnd.spring-boot.actuator.v2+json || application/json]}" onto public org.spr
Mapped "{[/application/info || /application/info.json],methods=[GET],produces=[application/vnd.spring-boot.actuator.v2+json || application/json]}" onto publ
Mapped "{[/application/beans || /application/beans.json],methods=[GET],produces=[application/vnd.spring-boot.actuator.v2+json || application/json]}" onto pu
Mapped "{[/application/heapdump || /application/heapdump.json],methods=[GET],produces=[application/octet-stream]}" onto public void org.springframework.boot
Mapped "{[/application/auditevents || /application/auditevents.json],methods=[GET],produces=[application/vnd.spring-boot.actuator.v2+json || application/jso
Mapped "{[/application/env/{name:.*}],methods=[GET],produces=[application/vnd.spring-boot.actuator.v2+json || application/json]}" onto public java.lang.Obje
Mapped "{[/application/env || /application/env.json],methods=[GET],produces=[application/vnd.spring-boot.actuator.v2+json || application/json]}" onto public
Mapped "{[/application/configprops || /application/configprops.json],methods=[GET],produces=[application/vnd.spring-boot.actuator.v2+json || application/jso
Mapped "{[/application/dump || /application/dump.json],methods=[GET],produces=[application/vnd.spring-boot.actuator.v2+json || application/json]}" onto publ
Mapped "{[/application/autoconfig || /application/autoconfig.json],methods=[GET],produces=[application/vnd.spring-boot.actuator.v2+json || application/json]
```

The actuator exposes a number of endpoints. The actuator endpoint (http://localhost:8080/application) acts as a discovery for all other endpoints. The following screenshot shows the response when we execute the request from a Postman:

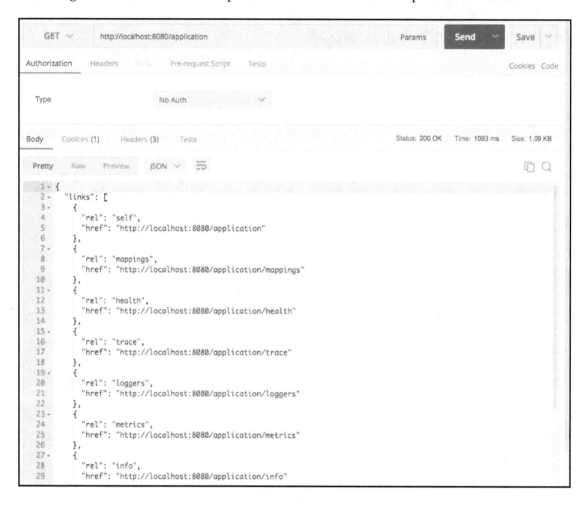

HAL Browser

A number of these endpoints expose a lot of data. To be able to visualize the information better, we will add an **HAL Browser** to our application:

```
<dependency>
  <groupId>org.springframework.data</groupId>
  <artifactId>spring-data-rest-hal-browser</artifactId>
</dependency>
```

Spring Boot Actuator exposes REST APIs around all the data captured from the Spring Boot application and environment. The HAL Browser enables visual representation around the Spring Boot Actuator API:

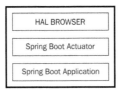

When we launch `http://localhost:8080/application` in the browser, we can see all the URLs exposed by actuator.

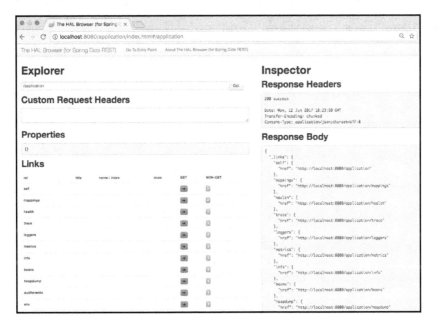

Let's browse all the information exposed by actuator as part of different endpoints through the HAL Browser.

Configuration properties

The `configprops` endpoint provides information about configuration options that can be configured through application properties. It basically is a collated list of all `@ConfigurationProperties`. The following screenshot shows configprops in HAL Browser:

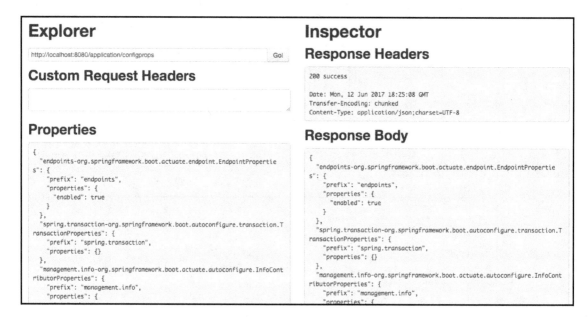

To illustrate a known example, the following section from the service response shows the configuration options available for Spring MVC:

```
"spring.mvc-  org.springframework.boot.autoconfigure.web.WebMvcProperties":
{
    "prefix": "spring.mvc",
    "properties": {
                   "dateFormat": null,
                   "servlet": {
                      "loadOnStartup": -1
                   },
    "staticPathPattern": "/**",
    "dispatchOptionsRequest": true,
    "dispatchTraceRequest": false,
    "locale": null,
    "ignoreDefaultModelOnRedirect": true,
    "logResolvedException": true,
    "async": {
                "requestTimeout": null
             },
    "messageCodesResolverFormat": null,
    "mediaTypes": {},
    "view": {
              "prefix": null,
              "suffix": null
           },
    "localeResolver": "ACCEPT_HEADER",
    "throwExceptionIfNoHandlerFound": false
    }
}
```

 To provide configuration for Spring MVC, we combine the prefix with the path in properties. For example, to configure loadOnStartup, we use a property with the name spring.mvc.servlet.loadOnStartup.

Environment details

The **environment** (**env**) endpoint provides information about the operating system, JVM installation, classpath, system environment variable, and the values configured in various application properties files. The following screenshot shows the environment endpoint in the HAL Browser:

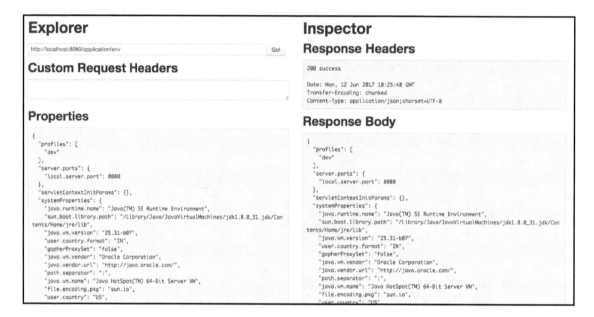

An extract from the response from the `/application/env` service is shown here. It shows a few system details as well as the details from application configuration:

```
"systemEnvironment": {
    "JAVA_MAIN_CLASS_13377": "com.mastering.spring.springboot.Application",
    "PATH": "/usr/bin:/bin:/usr/sbin:/sbin",
    "SHELL": "/bin/bash",
    "JAVA_STARTED_ON_FIRST_THREAD_13019": "1",
    "APP_ICON_13041": "../Resources/Eclipse.icns",
    "USER": "rangaraokaranam",
    "TMPDIR": "/var/folders/y_/x4jdvdkx7w94q5qsh745gzz00000gn/T/",
    "SSH_AUTH_SOCK": "/private/tmp/com.apple.launchd.IcESePQCLV/Listeners",
    "XPC_FLAGS": "0x0",
    "JAVA_STARTED_ON_FIRST_THREAD_13041": "1",
    "APP_ICON_11624": "../Resources/Eclipse.icns",
    "LOGNAME": "rangaraokaranam",
    "XPC_SERVICE_NAME": "0",
    "HOME": "/Users/rangaraokaranam"
  },
  "applicationConfig: [classpath:/application-prod.properties]": {
    "application.service1Timeout": "250",
    "application.service1Url": "http://abc-
prod.service.com/somethingelse",
    "application.enableSwitchForService1": "false"
  },
```

Health

The health service provides details of the disk space and status of the application. The following screenshot shows the service executed from the HAL Browser:

Mappings

The mappings endpoint provides information about different service endpoints that are exposed from the application:

- URI
- Request methods
- Bean
- Controller methods exposing the service

Mappings provides a collated list of all `@RequestMapping` paths. An extract from the response of the `/application/mappings` endpoint is shown here. We can see mappings of the different controller methods that were created earlier in this book:

```
"{[/welcome-internationalized],methods=[GET]}": {
    "bean": "requestMappingHandlerMapping",
    "method": "public java.lang.String
    com.mastering.spring.springboot.controller.
    BasicController.msg(java.uti l.Locale)"
},
"{[/welcome],methods=[GET]}": {
    "bean": "requestMappingHandlerMapping",
    "method": "public java.lang.String
     com.mastering.spring.springboot.controller.
     BasicController.welcome()"
},
"{[/welcome-with-object],methods=[GET]}": {
     "bean": "requestMappingHandlerMapping",
     "method": "public com.mastering.spring.springboot.
      bean.WelcomeBeancom.mastering.spring.springboot.
      controller.BasicController.welcomeWithObject()"
},
"{[/welcome-with-parameter/name/{name}],methods=[GET]}": {
     "bean": "requestMappingHandlerMapping",
     "method": "public
      com.mastering.spring.springboot.bean.WelcomeBean
      com.mastering.spring.springboot.controller.
      BasicController.welcomeWithParameter(java.lang.String)"
},
"{[/users/{name}/todos],methods=[POST]}": {
     "bean": "requestMappingHandlerMapping",
     "method": "org.springframework.http.ResponseEntity<?>
      com.mastering.spring.springboot.controller.
      TodoController.add(java.lang.String,com.mastering.spring.
      springboot.bean.Todo)"
},
```

```
"{[/users/{name}/todos],methods=[GET]}": {
        "bean": "requestMappingHandlerMapping",
        "method": "public java.util.List<com.mastering.spring.
         springboot.bean.Todo>
         com.mastering.spring.springboot.controller.
         TodoController.retrieveTodos(java.lang.String)"
},
"{[/users/{name}/todos/{id}],methods=[GET]}": {
        "bean": "requestMappingHandlerMapping",
        "method": "public
         org.springframework.hateoas.Resource<com.mastering.
         spring.springboot.bean.Todo>
         com.mastering.spring.springboot.controller.
         TodoController.retrieveTodo(java.lang.String,int)"
},
```

Beans

The beans endpoint provides the details about the beans that are loaded into the Spring context. This is useful in debugging any problems related to Spring context.

An extract from the response of the /application/beans endpoint is shown below:

```
{
    "bean": "basicController",
    "aliases": [],
    "scope": "singleton",
    "type": "com.mastering.spring.springboot.
     controller.BasicController",
    "resource": "file [/in28Minutes/Workspaces/
     SpringTutorial/mastering-spring-chapter-5-6-
     7/target/classes/com/mastering/spring/springboot/
     controller/BasicController.class]",
    "dependencies": [
                    "messageSource"
                    ]
},
{
    "bean": "todoController",
    "aliases": [],
    "scope": "singleton",
    "type": "com.mastering.spring.springboot.
     controller.TodoController",
     "resource": "file [/in28Minutes/Workspaces/SpringTutorial/
     mastering-spring-chapter-5-6-
     7/target/classes/com/mastering/spring/
```

```
                springboot/controller/TodoController.class]",
            "dependencies": [
                        "todoService"
                    ]
    }
```

It shows the details for two beans: `basicController` and `todoController`. You can see the following details for all the beans:

- The name of the bean and its aliases
- The scope of the bean
- The type of the bean
- The exact location of the class from which this bean is created
- Dependencies of the bean

Metrics

The metrics endpoint shows some of the important metrics about the following:

- Server--free memory, processors, uptime, and so on
- JVM--details about the heap, threads, garbage collection, sessions, and so on
- Responses provided by application services

An extract from the response of the `/application/metrics` endpoint is shown as follows:

```
{
    "mem": 481449,
    "mem.free": 178878,
    "processors": 4,
    "instance.uptime": 1853761,
    "uptime": 1863728,
    "systemload.average": 2.3349609375,
    "heap.committed": 413696,
    "heap.init": 65536,
    "heap.used": 234817,
    "heap": 932352,
    "nonheap.committed": 69248,
    "nonheap.init": 2496,
    "nonheap.used": 67754,
    "nonheap": 0,
    "threads.peak": 23,
    "threads.daemon": 21,
    "threads.totalStarted": 30,
    "threads": 23,
```

```
"classes": 8077,
"classes.loaded": 8078,
"classes.unloaded": 1,
"gc.ps_scavenge.count": 15,
"gc.ps_scavenge.time": 242,
"gc.ps_marksweep.count": 3,
"gc.ps_marksweep.time": 543,
"httpsessions.max": -1,
"httpsessions.active": 0,
"gauge.response.actuator": 8,
"gauge.response.mappings": 12,
"gauge.response.beans": 83,
"gauge.response.health": 14,
"gauge.response.root": 9,
"gauge.response.heapdump": 4694,
"gauge.response.env": 6,
"gauge.response.profile": 12,
"gauge.response.browser.star-star": 10,
"gauge.response.actuator.root": 2,
"gauge.response.configprops": 272,
"gauge.response.actuator.star-star": 13,
"counter.status.200.profile": 1,
"counter.status.200.actuator": 8,
"counter.status.200.mappings": 1,
"counter.status.200.root": 5,
"counter.status.200.configprops": 1,
"counter.status.404.actuator.star-star": 3,
"counter.status.200.heapdump": 1,
"counter.status.200.health": 1,
"counter.status.304.browser.star-star": 132,
"counter.status.302.actuator.root": 4,
"counter.status.200.browser.star-star": 37,
"counter.status.200.env": 2,
"counter.status.302.root": 5,
"counter.status.200.beans": 1,
"counter.status.200.actuator.star-star": 210,
"counter.status.302.actuator": 1
}
```

Auto-configuration

Auto-configuration is one of the most important features of Spring Boot. The auto-configuration endpoint (`/application/autoconfig`) exposes the details related to auto-configuration. It shows both positive matches and negative matches with details about why a particular auto-configuration succeeded or failed.

The following extract shows some of the positive matches from the response:

```
"positiveMatches": {
  "AuditAutoConfiguration#auditListener": [
    {
      "condition": "OnBeanCondition",
      "message": "@ConditionalOnMissingBean (types:
      org.springframework.boot.actuate.audit.
      listener.AbstractAuditListener; SearchStrategy: all) did not find
      any beans"
    }
  ],
  "AuditAutoConfiguration#authenticationAuditListener": [
  {
    "condition": "OnClassCondition",
    "message": "@ConditionalOnClass found required class
    'org.springframework.security.authentication.
    event.AbstractAuthenticationEvent'"
  },
```

The following extract shows some of the negative matches from the response:

```
"negativeMatches": {
  "CacheStatisticsAutoConfiguration.
  CaffeineCacheStatisticsProviderConfiguration": [
  {
    "condition": "OnClassCondition",
    "message": "@ConditionalOnClass did not find required class
    'com.github.benmanes.caffeine.cache.Caffeine'"
  }
  ],
  "CacheStatisticsAutoConfiguration.
  EhCacheCacheStatisticsProviderConfiguration": [
  {
    "condition": "OnClassCondition",
    "message": "@ConditionalOnClass did not find required classes
    'net.sf.ehcache.Ehcache',
    'net.sf.ehcache.statistics.StatisticsGateway'"
  }
  ],
```

All these details are very useful in order to debug auto-configuration.

Debugging

Three of the actuator endpoints are useful when debugging problems:

- `/application/heapdump`: Provides a heap dump
- `/application/trace`: Provides a trace of the last few requests serviced by the application
- `/application/dump`: Provides a thread dump

Deploying an application to Cloud

Spring Boot has great support for most popular Cloud **Platform as a Service** (**PaaS**) providers.

Some of the popular ones are as follows:

- Cloud Foundry
- Heroku
- OpenShift
- **Amazon Web Services** (**AWS**)

In this section, we will focus on deploying our application to Cloud Foundry.

Cloud Foundry

The Cloud Foundry Java buildpack has excellent support for Spring Boot. We can deploy standalone applications based on JARs as well as the traditional Java EE WAR applications.

Cloud Foundry provides a Maven plugin to deploy applications:

```
<build>
    <plugins>
        <plugin>
            <groupId>org.cloudfoundry</groupId>
            <artifactId>cf-maven-plugin</artifactId>
            <version>1.1.2</version>
        </plugin>
    </plugins>
</build>
```

Before we can deploy our application, we need to configure the application with a target and a space to deploy the application to.

The following are the steps involved:

1. We need to create a pivotal Cloud Foundry account at `https://account.run.pivotal.io/sign-up`.
2. Once we have an account, we can log in at `https://run.pivotal.io` to create an organization and space. Have the org and space details ready as we need them in order to deploy the application.

We can update the plugin with the configuration of `org` and `space`:

```
<build>
    <plugins>
        <plugin>
            <groupId>org.cloudfoundry</groupId>
            <artifactId>cf-maven-plugin</artifactId>
            <version>1.1.2</version>
            <configuration>
                <target>http://api.run.pivotal.io</target>
                <org>in28minutes</org>
                <space>development</space>
                <memory>512</memory>
                <env>
                    <ENV-VAR-NAME>prod</ENV-VAR-NAME>
                </env>
            </configuration>
        </plugin>
    </plugins>
</build>
```

We need to log in to Cloud Foundry using the Maven plugin on command prompt or terminal:

```
mvn cf:login -Dcf.username=<<YOUR-USER-ID>> -Dcf.password=<<YOUR-PASSWORD>>
```

If everything is successful, you will see a message, as shown here:

```
[INFO] -----------------------------------------------------------------
[INFO] Building Your First Spring Boot Example 0.0.1-SNAPSHOT
[INFO] -----------------------------------------------------------------
[INFO]
[INFO] --- cf-maven-plugin:1.1.2:login (default-cli) @ springboot-for-
beginners-example ---
[INFO] Authentication successful
[INFO] -----------------------------------------------------------------
```

```
[INFO] BUILD SUCCESS
[INFO] ------------------------------------------------------------
[INFO] Total time: 14.897 s
[INFO] Finished at: 2017-02-05T16:49:52+05:30
[INFO] Final Memory: 22M/101M
[INFO] ------------------------------------------------------------
```

Once you are able to log in, you can push the application to Cloud Foundry:

```
mvn cf:push
```

Once we execute the command, Maven will compile, run tests, build the application JAR or WAR, and then deploy it to the Cloud:

```
[INFO] Building jar: /in28Minutes/Workspaces/SpringTutorial/springboot-for-
beginners-example-rest-service/target/springboot-for-beginners-
example-0.0.1-SNAPSHOT.jar
 [INFO]
 [INFO] --- spring-boot-maven-plugin:1.4.0.RELEASE:repackage (default) @
springboot-for-beginners-example ---
 [INFO]
 [INFO] <<< cf-maven-plugin:1.1.2:push (default-cli) < package @
springboot-for-beginners-example <<<
 [INFO]
 [INFO] --- cf-maven-plugin:1.1.2:push (default-cli) @ springboot-for-
beginners-example ---
 [INFO] Creating application 'springboot-for-beginners-example'
 [INFO] Uploading '/in28Minutes/Workspaces/SpringTutorial/springboot-for-
beginners-example-rest-service/target/springboot-for-beginners-
example-0.0.1-SNAPSHOT.jar'
 [INFO] Starting application
 [INFO] Checking status of application 'springboot-for-beginners-example'
 [INFO] 1 of 1 instances running (1 running)
 [INFO] Application 'springboot-for-beginners-example' is available at
'http://springboot-for-beginners-example.cfapps.io'
 [INFO] ------------------------------------------------------------
[INFO] BUILD SUCCESS
 [INFO] ------------------------------------------------------------
 [INFO] Total time: 02:21 min
 [INFO] Finished at: 2017-02-05T16:54:55+05:30
 [INFO] Final Memory: 29M/102M
 [INFO] ------------------------------------------------------------
```

Once the application is up and running on the Cloud, we can use the URL from the log to launch the application: http://springboot-for-beginners-example.cfapps.io.

You can find more information about the Java Build Pack of Cloud Foundry at `https://docs.run.pivotal.io/buildpacks/java/build-tool-int.html#maven`.

Summary

Spring Boot makes developing Spring-based applications easy. It enables us to create production-ready applications very quickly.

In this chapter, we understood the different external configuration options provided by Spring Boot. We looked at embedded servers and deployed a test application to a PaaS Cloud platform--Cloud Foundry. We explored how to monitor our application in the production using Spring Boot Actuator. At the end, we looked at the features that make a developer more productive--Spring Boot developer tools and live reload.

In the next chapter, we will shift our attention toward data. We will cover Spring Data and take a look at how it makes integration with JPA and providing Rest services easier.

8
Spring Data

In *Chapter 7*, *Advanced Spring Boot Features*, we discussed advanced Spring Boot features, such as externalized configuration, monitoring, embedded servers, and deploying to the Cloud. In this chapter, let's turn our attention to data. Where we store our data and how we store data has been in rapid evolution during the last decade. After a few decades of stability with relational databases, in the last decade, a number of unstructured, nonrelational databases are taking firm ground. With a variety of data stores in play, the frameworks that talk to these data stores are becoming more important. While JPA made it easy to talk to relational databases, Spring Data aims to bring in a common approach to talk to a wider variety of data stores--relational or otherwise.

The following are some of the questions we will answer during this chapter:

- What is Spring Data?
- What are the aims of Spring Data?
- How do you talk to a relational database using Spring Data and Spring Data JPA?
- How do you talk to a nonrelational database such as MongoDB using Spring Data?

Background - data stores

Most applications talk to a variety of data stores. There has been a considerable evolution in how applications talk to a data store. The most basic API provided by Java EE is **JDBC (Java Database Connectivity)**. JDBC is used to talk to relational databases from the first version of Java EE. JDBC is based on using SQL queries to manipulate data. The following is an example of typical JDBC code:

```
PreparedStatement st = null;
st = conn.prepareStatement(INSERT_TODO_QUERY);
```

```
st.setString(1, bean.getDescription());
st.setBoolean(2, bean.isDone());
st.execute();
```

Typical JDBC code contains the following:

- The query (or stored procedure) to execute
- The code to set parameters for query into statement objects
- The code to liquidate ResultSet (the result of executing the query) into beans

Typical projects involved thousands of lines of JDBC code. JDBC code was cumbersome to write and maintain. Two frameworks became popular in an effort to provide an additional layer on top of JDBC:

- **myBatis** (earlier called iBatis): MyBatis removes the need for manually writing code to set parameters and retrieve results. It provides simple XML or annotation-based configuration to map Java POJOs to a database.
- **Hibernate**: Hibernate is an **ORM (Object/Relational Mapping)** framework. An ORM framework helps you to map your objects to tables in relational databases. The great thing about Hibernate is that developers do not need to write queries manually. Once the relationships between the objects and tables are mapped, Hibernate uses the mappings to create queries and populate/retrieve data.

Java EE came up with an API called **JPA** (Java Persistence API) that was roughly defined based on the popular ORM implementation at that time--the Hibernate framework. Hibernate (since 3.4.0.GA) supports/implements JPA.

In relational databases, data is stored in normalized, well-defined tables. While Java EE tried to solve the challenge of talking a relational data store, several other data stores became popular during the last decade. With the evolution of big data and real-time data needs, new and more unstructured forms of storing data came into existence. These kinds of databases are typically grouped under NoSQL databases. Examples are Cassandra (column), MongoDB (document), and Hadoop.

Spring Data

Each of the data stores have different ways to connect and retrieve/update data. Spring Data aims to provide a consistent model--another level of abstraction - to access data from different kinds of data stores.

Some of the important Spring Data features are listed as follows:

- Easy integration with multiple data stores through various repositories
- The ability to parse and form queries based on repository method names
- Provides the default CRUD functionality
- Basic support for auditing, such as created by user and last changed by user
- Powerful integration with Spring
- Great integration with Spring MVC to expose REST controllers through **Spring Data Rest**

Spring Data is an umbrella project made up of a number of modules. A few of the important Spring Data modules are listed as follows:

- **Spring Data Commons**: Defines the common concepts for all Spring Data modules--repository and query methods
- **Spring Data JPA**: Provides easy integration with JPA repositories
- **Spring Data MongoDB**: Provides easy integration with MongoDB--a document-based data store
- **Spring Data REST**: Provides the functionality to expose Spring Data repositories as REST services with minimal code
- **Spring Data for Apache Cassandra**: Provides easy integration with Cassandra
- **Spring for Apache Hadoop**: Provides easy integration with Hadoop

In this chapter, we will take an in-depth look at the common concepts behind Spring Data, repository, and query methods. In the initial examples, we will use Spring Data JPA to illustrate these concepts. We will also take a look at a sample integration with MongoDB later in the chapter.

Spring Data Commons

Spring Data Commons provides the basic abstractions behind Spring Data modules. We will use Spring Data JPA as an example to illustrate these abstractions.

Some of the important interfaces in Spring Data Commons are listed as follows:

```
Repository<T, ID extends Serializable>
CrudRepository<T, ID extends Serializable> extends Repository<T, ID>
PagingAndSortingRepository<T, ID extends Serializable> extends
CrudRepository<T, ID>
```

Repository

Repository is the core interface of Spring Data. It is a **marker interface**.

The CrudRepository interface

The CrudRepository defines the basic Create, Read, Update, and Delete methods. The important methods in CrudRepository are shown in the following code:

```
public interface CrudRepository<T, ID extends Serializable>
    extends Repository<T, ID> {
    <S extends T> S save(S entity);
    findOne(ID primaryKey);
    Iterable<T> findAll();
    Long count();
    void delete(T entity);
    boolean exists(ID primaryKey);
    // ... more functionality omitted.
}
```

The PagingAndSortingRepository interface

The PagingAndSortingRepository defines methods that provide the functionality to divide the ResultSet into pages as well as sort the results:

```
public interface PagingAndSortingRepository<T, ID extends
    Serializable>
    extends CrudRepository<T, ID> {
      Iterable<T> findAll(Sort sort);
      Page<T> findAll(Pageable pageable);
}
```

We will look at examples of using the Sort class and Page, Pageable interfaces in the section on Spring Data JPA.

Spring Data JPA

Spring Data JPA implements the core functionality defined in Spring Data Common interfaces.

JpaRepository is the JPA-specific repository interface:

```
public interface JpaRepository<T, ID extends Serializable>
extends PagingAndSortingRepository<T, ID>,
QueryByExampleExecutor<T>      {
```

SimpleJpaRepository is the default implementation of the CrudRepository interface for JPA:

```
public class SimpleJpaRepository<T, ID extends Serializable>
implements JpaRepository<T, ID>, JpaSpecificationExecutor<T>
```

Spring Data JPA example

Let's set up a simple project to understand the different concepts related to Spring Data Commons and Spring Data JPA.

The following are the steps involved:

1. Create a new project with `spring-boot-starter-data-jpa` as a dependency.
2. Add entities.
3. Add the `SpringBootApplication` class to run the application.
4. Create repositories.

New project with Starter Data JPA

We will create a simple Spring Boot Maven project using the following dependencies:

```xml
<dependency>
    <groupId>org.springframework.boot</groupId>
    <artifactId>spring-boot-starter-data-jpa</artifactId>
</dependency>
<dependency>
    <groupId>com.h2database</groupId>
    <artifactId>h2</artifactId>
    <scope>runtime</scope>
</dependency>
<dependency>
    <groupId>org.springframework.boot</groupId>
    <artifactId>spring-boot-starter-test</artifactId>
    <scope>test</scope>
</dependency>
```

`spring-boot-starter-data-jpa` is the Spring Boot starter project for Spring Data JPA. Important dependencies that `spring-boot-starter-data-jpa` brings in are **JTA (Java Transaction API)**, Hibernate Core, and Entity Manager (Default JPA Implementation). Some of the other important dependencies are shown in the following screenshot:

Entities

Let's define a couple of entities to use in our example. We will create an entity `Todo` to manage todos. A simple example is shown as follows:

```
@Entity
public class Todo {
  @Id
  @GeneratedValue(strategy = GenerationType.AUTO)
  private Long id;
  @ManyToOne(fetch = FetchType.LAZY)
  @JoinColumn(name = "userid")
  private User user;
  private String title;
  private String description;
  private Date targetDate;
  private boolean isDone;
  public Todo() {// Make JPA Happy
  }
}
```

Important things to note are as follows:

- `Todo` has a title, a description, a target date, and a completion indicator (`isDone`). JPA needs a constructor.
- `@Entity`: The annotation specifies that the class is an entity.
- `@Id`: Specifies that ID is the primary key of the entity.
- `@GeneratedValue(strategy = GenerationType.AUTO)`: The `GeneratedValue` annotation is used to specify how the primary key is generated. In this example, we are using a strategy of `GenerationType.AUTO`. This indicates that we would want the persistence provider to choose the right strategy.
- `@ManyToOne(fetch = FetchType.LAZY)`: Indicates a many-to-one relationship between `User` and `Todo`. A `@ManyToOne` relationship is used on one side of the relationship. `FetchType.Lazy` indicates that the data can be lazily fetched.
- `@JoinColumn(name = "userid")`: The `JoinColumn` annotation specifies the name of the foreign key column.

The following snippet shows the `User` entity:

```
@Entity
public class User {
  @Id
  @GeneratedValue(strategy = GenerationType.AUTO)
  private Long id;
  private String userid;
  private String name;
  @OneToMany(mappedBy = "user")
  private List<Todo> todos;
  public User() {// Make JPA Happy
  }
}
```

Important things to note are as follows:

- The user is defined as an entity with the `userid` and `name` attributes. The ID is the primary key, which is autogenerated.
- The `@OneToMany(mappedBy = "user")`: `OneToMany` annotation is used on the many side of a many-to-one relationship. The `mappedBy` attribute indicates the property of the owner entity of the relationship.

The SpringBootApplication class

Let's create a `SpringBootApplication` class to be able to run the Spring Boot application. The following snippet shows a simple example:

```
@SpringBootApplication
public class SpringDataJpaFirstExampleApplication {
  public static void main(String[] args) {
    SpringApplication.run(
      SpringDataJpaFirstExampleApplication.class, args);
  }
}
```

The following snippet shows some of the logs generated when we run `SpringDataJpaFirstExampleApplication` as a Java application:

```
LocalContainerEntityManagerFactoryBean : Building JPA container
EntityManagerFactory for persistence unit 'default'
org.hibernate.Version : HHH000412: Hibernate Core {5.0.11.Final}
org.hibernate.dialect.Dialect : HHH000400: Using dialect:
org.hibernate.dialect.H2Dialect
org.hibernate.tool.hbm2ddl.SchemaExport : HHH000227: Running hbm2ddl schema
export
org.hibernate.tool.hbm2ddl.SchemaExport : HHH000230: Schema export complete
j.LocalContainerEntityManagerFactoryBean : Initialized JPA
EntityManagerFactory for persistence unit 'default'
```

Some of the important observations are as follows:

- `HHH000412: Hibernate Core {5.0.11.Final}`: The Hibernate framework is initialized
- `HHH000400: Using dialect: org.hibernate.dialect.H2Dialect`: The H2 in-memory database is initialized
- `HHH000227: Running hbm2ddl schema export`: Based on the entities available (`Todo` and `User`) and the relationship between them, a schema is created

A lot of magic happened in the previous execution. Let's look at some of the important questions:

1. How does the Hibernate framework come into the picture even though we did not explicitly declare a dependency in pom.xml?
2. How is the H2 in-memory database used?
3. What is the schema that is created?

Let's now answer each of these questions.

How does the Hibernate framework come into the picture even though we did not explicitly declare a dependency in pom.xml?

- Hibernate is one of the dependencies of Spring Boot Starter JPA. So, it is the default JPA implementation used.

How is the H2 in-memory database used?

- In our dependencies, we included an H2 dependency with scope runtime. When Spring Boot Data JPA auto-configuration runs, it notices that we have not included any data source in our configuration (actually, we have no configuration at all). Spring Boot Data JPA then tries to auto-configure an in-memory database. It sees H2 on the classpath. Therefore, it initializes an in-memory H2 database.

What is the schema that is created?

The following snippet shows the schema that is created based on the Entity classes and the relationships we declared. This is auto-created by Spring Boot Data JPA auto-configuration:

```
create table todo (
    id bigint generated by default as identity,
    description varchar(255),
    is_done boolean not null,
    target_date timestamp,
    title varchar(255),
    userid bigint,
    primary key (id)
)
create table user (
    id bigint generated by default as identity,
    name varchar(255),
    userid varchar(255),
    primary key (id)
)
```

```
    alter table todo
    add constraint FK4wek6l19imiccm4ypjj5hfn2g
foreign key (userid)
references user
```

The `todo` table has a foreign key user ID for the user table.

Populating some data

To be able to test the repositories that we will create, we will populate some test data into these tables. All that we need to do is include the file called `data.sql` with the following statements in `src\main\resources`:

```
insert into user (id, name, userid)
 values (1, 'User Name 1', 'UserId1');
insert into user (id, name, userid)
 values (2, 'User Name 2', 'UserId2');
insert into user (id, name, userid)
 values (3, 'User Name 3', 'UserId3');
insert into user (id, name, userid)
 values (4, 'User Name 4', 'UserId4');
insert into todo (id, title, description, is_done, target_date, userid)
 values (101, 'Todo Title 1', 'Todo Desc 1', false, CURRENT_DATE(), 1);
insert into todo (id, title, description, is_done, target_date, userid)
 values (102, 'Todo Title 2', 'Todo Desc 2', false, CURRENT_DATE(), 1);
insert into todo (id, title, description, is_done, target_date, userid)
 values (103, 'Todo Title 3', 'Todo Desc 3', false, CURRENT_DATE(), 2);
```

These are simple insert statements. We are creating a total of four users - the first user has two todos, the second user has one todo, and the last two users have none.

When you run `SpringDataJpaFirstExampleApplication` as Java application again, you will see a few extra statements in the log:

```
ScriptUtils : Executing SQL script from URL
[file:/in28Minutes/Workspaces/SpringDataJPA-Preparation/Spring-Data-JPA-
Trial-Run/target/classes/data.sql]

ScriptUtils : Executed SQL script from URL
[file:/in28Minutes/Workspaces/SpringDataJPA-Preparation/Spring-Data-JPA-
Trial-Run/target/classes/data.sql] in 42 ms.
```

The log statements confirm that the data is being populated into the H2 in-memory database. Let's turn our attention to creating repositories to access and manipulate the data from the Java code.

A simple repository

A custom repository can be created by extending the repository marker interface. In the following example, we extend the repository interface with two methods--findAll and count:

```
import org.springframework.data.repository.Repository;
public interface TodoRepository extends Repository<Todo, Long> {
  Iterable<Todo> findAll();
  long count();
}
```

A few important things to note are as follows:

- `public interface TodoRepository extends Repository<Todo, Long>`: The TodoRepository interface extends the Repository interface. The two generic types indicate the entity being managed--Todo and the type of the primary key, that is, Long.
- `Iterable<Todo> findAll()`: Used to list all the todos. Note that the name of the method should match what's defined in CrudRepository.
- `long count()`: Used to find the count of all todos.

Unit test

Let's write a simple unit test to test whether we are able to access the todo data using TodoRepository. The following snippet shows the important details:

```
@DataJpaTest
@RunWith(SpringRunner.class)
public class TodoRepositoryTest {
  @Autowired
  TodoRepository todoRepository;
  @Test
  public void check_todo_count() {
    assertEquals(3, todoRepository.count());
  }
}
```

A few important things to note are as follows:

- `@DataJpaTest`: The `DataJpaTest` annotation is typically used along with `SpringRunner` in JPA repository unit tests. This annotation will enable only JPA-related auto-configuration. The test would use an in-memory database by default.
- `@RunWith(SpringRunner.class)`: `SpringRunner` is a simple alias for `SpringJUnit4ClassRunner`. It launches a Spring context.
- `@Autowired TodoRepository todoRepository`: Autowires `TodoRepository` to be used in the test.
- `assertEquals(3, todoRepository.count())`: Checks whether the count returned is 3. Remember that we inserted three todos in `data.sql`.

A word of caution: We are taking a shortcut to write a unit test in the preceding example. Ideally, a unit test should not depend on already-created data in the database. We will fix this in our future tests.

The `Extending Repository` interface helps us in exposing selected methods on entities.

The CrudRepository interface

We can extend `CrudRepository` to expose all create, read, update, and delete methods on an entity. The following snippet shows `TodoRepository` extending `CrudRepository`:

```
public interface TodoRepository extends CrudRepository<Todo, Long>
  {
  }
```

`TodoRepository` can be used to perform all methods exposed by the `CrudRepository` interface. Let's write a few unit tests to test some of these methods.

Unit test

The `findById()` method can be used to query using the primary key. The following snippet shows an example:

```
@Test
public void findOne() {
  Optional<Todo> todo = todoRepository.findById(101L);
  assertEquals("Todo Desc 1", todo.get().getDescription());
}
```

`Optional` represents a container object for an object that can be null. Some of the important methods in `Optional` are listed below:

- `isPresent()`: Check if `Optional` contains a non-null value.
- `orElse()`: Default value if the object contained is null.
- `ifPresent()`: Code in `ifPresent` is executed if the object contained is not null.
- `get()`: To retrieve the contained object.

The `existsById()` method can be used to check whether an entity with the given ID exists. The following example shows how it can be done:

```
@Test
public void exists() {
    assertFalse(todoRepository.existsById(105L));
    assertTrue(todoRepository.existsById(101L));
}
```

The `deleteById()` method is used to delete an entity with a specific ID. In the following example, we are deleting one of the `todos`, reducing the available todos from three to two:

```
@Test
public void delete() {
    todoRepository.deleteById(101L);
    assertEquals(2,todoRepository.count());
}
```

The `deleteAll()` method is used to delete all the entities managed by the specific repository. In the specific example here, all the `todos` from the `todo` table are deleted:

```
@Test
public void deleteAll() {
    todoRepository.deleteAll();
    assertEquals(0,todoRepository.count());
}
```

The `save()` method can be used to update or insert an entity. The following example shows how the description of a `todo` can be updated. The following test uses `TestEntityManager` to flush the data before retrieving it. `TestEntityManager` is autowired as part of the functionality of `@DataJpaTest` Annotation:

```
@Autowired
TestEntityManager entityManager;
@Test
public void save() {
    Todo todo = todoRepository.findById(101L).get();
```

```
todo.setDescription("Todo Desc Updated");
todoRepository.save(todo);
entityManager.flush();
Todo updatedTodo = todoRepository.findById(101L).get();
assertEquals("Todo Desc Updated",updatedTodo.getDescription());
}
```

The PagingAndSortingRepository interface

PagingAndSortingRepository extends CrudRepository and provides methods in order to retrieve entities with pagination and a specified sort mechanism. Take a look at the following example:

```
public interface UserRepository
extends PagingAndSortingRepository<User, Long> {
    }
```

Important things to note are as follows:

- public interface UserRepository extends PagingAndSortingRepository : The UserRepository interface extends the PagingAndSortingRepository interface
- <User, Long>: Entities are of type User and have an ID field of type Long

Unit tests

Let's write a few tests to use the sorting and pagination capabilities of UserRepository. The base of the test is very similar to TodoRepositoryTest:

```
@DataJpaTest
@RunWith(SpringRunner.class)
public class UserRepositoryTest {
  @Autowired
  UserRepository userRepository;
  @Autowired
  TestEntityManager entityManager;
}
```

Let's write a simple test to sort users and print the users to the log:

```
@Test
public void testing_sort_stuff() {
  Sort sort = new Sort(Sort.Direction.DESC, "name")
  .and(new Sort(Sort.Direction.ASC, "userid"));
  Iterable<User> users = userRepository.findAll(sort);
```

```
    for (User user : users) {
        System.out.println(user);
        }
    }
```

Important things to note are as follows:

- new Sort(Sort.Direction.DESC, "name"): We would want to sort by name in descending order.
- and(new Sort(Sort.Direction.ASC, "userid")): The and() method is a conjunction method to combine different sort configurations. In this example, we are adding secondary criteria to sort by user ID in the ascending order.
- userRepository.findAll(sort): The sort criteria are passed as a parameter to the findAll() method.

The output of the preceding test is as shown as follows. The users are sorted in descending order by name:

```
User [id=4, userid=UserId4, name=User Name 4, todos=0]
User [id=3, userid=UserId3, name=User Name 3, todos=0]
User [id=2, userid=UserId2, name=User Name 2, todos=1]
User [id=1, userid=UserId1, name=User Name 1, todos=2]
```

The test for the pageable is shown as follows:

```
@Test
public void using_pageable_stuff() {
    PageRequest pageable = new PageRequest(0, 2);
    Page<User> userPage = userRepository.findAll(pageable);
    System.out.println(userPage);
    System.out.println(userPage.getContent());
}
```

The output of the test is shown as follows:

```
Page 1 of 2 containing com.in28minutes.model.User instances
[User [id=1, userid=UserId1, name=User Name 1, todos=2],
User [id=2, userid=UserId2, name=User Name 2, todos=1]]
```

Important things to note are as follows:

- new PageRequest(0, 2): We are requesting the first page (index 0) and setting the size of each page to two
- userRepository.findAll(pageable): The PageRequest object is sent as a parameter to the findAll method

- `Page 1 of 2`: The output shows that we are looking at the first page in a total of two pages

A couple of important things to note about `PageRequest` are as follows:

- The `PageRequest` object has the `next()`, `previous()`, and `first()` methods to traverse the pages
- The `PageRequest` constructor (`public PageRequest(int page, int size, Sort sort)`) also accepts a third parameter--`Sort` order

Important methods in Page and its child interface, Slice, are listed as follows:

- `int getTotalPages()`: Returns the number of result pages
- `long getTotalElements()`: Returns the total number of elements in all pages
- `int getNumber()`: Returns the number of the current page
- `int getNumberOfElements()`: Returns the number of elements in the current page
- `List<T> getContent()`: Gets the content of the current slice (or page) as a list
- `boolean hasContent()`: Returns if the current slice has any elements
- `boolean isFirst()`: Returns if this is the first slice
- `boolean isLast()`: Returns if this is the last slice
- `boolean hasNext()`: Returns if there is a next slice
- `boolean hasPrevious()`: Returns if there is a previous slice
- `Pageable nextPageable()`: Gets access to the next slice
- `Pageable previousPageable()`: Gets access to the previous slice

Query methods

In the previous sections, we looked at the `CrudRepository` and `PagingAndSortingRepository` interfaces. We looked at the different methods that they provided by default. Spring Data does not stop here. It defines a few patterns that allow you to define custom query methods. In this section, we will look at examples of some of the options Spring Data provides to customize your query methods.

We will start with examples related to finding rows matching specific attribute values. The following example shows different methods in order to search for the `User` by their name:

```
public interface UserRepository
extends PagingAndSortingRepository<User, Long> {
  List<User> findByName(String name);
  List<User> findByName(String name, Sort sort);
  List<User> findByName(String name, Pageable pageable);
  Long countByName(String name);
  Long deleteByName(String name);
  List<User> removeByName(String name);
}
```

Important things to note are as follows:

- `List<User> findByName(String name)`: The pattern is `findBy`, followed by the name of the attribute that you would want to query by. The value of the attribute is passed in as a parameter.
- `List<User> findByName(String name, Sort sort)`: This method allows you to specify a specific sort order.
- `List<User> findByName(String name, Pageable pageable)`: This method allows the use of pagination.
- Instead of find we can also use read, query or get to name the methods. For example, queryByName instead of findByName.
- Similar to find..By we can use count..By to find the count, and delete..By (or remove..By) to delete records.

The following example shows how to search by attributes of a containing element:

```
List<User> findByTodosTitle(String title);
```

The user contains `Todos`. `Todo` has `title` attribute. To create a method to search a user based on the title of the todo, we can create a method by the name `findByTodosTitle` in `UserRepository`.

The following examples show a few more variations that are possible with `findBy`:

```
public interface TodoRepository extends CrudRepository<Todo, Long>
{
  List<Todo> findByTitleAndDescription
  (String title, String description);
  List<Todo> findDistinctTodoByTitleOrDescription
  (String title,String description);
  List<Todo> findByTitleIgnoreCase(String title, String
  description);
```

```
    List<Todo> findByTitleOrderByIdDesc(String lastname);
    List<Todo> findByIsDoneTrue(String lastname);
}
```

Important things to note are as follows:

- `findByTitleAndDescription`: Multiple attributes can be used to query
- `findDistinctTodoByTitleOrDescription`: Find distinct rows that match either title or description
- `findByTitleIgnoreCase`: Illustrates the use of the ignore case
- `findByTitleOrderByIdDesc`: Illustrates an example of specifying a specific sort order

The following example shows how to find a specific subset of records using find:

```
public interface UserRepository
extends PagingAndSortingRepository<User, Long> {
    User findFirstByName(String name);
    User findTopByName(String name);
    List<User> findTop3ByName(String name);
    List<User> findFirst3ByName(String name);
}
```

Important things to note are as follows:

- `findFirstByName, findTopByName`: Queries for the first user
- `findTop3ByName, findFirst3ByName`: Finds the top three users

Queries

Spring Data JPA also provides options to write custom queries. The following snippet shows a simple example:

```
@Query("select u from User u where u.name = ?1")
List<User> findUsersByNameUsingQuery(String name);
```

Important things to note are as follows:

- `@Query`: The annotation to define queries for repository methods
- `select u from User u where u.name = ?1`: Query to be executed. `?1` represents the first parameter
- `findUsersByNameUsingQuery`: When this method is called, the query specified is executed with the name as the parameter

Named Parameters

We can use named parameters to make the query more readable. The following snippet from UserRepository shows an example:

```
@Query("select u from User u where u.name = :name")
List<User> findUsersByNameUsingNamedParameters
(@Param("name") String name);
```

Important things to note are as follows:

- `select u from User u where u.name = :name` : Defines a named parameter `"name"` in the query
- `findUsersByNameUsingNamedParameters(@Param("name") String name)`: `@Param("name")` defines the named parameter in the arguments list

Named Query

Another option is to use named queries defined on the entity itself. The following example shows how to define a named query on the User entity:

```
@Entity
@NamedQuery(name = "User.findUsersWithNameUsingNamedQuery",
query = "select u from User u where u.name = ?1")
public class User {
```

To use this query in a repository, we would need to create a method with the same name as the named query. The following snippet shows the corresponding method in UserRepository:

```
List<User> findUsersWithNameUsingNamedQuery(String name);
```

Note that the name of the named query is `User.findUsersWithNameUsingNamedQuery`. So, the name of the method in the repository should be `findUsersWithNameUsingNamedQuery`.

Native query

Spring Data JPA provides the option to execute native queries as well. The following example demonstrates a simple native query in `UserRepository`:

```
@Query(value = "SELECT * FROM USERS WHERE u.name = ?1",
 nativeQuery = true)
List<User> findUsersByNameNativeQuery(String name);
```

Important things to note are as follows:

- `SELECT * FROM USERS WHERE u.name = ?1`: This is the native query to be executed. Note that we are not referring to the User entity but are using the table name users in the query.
- `nativeQuery = true`: This attribute ensures that the query is executed as a native query.

Spring Data Rest

Spring Data Rest provides a very simple option to expose CRUD RESTful services around data repositories.

Some of the important features of Spring Data Rest include the following:

- Exposing the REST API around Spring Data repositories
- Support for pagination and filtering
- Understanding query methods in Spring Data repositories and exposing them as search resources
- Among the frameworks supported are JPA, MongoDB, and Cassandra
- Options to customize the resources are exposed by default

We will start by including the Spring Boot Data Rest starter in our `pom.xml`:

```
<dependency>
 <groupId>org.springframework.boot</groupId>
 <artifactId>spring-boot-starter-data-rest</artifactId>
</dependency>
```

We can make `UserRepository` expose the REST service by adding a simple annotation, as shown in the following snippet:

```
@RepositoryRestResource(collectionResourceRel = "users", path =
 "users")
public interface UserRepository
extends PagingAndSortingRepository<User, Long> {
```

Important things to note are as follows:

- @RepositoryRestResource: The annotation used to expose a repository using REST
- collectionResourceRel = "users": The collectionResourceRel value to be used in the generated links
- path = "users": The path under which the resource has to be exposed

When we launch SpringDataJpaFirstExampleApplication as a Java application, the following can be seen in the log:

```
s.b.c.e.t.TomcatEmbeddedServletContainer : Tomcat initialized with port(s):
8080 (http)
o.s.b.w.servlet.ServletRegistrationBean : Mapping servlet:
'dispatcherServlet' to [/]
o.s.b.w.servlet.FilterRegistrationBean : Mapping filter:
'characterEncodingFilter' to: [/*]
s.w.s.m.m.a.RequestMappingHandlerMapping : Mapped "{[/error]}" onto ****
o.s.d.r.w.RepositoryRestHandlerMapping : Mapped "{[/{repository}],
methods=[OPTIONS]
o.s.d.r.w.RepositoryRestHandlerMapping : Mapped "{[/{repository}],
methods=[HEAD]
o.s.d.r.w.RepositoryRestHandlerMapping : Mapped "{[/{repository}],
methods=[GET]
o.s.d.r.w.RepositoryRestHandlerMapping : Mapped "{[/{repository}],
methods=[POST]
o.s.d.r.w.RepositoryRestHandlerMapping : Mapped "{[/{repository}/{id}],
methods=[OPTIONS]
o.s.d.r.w.RepositoryRestHandlerMapping : Mapped
"{[/{repository}/{id}/{property}]
o.s.d.r.w.RepositoryRestHandlerMapping : Mapped "{[/{repository}/search],
methods=[GET]
```

The preceding log shows that the Spring MVC DispatcherServlet is launched and ready to serve different request methods and URIs.

The GET method

When we send a GET request to `http://localhost:8080/users`, we get the response shown here. The response is edited to remove the details of UserId2, UserId3 and UserId4 for brevity:

```json
{
  "_embedded" : {
  "users" : [ {
            "userid" : "UserId1",
            "name" : "User Name 1",
            "_links" : {
              "self" : {
                "href" : "http://localhost:8080/users/1"
                },
              "user" : {
                "href" : "http://localhost:8080/users/1"
                },
              "todos" : {
                  "href" : "http://localhost:8080/users/1/todos"
                }
            }
        } ]
    },
  "_links" : {

    "self" : {
            "href" : "http://localhost:8080/users"
            },
          "profile" : {
                "href" : "http://localhost:8080/profile/users"
                },
          "search" : {
                "href" : "http://localhost:8080/users/search"
            }
        }
    },
  "page" : {
          "size" : 20,
          "totalElements" : 4,
          "totalPages" : 1,
          "number" : 0
        }
    }
```

The POST method

The following screenshot shows how to fire a POST request to create a new user:

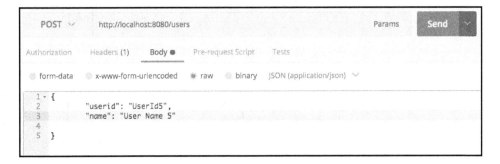

The following snippet shows the response:

```
{
  "userid": "UserId5",
  "name": "User Name 5",
  "_links": {
    "self": {
      "href": "http://localhost:8080/users/5"
        },
    "user": {
      "href": "http://localhost:8080/users/5"
        },
    "todos": {
      "href": "http://localhost:8080/users/5/todos"
      }
    }
}
```

The response contains the URI of the created
resource--http://localhost:8080/users/5.

The search resource

Spring Data Rest exposes search resources for other methods in the repository. For example, the findUsersByNameUsingNamedParameters method is exposed at http://localhost:8080/users/search/findUsersByNameUsingNamedParameters? name=User%20Name%201. The following snippet shows the response of a Get request to the preceding URL:

```
{
   "_embedded": {
      "users": [
         {
            "userid": "UserId1",
            "name": "User Name 1",
            "_links": {
               "self": {
                  "href": "http://localhost:8080/users/1"
               },
               "user": {
                  "href": "http://localhost:8080/users/1"
               },
               "todos": {
                  "href":
   "http://localhost:8080/users/1/todos"
               }
            }
         }
      ]
   },
   "_links": {
      "self": {
         "href":"http://localhost:8080/users/search/
      findUsersByNameUsingNamedParameters?name=User%20Name%201"
      }
   }
}
```

Big Data

As we discussed in the introduction to the chapter, there are a variety of data stores that are providing alternatives to traditional databases. The term **Big Data** has become popular in the last few years. While there is no agreed definition of Big Data, there are a few shared characteristics:

- **Unstructured Data**: There is no specific structure to the data
- **Large Volumes**: Typically, more volumes than that can be processed by traditional databases, for example, log streams, Facebook posts, tweets
- **Easily Scalable**: Typically provides options to scale horizontally and vertically

Hadoop, Cassandra, and MongoDB are among the popular options.

In this section, we will take MongoDB as an example to connect using Spring Data.

MongoDB

 Follow the instructions at `http://docs.mongodb.org/manual/installat ion/` to install MongoDB on your specific operating system.

To get started with connecting to MongoDB, include the dependency for Spring Boot MongoDB starter in the `pom.xml`:

```
<dependency>
  <groupId>org.springframework.boot</groupId>
  <artifactId>spring-boot-starter-data-mongodb</artifactId>
</dependency>
```

Let's create a new Entity class `Person` to store to MongoDB. The following snippet shows a `Person` class with an ID and a name:

```
public class Person {
  @Id
  private String id;
  private String name;
  public Person() {// Make JPA Happy
  }
public Person(String name) {
  super();
  this.name = name;
  }
}
```

We would want to store the `Person` entities to MongoDB. We would need to create a new repository. The following snippet shows a MongoDB repository:

```
public interface PersonMongoDbRepository
extends MongoRepository<Person, String> {
  List<Person> findByName(String name);
  Long countByName(String name);
}
```

Important things to note are as follows:

- `PersonMongoDbRepository extends MongoRepository`: `MongoRepository` is a MongoDB-specific Repository interface
- `MongoRepository<Person, String>`: We would want to store `Person` entities that have a key of type String
- `List<Person> findByName(String name)`: A simple method to find a person by name

Unit test

We will write a simple unit test to test this repository. The code for the unit test is shown as follows:

```
@DataMongoTest
@RunWith(SpringRunner.class)
public class PersonMongoDbRepositoryTest {
  @Autowired
  PersonMongoDbRepository personRepository;
  @Test
  public void simpleTest(){
    personRepository.deleteAll();
    personRepository.save(new Person( "name1"));
    personRepository.save(new Person( "name2"));
    for (Person person : personRepository.findAll()) {
      System.out.println(person);
    }
    System.out.println(personRepository.findByName("name1"));
    System.out.println(personRepository.count());
  }
}
```

Some important things to note are as follows:

- Make sure that MongoDB is running when your run the test.
- `@DataMongoTest`: The `DataMongoTest` annotation is used in combination with `SpringRunner` for a typical MongoDB unit test. This disables auto-configuration for everything except things related to MongoDB.
- `@Autowired PersonMongoDbRepository personRepository`: Autowires the MongoDB repository to be tested.

An important thing to note is that all the code in the test is very similar to the code written for Spring Data JPA. This example show how simple Spring Data makes it to connect to different kinds of data stores. The code to interact with a nonrelational Big Data data store is similar to the code that talks to a relational database. That's the magic of Spring Data.

Summary

Spring Boot makes the development of Spring-based applications easy. Spring Data makes it easy to connect to different data stores.

In this chapter, we looked at how Spring Data makes it easy to connect to different data stores through simple concepts such as repository. We also came to know how to use Spring Data in combination with Spring Data JPA to connect to an in-memory relational database and how to use Spring Data MongoDB to connect and save data to a Big Data store, such as MongoDB.

In the next chapter, we will shift our attention toward the cloud. We will learn about Spring Cloud and how it solves the problems of the Cloud.

9
Spring Cloud

In this chapter, we will look at some of the important patterns related to developing Cloud-Native applications and implementing them using projects under the umbrella of Spring Cloud. We will look at the following features:

- Implementing centralized microservice configuration with Spring Cloud Config Server
- Using Spring Cloud Bus to synchronize configuration across microservice instances
- Using Feign to create declarative REST clients
- Implementing client-side load balancing using Ribbon
- Implementing the Name server using Eureka
- Implementing API Gateway using Zuul
- Implementing distributed tracing using Spring Cloud Sleuth and Zipkin
- Using Hystrix to implement fault tolerance

Introducing Spring Cloud

In `Chapter 4`, *Evolution toward Microservices and Cloud-Native Applications*, we discussed the problems with monolithic applications and how architectures evolved toward microservices. However, microservices have their own sets of challenges:

- Organizations adopting microservice architectures also need to make challenging decisions around the consistency of microservices without affecting the innovation capabilities of the microservice teams.
- Smaller applications mean more builds, releases, and deployments. This is usually addressed using more automation.

- Microservice architectures are built based on a large number of smaller, fine-grained services. There are challenges associated with managing configuration and availability of these services.
- Debugging issues becomes more difficult because of the distributed nature of applications.

To reap maximum benefits from microservice architectures, microservices should be Cloud-Native--easily deployable on the Cloud. In `Chapter 4`, *Evolution toward Microservices and Cloud-Native Applications*, we discussed the characteristics of Twelve-Factor Apps--patterns that are typically considered good practices in Cloud-Native applications.

Spring Cloud aims to provide solutions to some commonly encountered patterns when building systems on the Cloud. Some of the important features include the following:

- Solutions to manage distributed microservice configuration
- Service registration and discovery using Name servers
- Load balancing across multiple instances of microservices
- More fault-tolerant services using circuit breakers
- API Gateways for aggregation, routing, and caching
- Distributed tracing across microservices

It is important to understand that Spring Cloud is not a single project. It is a group of subprojects aimed at solving the problems associated with applications deployed on the Cloud.

Some important Spring Cloud subprojects are as follows:

- **Spring Cloud Config**: Enables centralized external configuration across different microservices across different environments.
- **Spring Cloud Netflix**: Netflix is one of the early adopters of microservice architecture. A number of internal Netflix projects were open sourced under the umbrella of Spring Cloud Netflix. Examples include Eureka, Hystrix, and Zuul.
- **Spring Cloud Bus**: Makes it easier to build the integration of microservices with a lightweight message broker.
- **Spring Cloud Sleuth**: Along with Zipkin, this provides distributed tracing solutions.
- **Spring Cloud Data Flow**: Provides capabilities for building orchestration around microservice applications. Provides a DSL, GUI, and REST API.
- **Spring Cloud Stream**: Provides a simple declarative framework to integrate Spring-based (and Spring Boot)-based applications with message brokers such as Apache Kafka or RabbitMQ.

A few things are common to all projects under the Spring Cloud umbrella:

- They solve some of the common problems with developing applications on the Cloud
- They provide great integration with Spring Boot
- They are typically configured with simple annotations
- They make extensive use of auto-configuration

Spring Cloud Netflix

Netflix is one of the first organizations to start making the switch from monolithic to microservice architectures. Netflix has been very open about documenting this experience. Some of the internal Netflix frameworks are open sourced under the umbrella of Spring Cloud Netflix. As defined on the Spring Cloud Netflix website (`https://cloud.spring.io /spring-cloud-netflix/`):

> *Spring Cloud Netflix provides Netflix OSS integrations for Spring Boot apps through autoconfiguration and binding to the Spring environment and other Spring programming model idioms.*

Some of the important projects under the Spring Cloud Netflix umbrella are as follows:

- **Eureka**: The Name server that provides service registration and discovery capabilities for microservices.
- **Hystrix**: Capabilities to build fault-tolerant microservices through circuit breakers. Also provides a dashboard.
- **Feign**: Declarative REST Client makes it easy to call services created with JAX-RS and Spring MVC.
- **Ribbon**: Provides client-side load balancing capabilities.
- **Zuul**: Provides typical API Gateways capabilities, such as routing, filtering, authentication, and security. It can be extended with custom rules and filters.

Demo microservices setup

We will use two microservices to demonstrate concepts in this chapter:

- **Microservice A**: A simple microservice exposing two services--one to retrieve a message from the configuration file and another `random service` providing a list of random numbers.
- **Service consumer microservice**: A simple microservice exposing a simple calculation service called the `add` service. The `add` service consumes the `random service` from **Microservice A** and adds the numbers up.

The following figure shows the relationship between the microservices and the services that are exposed:

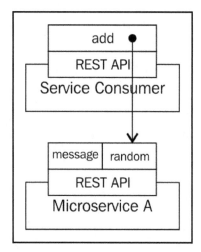

Let's quickly set up these microservices.

Microservice A

Let's use Spring Initializr (`https://start.spring.io`) to get started with Microservice A. Choose **GroupId**, **ArtifactId**, and the frameworks, as shown in the following screenshot:

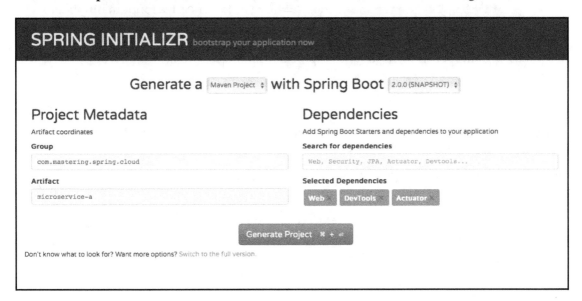

We will create a service to expose a set of random numbers:

```
@RestController
public class RandomNumberController {
  private Log log =
    LogFactory.getLog(RandomNumberController.class);
  @RequestMapping("/random")
  public List<Integer> random() {
    List<Integer> numbers = new ArrayList<Integer>();
    for (int i = 1; i <= 5; i++) {
      numbers.add(generateRandomNumber());
    }
    log.warn("Returning " + numbers);
    return numbers;
  }
  private int generateRandomNumber() {
    return (int) (Math.random() * 1000);
  }
}
```

Important things to note are as follows:

- `@RequestMapping("/random") public List<Integer> random():` Random service returns a list of random numbers
- `private int generateRandomNumber() {:` Generates random numbers between 0 and 1000

The following snippet shows a sample response from the service at `http://localhost:8080/random:`

```
[666,257,306,204,992]
```

Next, we would want to create a service to return a simple message from the application configuration in `application.properties`.

Let's define a simple application configuration with one property--`message`:

```
@Component
@ConfigurationProperties("application")
public class ApplicationConfiguration {
  private String message;
  public String getMessage() {
    return message;
  }
  public void setMessage(String message) {
    this.message = message;
  }
}
```

A few important things to note are as follows:

- `@ConfigurationProperties("application"):` Defines a class defining `application.properties`.
- `private String message:` Defines one property--`message`. The value can be configured in `application.properties` with `application.message` as the key.

Let's configure `application.properties`, as shown in the following snippet:

```
spring.application.name=microservice-a
application.message=Default Message
```

A couple of important things to note are as follows:

- `spring.application.name=microservice-a`: `spring.application.name` is used to give a name to the application
- `application.message=Default Message`: Configures a default message for `application.message`

Let's create a controller to read the message and return it, as shown in the following snippet:

```
@RestController
public class MessageController {
  @Autowired
  private ApplicationConfiguration configuration;
  @RequestMapping("/message")
  public Map<String, String> welcome() {
    Map<String, String> map = new HashMap<String, String>();
    map.put("message", configuration.getMessage());
    return map;
  }
}
```

Important things to note are as follows:

- `@Autowired private ApplicationConfiguration configuration`: Autowires `ApplicationConfiguration` to enable reading the configured message value.
- `@RequestMapping("/message") public Map<String, String> welcome()`: Exposes a simple service at the URI/message.
- `map.put("message", configuration.getMessage())`: The service returns a map with one entry. It has a key message and the value is picked up from the `ApplicationConfiguration`.

When the service is executed at `http://localhost:8080/message`, we get the following response:

```
{"message":"Default Message"}
```

Service consumer

Let's set up another simple microservice to consume the `random service` exposed by Microservice A. Let's use Spring Initializr (`https://start.spring.io`) to initialize the microservice, as shown in the following screenshot:

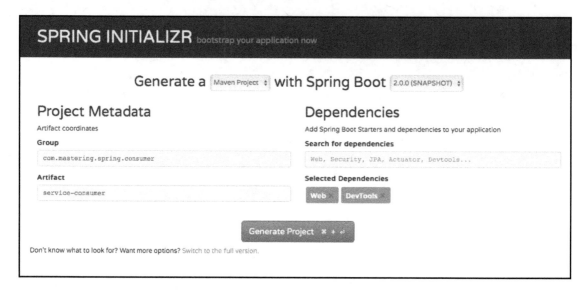

Let's add the service to consume `random service`:

```java
@RestController
public class NumberAdderController {
  private Log log = LogFactory.getLog(
    NumberAdderController.class);
  @Value("${number.service.url}")
  private String numberServiceUrl;
  @RequestMapping("/add")
  public Long add() {
    long sum = 0;
    ResponseEntity<Integer[]> responseEntity =
      new RestTemplate()
      .getForEntity(numberServiceUrl, Integer[].class);
    Integer[] numbers = responseEntity.getBody();
    for (int number : numbers) {
      sum += number;
    }
    log.warn("Returning " + sum);
    return sum;
  }
}
```

Important things to note are as follows:

- `@Value("${number.service.url}") private String numberServiceUrl`: We would want the number service URL to be configurable in application properties.
- `@RequestMapping("/add") public Long add()`: Exposes a service at the URI `/add`. The `add` method calls the number service using `RestTemplate` and has the logic to sum the numbers returned in the response.

Let's configure `application.properties`, as shown in the following snippet:

```
spring.application.name=service-consumer
server.port=8100
number.service.url=http://localhost:8080/random
```

Important things to note are as follows:

- `spring.application.name=service-consumer`: Configures a name for the Spring Boot application
- `server.port=8100`: Uses `8100` as the port for service consumer
- `number.service.url=http://localhost:8080/random`: Configures the number service URL for use in the add service

When the service is called at the URL `http://localhost:8100/add`, the following response is returned:

```
2890
```

The following is an extract from the log of Microservice A:

```
c.m.s.c.c.RandomNumberController : Returning [752,
   119, 493, 871, 445]
```

The log shows that `random service` from Microservice A returned `5` numbers. The `add` service in the service consumer added them up and returned a result `2890`.

We now have our example microservices ready. In the next steps, we will add Cloud-Native features to these microservices.

Ports

In this chapter, we will create six different microservices applications and components. To keep things simple, we will use specific ports for specific applications.

The following table shows the ports that we would reserve for use by the different applications created in this chapter:

Microservice component	Port(s) used
Microservice A	8080 and 8081
Service consumer microservice	8100
Config Server (Spring Cloud Config)	8888
Eureka server (Name server)	8761
Zuul API Gateway Server	8765
Zipkin Distributed Tracing Server	9411

We have two of our microservices ready. We are ready to Cloud-enable our microservices.

Centralized microservice configuration

Spring Cloud Config provides solutions to externalize the configuration of a microservice. Let's first understand the need to externalize microservice configuration.

Problem statement

In microservice architectures, we typically have a number of small microservices interacting with each other instead of a set of big monolithic applications. Each microservice is typically deployed in multiple environments--development, testing, load test, staging, and production. In addition, there can be multiple instances of microservices in different environments. For example, a specific microservice might be handling heavy load. There might be multiple production instances for that microservice in production.

The configuration of an application typically contains the following:

- **Database configuration**: Details needed to connect to the database
- **Message broker configuration**: Any configuration needed to connect to AMQP or similar resources
- **External services configuration**: Other services that the microservice needs
- **Microservice configuration**: Typical configuration related to the business logic of the microservice

Each instance of a microservice can have its own configuration--different databases, different external services it consumes, among others. For example, if a microservice is deployed in five environments and there are four instances in each environment, the microservice can have a total of 20 different configurations.

The following figure shows typical configurations needed for Microservice A. We are looking at two instances in development, three instances in QA, one instance in the stage, and four instances in production:

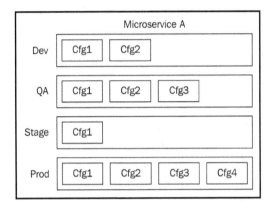

Solution

Maintaining configurations for different microservices separately would make it difficult for the operations team. The solution, as shown in the following figure, is to create a centralized **Configuration Server:**

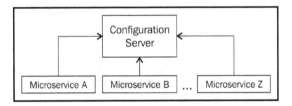

The centralized **Configuration Server** holds all the configuration belonging to all the different microservices. This helps in keeping the configuration separate from the application deployable.

The same deployable (EAR or WAR) can be used in different environments. However, all configuration (things that vary between different environments) will be stored in the centralized configuration server.

An important decision that needs to be made would be to decide whether there are separate instances of centralized configuration servers for different environments. Typically, you would want access to your production configuration to be more restrictive compared to other environments. At a minimum, we recommend a separate centralized configuration server for production. Other environments can share one instance of the configuration server.

Options

The following screenshot shows the options provided in Spring Initializer for Cloud Config Servers:

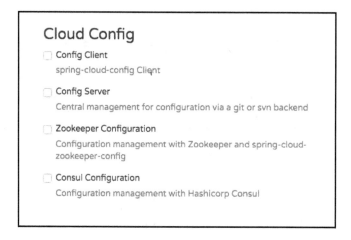

In this chapter, we will configure a Cloud Config Server using Spring Cloud Config.

Spring Cloud Config

Spring Cloud Config provides support for centralized microservice configuration. It is a combination of two important components:

- **Spring Cloud Config Server**: Provides support for exposing centralized configuration backed up by a version control repository--GIT or subversion
- **Spring Cloud Config Client**: Provides support for applications to connect to Spring Cloud Config Server

The following figure shows a typical microservice architecture using Spring Cloud Config. The configuration for multiple microservices is stored in a single **GIT** repository:

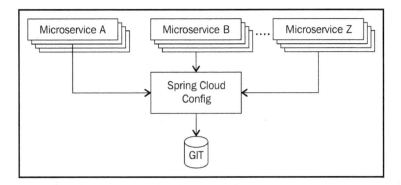

Implementing Spring Cloud Config Server

The following figure shows the updated implementation of Microservice A and service consumer with Spring Cloud Config. In the following figure, we will integrate Microservice A with Spring Cloud Config in order to retrieve its configuration from the local Git repository:

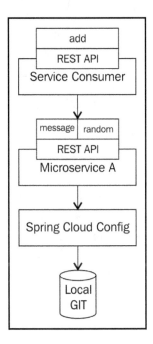

Implementing Spring Cloud Config needs the following:

1. Setting up the Spring Cloud Config server.
2. Setting up a local Git repository and connecting it to Spring Cloud Config server.
3. Updating Microservice A to use the configuration from Cloud Config Server-- using Spring Cloud Config Client.

Setting up Spring Cloud Config Server

Let's set up the Cloud Config Server using Spring Initializr (`http://start.spring.io`). The following screenshot shows **GroupId** and **ArtifactId** to choose. Make sure that you select **Config Server** as a dependency:

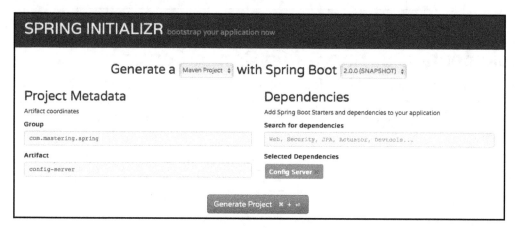

If you want to add the Config Server to an existing application, use the dependency shown here:

```
<dependency>
  <groupId>org.springframework.cloud</groupId>
  <artifactId>spring-cloud-config-server</artifactId>
</dependency>
```

Once the project is created, the first step is to add the `EnableConfigServer` annotation. The following snippet shows the annotation added to `ConfigServerApplication`:

```
@EnableConfigServer
@SpringBootApplication
public class ConfigServerApplication {
```

Connecting Spring Cloud Config Server to a local Git repository

The Config Server needs to be connected to a Git repository. To keep things simple, let's connect to a local Git repository.

 You can install Git for your specific operating system from `https://git-s cm.com`.

The following commands help you set a simple local Git repository.

Switch to a directory of your choice after installing Git. Execute the following commands on a terminal or Command Prompt:

```
mkdir git-localconfig-repo
cd git-localconfig-repo
git init
```

Create a file called `microservice-a.properties` in the `git-localconfig-repo` folder with the content shown here:

```
management.security.enabled=false
application.message=Message From Default Local Git Repository
```

Execute the following commands to add and commit `microservice-a.properties` to a local Git repository:

```
git add -A
git commit -m "default microservice a properties"
```

Now that we have the local Git repository ready with our configuration, we would need to connect the Config Server to it. Let's configure `application.properties` in `config-server`, as shown here:

```
spring.application.name=config-server
server.port=8888
spring.cloud.config.server.git.uri=file:///in28Minutes
/Books/MasteringSpring/git-localconfig-repo
```

Some important things to note are as follows:

- `server.port=8888`: Configures the port for Config Server. `8888` is typically the most commonly used port for Config Server.
- `spring.cloud.config.server.git.uri=file:///in28Minutes/Books/Ma steringSpring/git-localconfig-repo`: Configures the URI to the local Git repository. If you want to connect to a remote Git repository, you can configure the URI of the Git repository here.

Start the server. When you hit the URL `http://localhost:8888/microservice-a/default`, you will see the following response:

```
{
  "name":"microservice-a",
  "profiles":[
    "default"
  ],
  "label":null,
  "version":null,
  "state":null,
  "propertySources":[
    {
      "name":"file:///in28Minutes/Books/MasteringSpring
      /git-localconfig-repo/microservice-a.properties",
      "source":{
        "application.message":"Message From Default
        Local Git Repository"
      }
    }]
}
```

Some important things to understand are as follows:

- `http://localhost:8888/microservice-a/default`: The URI format is `/{application-name}/{profile}[/{label}]`. Here, the application-name is `microservice-a` and the profile is `default`.
- The service returns the configuration from `microservice-a.properties` since we are using the default profile. You can see it in the response in the `propertySources>name` field.
- `"source":{"application.message":"Message From Default Local Git Repository"}`: The content of the response is the content of the property file.

Creating an environment-specific configuration

Let's create a specific configuration for Microservice A for the `dev` environment.

Create a new file in `git-localconfig-repo` with the name `microservice-a-dev.properties` with the content shown here:

```
application.message=Message From Dev Git Repository
```

Execute the following commands to `add` and `commit microservice-a-dev.properties` to the local Git repository:

```
git add -A
git commit -m "default microservice a properties"
```

When you hit the URL `http://localhost:8888/microservice-a/dev`, you will see the following response:

```
{
  "name":"microservice-a",
  "profiles":[
    "dev"
  ],
  "label":null,
  "version":null,
  "state":null,
  "propertySources":[
  {
    "name":"file:///in28Minutes/Books/MasteringSpring
      /git-localconfig-repo/microservice-a-dev.properties",
    "source":{
      "application.message":"Message From Dev Git Repository"
    }
  },
  {
  "name":"file:///in28Minutes/Books/MasteringSpring
    /git-localconfig-repo/microservice-a.properties",
  "source":{
    "application.message":"Message From Default
      Local Git Repository"
  }}]
}
```

The response contains the `dev` configuration from `microservice-a-dev.properties`. The configuration from the default property file (`microservice-a.properties`) is also returned. Properties configured in `microservice-a-dev.properties` (environment-specific properties) have higher priority than the defaults configured in `microservice-a.properties`.

Similar to `dev`, a separate configuration for Microservice A can be created for different environments. If there is a need for multiple instances in a single environment, a tag can be used to differentiate. A URL of the format `http://localhost:8888/microservice-a/dev/{tag}` can be used to retrieve configuration based on the specific tag.

The next step is to connect Microservice A to the Config Server.

Spring Cloud Config Client

We will use Spring Cloud Config Client to connect `Microservice A` to `Config Server`. The dependency is shown here. Add the following code to the `pom.xml` file of `Microservice A`:

```
<dependency>
  <groupId>org.springframework.cloud</groupId>
  <artifactId>spring-cloud-starter-config</artifactId>
</dependency>
```

Dependencies for Spring Cloud are managed differently from Spring Boot. We will use dependency management to manage dependencies. The following snippet will ensure that the correct version of all Spring Cloud dependencies is used:

```
<dependencyManagement>
    <dependencies>
        <dependency>
            <groupId>org.springframework.cloud</groupId>
            <artifactId>spring-cloud-dependencies</artifactId>
            <version>Dalston.RC1</version>
            <type>pom</type>
            <scope>import</scope>
        </dependency>
    </dependencies>
</dependencyManagement>
```

Rename `application.properties` in `Microservice A` to `bootstrap.properties`.

Configure it as shown here:

```
spring.application.name=microservice-a
spring.cloud.config.uri=http://localhost:8888
```

Since we would want `Microservice A` to connect to `Config Server`, we provide the URI of `Config Server` using `spring.cloud.config.uri`. Cloud Config Server is used to retrieve the configuration for microservice A. Hence, the configuration is provided in `bootstrap.properties`.

 Spring Cloud Context: Spring Cloud introduces a few important concepts for the Spring application deployed in the Cloud. The Bootstrap Application Context is an important concept. It is the parent context for the microservice application. It is responsible for loading an external configuration (for example, from Spring Cloud Config Server) and Decrypting Configuration Files (external and local). The Bootstrap context is configured using bootstrap.yml or bootstrap.properties. We had to change the name of application.properties to bootstrap.properties in Microservice A earlier because we want Microservice A to use the Config Server for bootstrapping.

An extract from the log when Microservice A is restarted is shown here:

```
Fetching config from server at: http://localhost:8888
Located environment: name=microservice-a, profiles=[default],
label=null, version=null, state=null
Located property source: CompositePropertySource
[name='configService', propertySources=[MapPropertySource
[name='file:///in28Minutes/Books/MasteringSpring/git-localconfig-
repo/microservice-a.properties']]]
```

The `Microservice A` service is using the configuration from `Spring Config Server` at `http://localhost:8888`.

The following is the response when `Message Service` at `http://localhost:8080/message` is invoked:

```
{"message":"Message From Default Local Git Repository"}
```

The message is picked up from the `localconfig-repo/microservice-a.properties` file.

You can set the active profile to `dev` to pick up the dev configuration:

```
spring.profiles.active=dev
```

The configuration for the service consumer microservice can also be stored in `local-config-repo` and exposed using Spring Config Server.

Spring Cloud Bus

Spring Cloud Bus makes it seamless to connect microservices to lightweight message brokers, such as Kafka and RabbitMQ.

The need for Spring Cloud Bus

Consider an example of making a configuration change in a microservice. Let's assume that there are five instances of `Microservice A` running in production. We would need to make an emergency configuration change. For example, let's make a change in `localconfig-repo/microservice-a.properties`:

```
application.message=Message From Default Local
    Git Repository Changed
```

For `Microservice A` to pick up this configuration change, we need to invoke a POST request on `http://localhost:8080/refresh`. The following command can be executed at command prompt to send a POST request:

```
curl -X POST http://localhost:8080/refresh
```

You will see the configuration change reflected at `http://localhost:8080/message`. The following is the response from the service:

```
{"message":"Message From Default Local Git Repository Changed"}
```

We have five instances of Microservice A running. The change in configuration is reflected only for the instance of the Microservice A where the url is executed. The other four instances will not receive the configuration change until the refresh request is executed on them.

If there are a number of instances of a microservice, then executing the refresh URL for each instance becomes cumbersome since you would need to do this for every configuration change.

Propogating configuration changes using Spring Cloud Bus

The solution is to use Spring Cloud Bus to propagate the configuration change to multiple instances over a message broker such as RabbitMQ.

The following figure shows how different instances of a microservice (actually, they can be completely different microservices as well) are connected to a message broker using Spring Cloud Bus:

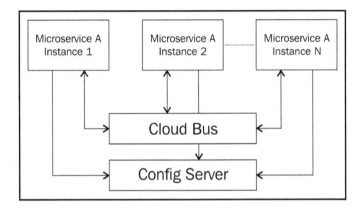

Each microservice instance will register with the Spring Cloud Bus at application startup.

When refresh is called on one of the microservice instances, Spring Cloud Bus will propagate a change event to all the microservice instances. The microservice instances will request the updated configuration from the configuration server on receiving the change event.

Implementation

We will use RabbitMQ as the message broker. Ensure that you have installed and started up RabbitMQ before proceeding further.

Installation instructions for RabbitMQ are provided at `https://www.rabb itmq.com/download.html`.

The next step is to add connectivity to Spring Cloud Bus for `Microservice A`. Let's add the following dependency in the `pom.xml` file of Microservice A:

```xml
<dependency>
  <groupId>org.springframework.cloud</groupId>
  <artifactId>spring-cloud-starter-bus-amqp</artifactId>
</dependency>
```

We can run `Microservice A` on different ports by providing the port as one of the startup VM arguments. The following screenshot shows how you can configure the server port as the VM argument in Eclipse. The value configured is `-Dserver.port=8081`:

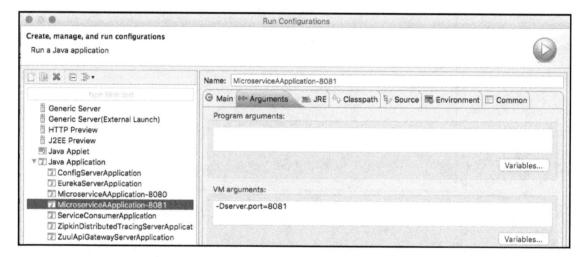

We will run Microservice A on ports `8080` (default) and `8081`. The following is an extract from the log when Microservice A is restarted:

```
o.s.integration.channel.DirectChannel : Channel 'microservice-
a.springCloudBusInput' has 1 subscriber(s).
Bean with name 'rabbitConnectionFactory' has been autodetected for JMX
exposure
Bean with name 'refreshBusEndpoint' has been autodetected for JMX exposure
Created new connection: SimpleConnection@6d12ea7c
[delegate=amqp://guest@127.0.0.1:5672/, localPort= 61741]
Channel 'microservice-a.springCloudBusOutput' has 1 subscriber(s).
 declaring queue for inbound: springCloudBus.anonymous.HK-
dFv8oRwGrhD4BvuhkFQ, bound to: springCloudBus
Adding {message-handler:inbound.springCloudBus.default} as a subscriber to
the 'bridge.springCloudBus' channel
```

All instances of `Microservice A` are registered with `Spring Cloud Bus` and listen to events on the Cloud Bus. The default configuration of RabbitMQ Connection is a result of the magic of autoconfiguration.

Let's update `microservice-a.properties` with a new message now:

```
application.message=Message From Default Local
  Git Repository Changed Again
```

Commit the file and fire a request to refresh the configuration on one of the instances, let's say port `8080`, using the URL `http://localhost:8080/bus/refresh`:

```
curl -X POST http://localhost:8080/bus/refresh
```

The following is an extract from the log of the second instance of `Microservice A` running on port `8081`:

```
Refreshing
org.springframework.context.annotation.AnnotationConfigApplicationContext@5
10cb933: startup date [Mon Mar 27 21:39:37 IST 2017]; root of context
hierarchy
Fetching config from server at: http://localhost:8888
Started application in 1.333 seconds (JVM running for 762.806)
Received remote refresh request. Keys refreshed [application.message]
```

You can see that even though the refresh URL is not called on port `8081`, the updated message is picked up from the Config Server. This is because all instances of Microservice A are listening on the Spring Cloud Bus for change events. As soon as the refresh URL is called on one of the instances, it triggers a change event and all other instances pick up the changed configuration.

You will see the configuration change reflect in both instances of Microservice A at `http://localhost:8080/message` and `http://localhost:8081/message`. The following is the response from the service:

```
{"message":"Message From Default Local
  Git Repository Changed Again"}
```

Declarative REST Client - Feign

Feign helps us create REST clients for REST services with minimum configuration and code. All you need to define is a simple interface and use proper annotations.

`RestTemplate` is typically used to make REST service calls. Feign helps us write REST clients without the need for `RestTemplate` and the logic around it.

Feign integrates well with Ribbon (client-side load balancing) and Eureka (Name server). We will look at this integration later in the chapter.

To use Feign, let's add the Feign starter to the `pom.xml` file of service consumer microservice:

```
<dependency>
  <groupId>org.springframework.cloud</groupId>
  <artifactId>spring-cloud-starter-feign</artifactId>
</dependency>
```

We need to add `dependencyManagement` for Spring Cloud to the `pom.xml` file as this is the first Cloud dependency that service consumer microservice is using:

```
<dependencyManagement>
    <dependencies>
      <dependency>
        <groupId>org.springframework.cloud</groupId>
        <artifactId>spring-cloud-dependencies</artifactId>
        <version>Dalston.RC1</version>
        <type>pom</type>
        <scope>import</scope>
      </dependency>
    </dependencies>
</dependencyManagement>
```

The next step is to add the annotation in order to enable scanning for Feign clients to `ServiceConsumerApplication`. The following snippet shows the usage of the `@EnableFeignClients` annotation:

```
@EnableFeignClients("com.mastering.spring.consumer")
public class ServiceConsumerApplication {
```

We need to define a simple interface to create a Feign client for a `random service`. The following snippet shows the details:

```
@FeignClient(name ="microservice-a", url="localhost:8080")
public interface RandomServiceProxy {
  @RequestMapping(value = "/random", method = RequestMethod.GET)
  public List<Integer> getRandomNumbers();
}
```

Some important things to note are as follows:

- `@FeignClient(name ="microservice-a", url="localhost:8080")`: The `FeignClient` annotation is used to declare that a REST client with the given interface needs to be created. We are hardcoding the URL of `Microservice A` for now. Later, we will look at how we can connect this to a Name server and eliminate the need for hardcoding.
- `@RequestMapping(value = "/random", method = RequestMethod.GET)`: This specific GET service method is exposed at the URI `/random`.
- `public List<Integer> getRandomNumbers()`: This defines the interface of the service method.

Let's update `NumberAdderController` to use `RandomServiceProxy` in order to call the service. The following snippet shows the important details:

```
@RestController
public class NumberAdderController {
  @Autowired
  private RandomServiceProxy randomServiceProxy;
  @RequestMapping("/add")
  public Long add() {
    long sum = 0;
    List<Integer> numbers = randomServiceProxy.getRandomNumbers();
    for (int number : numbers) {
      sum += number;
    }
    return sum;
  }
}
```

A couple of important things to note are as follows:

- `@Autowired private RandomServiceProxy randomServiceProxy`: `RandomServiceProxy` is autowired in.
- `List<Integer> numbers = randomServiceProxy.getRandomNumbers()`: Look at how simple it is to use the Feign client. No playing around with `RestTemplate` anymore.

When we invoke the `add` service in service consumer microservice at `http://localhost:8100/add`, you will get the following response:

```
2103
```

GZIP compression can be enabled on Feign requests by configuring it, as shown in the following snippet:

```
feign.compression.request.enabled=true
feign.compression.response.enabled=true
```

Load balancing

Microservices are the most important building blocks of Cloud-Native architectures. Microservice instances are scaled up and down based on the load of a specific microservice. How do we ensure that the load is equally distributed among the different instances of microservices? That's where the magic of load balancing comes in. Load balancing is important in order to ensure that the load is equally distributed among the different instances of microservices.

Ribbon

As shown in the following figure, Spring Cloud Netflix Ribbon provides client-side load balancing using round robin execution among the different instances of a microservice:

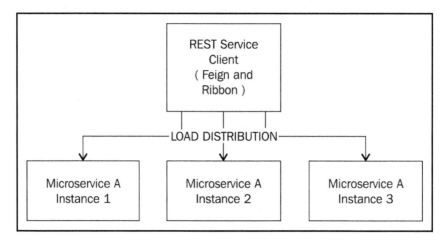

Implementation

We will add Ribbon to service consumer microservice. The service consumer microservice will distribute the load among two instances of Microservice A.

Let's start with adding the Ribbon dependency to the `pom.xml` file of service consumer microservice:

```
<dependency>
  <groupId>org.springframework.cloud</groupId>
  <artifactId>spring-cloud-starter-ribbon</artifactId>
</dependency>
```

Next, we can configure the URLs for the different instances of Microservice A. Add the following configuration to `application.properties` in service consumer microservice:

```
random-proxy.ribbon.listOfServers=
  http://localhost:8080,http://localhost:8081
```

We will then specify the `@RibbonClient` annotation on the service proxy--`RandomServiceProxy` in this example. The `@RibbonClient` annotation is used to specify declarative configuration for a ribbon client:

```
@FeignClient(name ="microservice-a")
@RibbonClient(name="microservice-a")
public interface RandomServiceProxy {
```

When you restart the service consumer microservice and hit the add service at `http://localhost:8100/add`, you will get the following response:

```
2705
```

This request is handled by an instance of `Microservice A` running on port `8080`, An extract from the log is shown here:

```
c.m.s.c.c.RandomNumberController : Returning [487,
  441, 407, 563, 807]
```

When we hit the add service again at the same URL, `http://localhost:8100/add` we get the following response:

```
3423
```

However, this time, the request is handled by an instance of `Microservice` A running on port `8081`. An extract from the log is shown here:

```
c.m.s.c.c.RandomNumberController : Returning [661,
    520, 256, 988, 998]
```

We have now successfully distributed the load among the different instances of `Microservice` A. While this can be improved further, this is a good start.

While round robin (`RoundRobinRule`) is the default algorithm used by Ribbon, there are other options available:

- `AvailabilityFilteringRule` will skip servers that are down and that have a number of concurrent connections.
- `WeightedResponseTimeRule` will pick the server based on the response times. If a server takes a long time to respond, it will get fewer requests.

The algorithm to be used can be specified in the application configuration:

```
microservice-a.ribbon.NFLoadBalancerRuleClassName =
    com.netflix.loadbalancer.WeightedResponseTimeRule
```

The `microservice-a` is the name of the service we specified in the `@RibbonClient(name="microservice-a")` annotation.

The following figure shows the architecture for the components we have set up already:

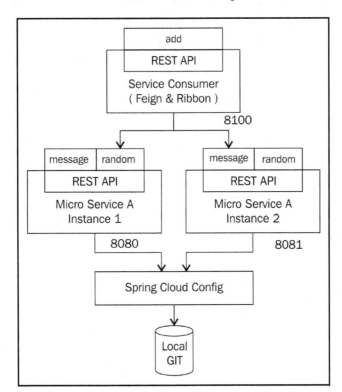

The Name server

Microservice architectures involve a number of smaller microservices interacting with each other. Adding to this, there can be multiple instances of each microservice. Maintaining the external service connections and configurations manually would be difficult as new instances of microservices are dynamically created and destroyed. Name servers provide features of service registration and service discovery. Name servers allow microservices to register themselves and also discover the URLs to other microservices they want to interact with.

Limitations of hard coding microservice URLs

In the previous example, we added the following configuration to
`application.properties` in the service consumer microservice:

```
random-proxy.ribbon.listOfServers=
    http://localhost:8080,http://localhost:8081
```

This configuration represents all instances of Microservice A. Take a look at these situations:

- A new instance of Microservice A is created
- An existing instance of Microservice A is no longer available
- Microservice A is moved to a different server

In all these instances, the configuration needs to be updated and the microservices refreshed
in order to pick up the changes.

Workings of Name server

The Name server is an ideal solution for the preceding situation. The following diagram
shows how Name servers work:

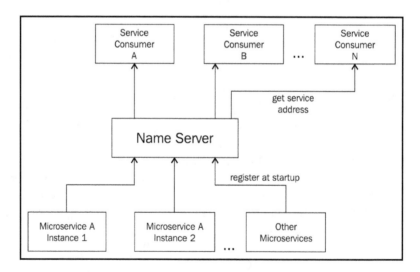

All microservices (different microservices and all their instances) will register themselves
with the Name server as each microservice starts up. When a service consumer wants to get
the location of a specific microservice, it requests the Name server.

A unique microservice ID is assigned to each microservice. This is used as a key in the register request and the lookup request.

Microservices can automatically register and unregister themselves. Whenever a service consumer looks up the Name server with a microservice ID, it will get the list of the instances of that specific microservice.

Options

The following screenshot shows the different options available for service discovery in Spring Initializr (`http://start.spring.io`):

We are going to use Eureka as the Name server for service discovery in our example.

Implementation

The implementation of Eureka for our example involves the following:

1. Setting up `Eureka Server`.
2. Updating `Microservice A` instances to register with `Eureka Server`.
3. Updating service consumer microservice to use the Microservice A instances registered with `Eureka Server`.

Setting up a Eureka Server

We will use Spring Initializr (`http://start.spring.io`) to set up a new project for Eureka Server. The following screenshot shows the **GroupId**, **ArtifactId**, and **Dependencies** to be selected:

The next step is to add the `EnableEurekaServer` annotation to the `SpringBootApplication` class. The following snippet shows the details:

```
@SpringBootApplication
@EnableEurekaServer
public class EurekaServerApplication {
```

The following snippet shows the configuration in `application.properties`:

```
server.port = 8761
eureka.client.registerWithEureka=false
eureka.client.fetchRegistry=false
```

We are using port 8761 for `Eureka Naming Server`. Launch `EurekaServerApplication`.

A screenshot of the Eureka dashboard at `http://localhost:8761` is shown here:

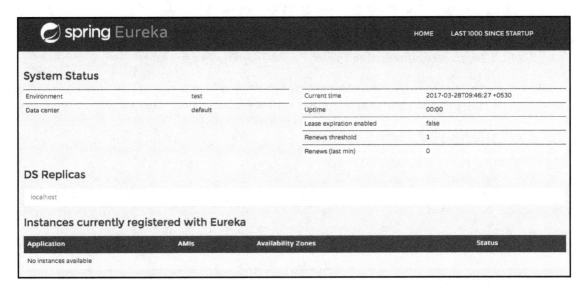

As of now, there are no applications registered with Eureka. In the next step, let's register `Microservice A` and other services with Eureka.

Registering microservices with Eureka

To register any microservice with the Eureka Name server, we would need to add the dependency on Eureka Starter project. The following dependency needs to be added to the `pom.xml` file of Microservice A:

```
<dependency>
    <groupId>org.springframework.cloud</groupId>
    <artifactId>spring-cloud-starter-eureka</artifactId>
</dependency>
```

The next step is to add `EnableDiscoveryClient` to the `SpringBootApplication` classes. An example of `MicroserviceAApplication` is shown here:

```
@SpringBootApplication
@EnableDiscoveryClient
public class MicroserviceAApplication {
```

Spring Cloud Commons hosts the common classes used in different Spring Cloud implementations. A good example is the `@EnableDiscoveryClient` annotation. Different implementations are provided by Spring Cloud Netflix Eureka, Spring Cloud Consul Discovery, and Spring Cloud Zookeeper Discovery.

We will configure the URL of the naming server in the application configuration. For Microservice A, the application configuration is in the local Git repository file, `git-localconfig-repomicroservice-a.properties`:

```
eureka.client.serviceUrl.defaultZone=
   http://localhost:8761/eureka
```

When both instances of `Microservice A` are restarted, you will see these messages in the log of `Eureka Server`:

```
Registered instance MICROSERVICE-A/192.168.1.5:microservice-a
   with status UP (replication=false)
Registered instance MICROSERVICE-A/192.168.1.5:microservice-a:
   8081 with status UP (replication=false)
```

A screenshot of the Eureka Dashboard at `http://localhost:8761` is shown as follows:

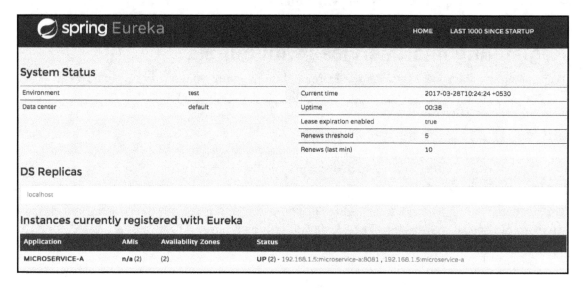

Two instances of `Microservice A` are now registered with `Eureka Server`. Similar updates can be done on `Config Server` in order to connect it to `Eureka Server`.

In the next step, we would want to connect the service consumer microservice to pick up URLs of instances of Microservice A from the Eureka server.

Connecting the service consumer microservice with Eureka

The Eureka starter project needs to be added as a dependency in the pom.xml file of the service consumer microservice:

```
<dependency>
  <groupId>org.springframework.cloud</groupId>
  <artifactId>spring-cloud-starter-eureka</artifactId>
</dependency>
```

Currently, the URLs of the different instances of Microservice A are hardcoded in the service consumer microservice, as shown here, in application.properties:

```
microservice-a.ribbon.listOfServers=
  http://localhost:8080,http://localhost:8081
```

However, now we would not want to hardcode Microservice A URLs. We would want the service consumer microservice to get the URLs from Eureka Server. We do that by configuring the URL of Eureka Server in the application.properties of the service consumer microservice. We will comment out the hardcoding of the Microservice A URLs:

```
#microservice-a.ribbon.listOfServers=
  http://localhost:8080,http://localhost:8081
eureka.client.serviceUrl.defaultZone=
  http://localhost:8761/eureka
```

Next, we will add EnableDiscoveryClient on the ServiceConsumerApplication class, as shown here:

```
@SpringBootApplication
@EnableFeignClients("com.mastering.spring.consumer")
@EnableDiscoveryClient
public class ServiceConsumerApplication {
```

Once the service consumer microservice is restarted, you will see that it will register itself with Eureka Server. The following is an extract from the log of Eureka Server:

```
Registered instance SERVICE-CONSUMER/192.168.1.5:
  service-consumer:8100 with status UP (replication=false)
```

In `RandomServiceProxy`, we have already configured a name for `microservice-a` on the Feign client, as shown here:

```
@FeignClient(name ="microservice-a")
@RibbonClient(name="microservice-a")
public interface RandomServiceProxy {
```

The service consumer microservice will use this ID (Microservice A) to query `Eureka Server` for instances. Once it gets the URLs from `Eureka Service`, it will invoke the service instance selected by Ribbon.

When the `add` service is invoked at `http://localhost:8100/add`, it returns an appropriate response.

Here's a quick review of the different steps involved:

1. As each instance of Microservice A starts up, it registers with `Eureka Name Server`.
2. The service consumer microservice requests `Eureka Name Server` for instances of Microservice A.
3. The service consumer microservice uses the Ribbon client-side load balancer to decide the specific instance of Microservice A to call.
4. The service consumer microservice calls a specific instance of Microservice A.

The biggest advantage of `Eureka Service` is that service consumer microservice is now decoupled from Microservice A. Whenever new instances of Microservice A come up or an existing instance goes down, the service consumer microservice does not need to be reconfigured.

API Gateways

Microservices have a number of cross-cutting concerns:

- **Authentication, authorization, and security**: How do we ensure that the microservice consumers are who they claim to be? How do we ensure that the consumers have the right access to microservices?
- **Rate limits** : There might be different kinds of API plans for consumers and different limits (the number of microservice invocations) for each plan. How do we enforce the limits on a specific consumer?

- **Dynamic routing**: Specific situations (for example, a microservice is down) might need dynamic routing.
- **Service aggregation**: The UI needs for a mobile are different from the desktop. Some microservice architectures have service aggregators tailored for a specific device.
- **Fault tolerance**: How do we ensure that failure in one microservice does not cause the entire system to crash?

When microservices talk directly with each other, these concerns have to be addressed by individual microservices. This kind of architecture might be difficult to maintain because each microservice might handle these concerns differently.

One of the most common solutions is to use an API Gateway. All service calls to and between microservices should go through an API Gateway. API Gateway typically provide these features for microservices:

- Authentication and security
- Rate limiting
- Insights and monitoring
- Dynamic routing and static response handling
- Load shedding
- Aggregation of responses from multiple services

Implementing client-side load balancing with Zuul

Zuul is part of the Spring Cloud Netflix project. It is an API Gateway service that provides the capabilities of dynamic routing, monitoring, filtering, security, and more.

Implementing Zuul as an API Gateway involves the following:

1. Setting up a new Zuul API Gateway Server.
2. Configuring Service Consumer to use Zuul API Gateway.

Setting up a new Zuul API Gateway Server

We will use Spring Initializr (`http://start.spring.io`) to set up a new project for Zuul API Gateway. The following screenshot shows the **GroupId**, **ArtifactId**, and **Dependencies** to be selected:

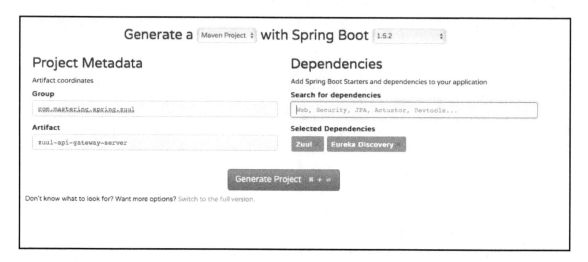

The next step is to enable Zuul proxy on the Spring Boot application. This is done by adding the `@EnableZuulProxy` annotation on the `ZuulApiGatewayServerApplication` class. The following snippet shows the details:

```
@EnableZuulProxy
@EnableDiscoveryClient
@SpringBootApplication
public class ZuulApiGatewayServerApplication {
```

We will run Zuul Proxy on port `8765`. The following snippet shows the configuration needed in `application.properties`:

```
spring.application.name=zuul-api-gateway
server.port=8765
eureka.client.serviceUrl.defaultZone=http://localhost:8761/eureka
```

We are configuring the port for Zuul proxy and connecting it to the Eureka Name server as well.

Zuul custom filters

Zuul provides options to create custom filters to implement typical API Gateway functionality, such as authentication, security, and tracing. In this example, we will create a simple logging filter to log every request. The following snippet shows the details:

```
@Component
public class SimpleLoggingFilter extends ZuulFilter {
  private static Logger log =
    LoggerFactory.getLogger(SimpleLoggingFilter.class);
  @Override
  public String filterType() {
    return "pre";
  }
  @Override
  public int filterOrder() {
    return 1;
  }
  @Override
  public boolean shouldFilter() {
    return true;
  }
  @Override
  public Object run() {
    RequestContext context = RequestContext.getCurrentContext();
    HttpServletRequest httpRequest = context.getRequest();
    log.info(String.format("Request Method : %s n URL: %s",
    httpRequest.getMethod(),
    httpRequest.getRequestURL().toString()));
    return null;
  }
}
```

A few important things to note are as follows:

- `SimpleLoggingFilter extends ZuulFilter`: `ZuulFilter` is the base abstract class to create filters for Zuul. Any filter should implement the four methods listed here.
- `public String filterType()`: Possible return values are `"pre"` for prerouting filtering, `"route"` for routing to an origin, `"post"` for postrouting filters, and `"error"` for error handling. In this example, we would want to filter before the request is executed. We return a value `"pre"`.
- `public int filterOrder()`: Defines the precedence for a filter.

- `public boolean shouldFilter()`: If the filter should only be executed in certain conditions, the logic can be implemented here. If you would want the filter to always be executed, return `true`.
- `public Object run()`: The method to implement the logic for the filter. In our example, we are logging the request method and the URL of the request.

When we start up the Zuul server by launching `ZuulApiGatewayServerApplication` as a Java application, you will see the following log in `Eureka Name Server`:

```
Registered instance ZUUL-API-GATEWAY/192.168.1.5:zuul-api-
    gateway:8765 with status UP (replication=false)
```

This shows that `Zuul API gateway` is up and running. `Zuul API gateway` is also registered with `Eureka Server`. This allows microservice consumers to talk to the Name server to get details about `Zuul API gateway`.

The following figure shows the Eureka dashboard at `http://localhost:8761`. You can see that instances of `Microservice A, service consumer,` and `Zuul API Gateway` are now registered with `Eureka Server`:

Instances currently registered with Eureka			
Application	**AMIs**	**Availability Zones**	**Status**
MICROSERVICE-A	n/a (1)	(1)	UP (1) - 192.168.1.5:microservice-a
SERVICE-CONSUMER	n/a (1)	(1)	UP (1) - 192.168.1.5:service-consumer:8100
ZUUL-API-GATEWAY	n/a (1)	(1)	UP (1) - 192.168.1.5:zuul-api-gateway:8765

The following is an extract from the `Zuul API gateway` log:

```
Mapped URL path [/microservice-a/**] onto handler of type [
class org.springframework.cloud.netflix.zuul.web.ZuulController]
Mapped URL path [/service-consumer/**] onto handler of type [
class org.springframework.cloud.netflix.zuul.web.ZuulController]
```

By default, all services in Microservice A and the service consumer microservice are enabled for reverse proxying by Zuul.

Invoking microservices through Zuul

Let's invoke `random service` through the service proxy now. The direct URL to a random microservice is `http://localhost:8080/random`. This is exposed by Microservice A, whose application name is `microservice-a`.

The URL structure to call a service through `Zuul API Gateway` is `http://localhost:{port}/{microservice-application-name}/{service-uri}`. So, the `Zuul API Gateway` URL for `random service` is `http://localhost:8765/microservice-a/random`. When you invoke `random service` through API Gateway, you get a response shown here. The response is similar to what you would typically get when directly calling the random service:

```
[73,671,339,354,211]
```

The following is an extract from the `Zuul Api Gateway` log. You can see that the `SimpleLoggingFilter` that we created in `Zuul API Gateway` is executed for the request:

```
c.m.s.z.filters.pre.SimpleLoggingFilter : Request Method : GET
URL: http://localhost:8765/microservice-a/random
```

The `add` service is exposed by service consumer, whose application name is service-consumer and the service URI is `/add`. So, the URL to execute the `add` service through the API Gateway is `http://localhost:8765/service-consumer/add`. The response from the service is shown here. The response is similar to what you would typically get when directly calling the `add` service:

```
2488
```

The following is an extract from the `Zuul API Gateway` log. You can see that the initial `add` service call is going through the API Gateway:

```
2017-03-28 14:05:17.514 INFO 83147 --- [nio-8765-exec-1]
c.m.s.z.filters.pre.SimpleLoggingFilter : Request Method : GET
URL: http://localhost:8765/service-consumer/add
```

The `add` service calls `random service` on `Microservice A`. While the initial call to add service goes through the API Gateway, the call from add service (service consumer microservice) to `random service` (Microservice A) is not routed through API Gateway. In an ideal world, we would want all the communication to take place through API Gateway.

In the next step, let's make the requests from the service consumer microservice go through the API Gateway as well.

Configuring service consumer to use Zuul API gateway

The following code shows the existing configuration of `RandomServiceProxy`, which is used to call `random service` on `Microservice A`. The name attribute in the `@FeignClient` annotation is configured to use the application name of Microservice A. The request mapping uses the `/random` URI:

```
@FeignClient(name ="microservice-a")
@RibbonClient(name="microservice-a")
public interface RandomServiceProxy {
@RequestMapping(value = "/random", method = RequestMethod.GET)
   public List<Integer> getRandomNumbers();
}
```

Now, we want the call to go through the API Gateway. We would need to use the application name of the API Gateway and the new URI of `random service` in the request mapping. The following snippet shows the updated `RandomServiceProxy` class:

```
@FeignClient(name="zuul-api-gateway")
//@FeignClient(name ="microservice-a")
@RibbonClient(name="microservice-a")
public interface RandomServiceProxy {
   @RequestMapping(value = "/microservice-a/random",
   method = RequestMethod.GET)
   //@RequestMapping(value = "/random", method = RequestMethod.GET)
   public List<Integer> getRandomNumbers();
}
```

When we invoke the add service at `http://localhost:8765/service-consumer/add`, we will see the typical response:

```
2254
```

However, now we will see more things happen on `Zuul API gateway`. The following is an extract from the `Zuul API gateway` log. You can see that the initial add service call on the service consumer, as well as the `random service` call on `Microservice A`, are now being routed through the API Gateway:

```
2017-03-28 14:10:16.093 INFO 83147 --- [nio-8765-exec-4]
c.m.s.z.filters.pre.SimpleLoggingFilter : Request Method : GET
URL: http://localhost:8765/service-consumer/add
2017-03-28 14:10:16.685 INFO 83147 --- [nio-8765-exec-5]
c.m.s.z.filters.pre.SimpleLoggingFilter : Request Method : GET
URL: http://192.168.1.5:8765/microservice-a/random
```

We saw a basic implementation of a simple logging filter on `Zuul API Gateway`. A similar approach can be used to implement filters for other cross-cutting concerns.

Distributed tracing

In typical microservice architectures, there are a number of components involved. A few of them are listed here:

- Different microservices
- API Gateway
- Naming server
- Configuration server

A typical call may involve more than four or five components. These are the important questions to ask:

- How can we debug issues?
- How can we find out the root cause of a specific problem?

A typical solution is centralized logging with a dashboard. Have all microservice logs consolidated in one place and offer a dashboard on top of it.

Distributed tracing options

The following screenshot shows the options for distributed tracing on the Spring Initializr website:

```
Cloud Tracing

☐ Sleuth
    Distributed tracing via logs with spring-cloud-sleuth

☐ Zipkin Client
    Distributed tracing with an existing Zipkin installation and spring-cloud-sleuth-
    zipkin. Alternatively, consider Sleuth Stream.

☐ Sleuth Stream
    Marshals Spring Cloud Sleuth Spans over a Spring Cloud Stream binder

☐ Zipkin Stream
    Consumes span data in messages from Spring Cloud Sleuth Stream and writes
    them to a Zipkin store

☐ Zipkin UI
    add the Zipkin UI module to the Zipkin server to get a Zipkin service that accepts
    Spans and provides visualization
```

In this example, we will use a combination of Spring Cloud Sleuth and Zipkin Server to implement Distributed Tracing.

Implementing Spring Cloud Sleuth and Zipkin

Spring Cloud Sleuth provides features to uniquely trace a service call across different microservice components. **Zipkin** is a distributed tracing system that's used to gather data needed to troubleshoot latency issues in microservices. We will be implementing a combination of Spring Cloud Sleuth and Zipkin to implement Distributed Tracing.

The following are the steps involved:

1. Integrate Microservice A, API Gateway, and the service consumer with Spring Cloud Sleuth.
2. Set up Zipkin Distributed Tracing Server.
3. Integrate Microservice A, API Gateway, and the service consumer with Zipkin.

Integrating microservice components with Spring Cloud Sleuth

When we call the add service on the service consumer, it will invoke Microservice A through API Gateway. To be able to track the service call across different components, we would need something unique assigned to the request flow across components.

Spring Cloud Sleuth provides options to track a service call across different components using a concept called **span**. Each span has a unique 64-bit ID. The unique ID can be used to trace the call across components.

The following snippet shows the dependency for `spring-cloud-starter-sleuth`:

```
<dependency>
  <groupId>org.springframework.cloud</groupId>
  <artifactId>spring-cloud-starter-sleuth</artifactId>
</dependency>
```

We need to add the preceding dependency on Spring Cloud Sleuth to the following three projects listed:

- Microservice A
- Service consumer
- Zuul API Gateway Server

We will start with tracing all the service requests across microservices. To be able to trace all the requests, we will need to configure an `AlwaysSampler` bean, as shown in the following snippet:

```
@Bean
public AlwaysSampler defaultSampler() {
  return new AlwaysSampler();
}
```

The `AlwaysSampler` bean needs to be configured in the following microservice application classes:

- `MicroserviceAApplication`
- `ServiceConsumerApplication`
- `ZuulApiGatewayServerApplication`

When we invoke the `add` service at `http://localhost:8765/service-consumer/add`, we will see the typical response:

```
1748
```

However, you will start to see a few more details in the log entries. A simple entry from the service consumer microservice log is shown here:

```
2017-03-28 20:53:45.582 INFO [service-
consumer,d8866b38c3a4d69c,d8866b38c3a4d69c,true] 89416 --- [1-api-
gateway-5] c.netflix.loadbalancer.BaseLoadBalancer : Client:zuul-api-
gateway instantiated a
LoadBalancer:DynamicServerListLoadBalancer:{NFLoadBalancer:name=zuul-api-
gateway,current list of Servers=[],Load balancer stats=Zone stats:
{},Server stats: []}ServerList:null
```

`[service-consumer,d8866b38c3a4d69c,d8866b38c3a4d69c,true]`: The first value `service-consumer` is the application name. The key part is the second value-- `d8866b38c3a4d69c`. This is the value that can be used to trace this request across other microservice components.

The following are some other entries from the `service consumer` log:

```
2017-03-28 20:53:45.593 INFO [service-
consumer,d8866b38c3a4d69c,d8866b38c3a4d69c,true] 89416 --- [1-api-
gateway-5] c.n.l.DynamicServerListLoadBalancer : Using serverListUpdater
PollingServerListUpdater
 2017-03-28 20:53:45.597 INFO [service-
consumer,d8866b38c3a4d69c,d8866b38c3a4d69c,true] 89416 --- [1-api-
gateway-5] c.netflix.config.ChainedDynamicProperty : Flipping property:
zuul-api-gateway.ribbon.ActiveConnectionsLimit to use NEXT property:
niws.loadbalancer.availabilityFilteringRule.activeConnectionsLimit =
2147483647
2017-03-28 20:53:45.599 INFO [service-
consumer,d8866b38c3a4d69c,d8866b38c3a4d69c,true] 89416 --- [1-api-
gateway-5] c.n.l.DynamicServerListLoadBalancer :
DynamicServerListLoadBalancer for client zuul-api-gateway initialized:
DynamicServerListLoadBalancer:{NFLoadBalancer:name=zuul-api-gateway,current
list of Servers=[192.168.1.5:8765],Load balancer stats=Zone stats:
{defaultzone=[Zone:defaultzone; Instance count:1; Active connections count:
0; Circuit breaker tripped count: 0; Active connections per server: 0.0;]
 [service-consumer,d8866b38c3a4d69c,d8866b38c3a4d69c,true] 89416 ---
[nio-8100-exec-1] c.m.s.c.service.NumberAdderController : Returning 1748
```

The following is an extract from the `Microservice A` log:

```
[microservice-a,d8866b38c3a4d69c,89d03889ebb02bee,true] 89404 ---
[nio-8080-exec-8] c.m.s.c.c.RandomNumberController : Returning [425, 55,
51, 751, 466]
```

The following is an extract from the `Zuul API Gateway` log:

```
[zuul-api-gateway,d8866b38c3a4d69c,89d03889ebb02bee,true] 89397 ---
[nio-8765-exec-8] c.m.s.z.filters.pre.SimpleLoggingFilter : Request Method
: GET
URL: http://192.168.1.5:8765/microservice-a/random
```

As you can see in the preceding log extracts, we can use the second value in the log--called span ID--to trace the service call across microservice components. In this example, the span ID is d8866b38c3a4d69c.

However, this requires searching through logs of all the microservice components. One option is to implement a centralized log using something like an ELK (Elasticsearch, Logstash, and Kibana) stack. We will take the simpler option of creating a Zipkin Distributed Tracing service in the next step.

Setting up Zipkin Distributed Tracing Server

We will use Spring Initializr (`http://start.spring.io`) to set up a new project. The following screenshot shows the **GroupId**, **ArtifactId**, and **Dependencies** to be selected:

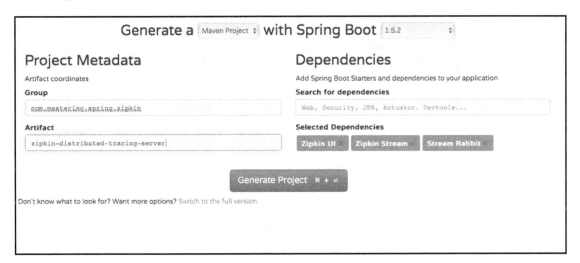

Dependencies include the following:

- **Zipkin Stream**: Multiple options exist to configure a Zipkin server. In this example, we will keep it simple by creating a standalone service listening on events and storing information in the memory.
- **Zipkin UI**: Provides a dashboard with the search functionality.
- **Stream Rabbit**: Used to bind the Zipkin stream with a RabbitMQ service.

In production, you would want to have a more robust infrastructure. One option is to connect a permanent data store to the Zipkin Stream Server.

Next, we will add the `@EnableZipkinServer` annotation to the `ZipkinDistributedTracingServerApplication` class to enable auto-configuration for the Zipkin server. The following snippet shows the details:

```
@EnableZipkinServer
@SpringBootApplication
public class ZipkinDistributedTracingServerApplication {
```

We will use port `9411` to run the tracing server. The following snippet shows the configuration that needs to be added in the `application.properties` file:

```
spring.application.name=zipkin-distributed-tracing-server
server.port=9411
```

You can launch the Zipkin UI dashboard at `http://localhost:9411/`. The following is a screenshot of that. There is no data shown, as none of the microservices are connected to Zipkin yet:

Integrating microservice components with Zipkin

We will need to connect all the microservice components that we want to trace with `Zipkin server`. Here is the list of components we will start with:

- Microservice A
- Service consumer
- Zuul API Gateway Server

All we need to do is add dependencies on `spring-cloud-sleuth-zipkin` and `spring-cloud-starter-bus-amqp` to the `pom.xml` file of the preceding projects:

```
<dependency>
   <groupId>org.springframework.cloud</groupId>
   <artifactId>spring-cloud-sleuth-zipkin</artifactId>
</dependency>
<dependency>
   <groupId>org.springframework.cloud</groupId>
   <artifactId>spring-cloud-starter-bus-amqp</artifactId>
</dependency>
```

Go ahead and execute the `add` service at `http://localhost:8100/add`. You can now see the details on the Zipkin dashboard. The following screenshot shows some of the details:

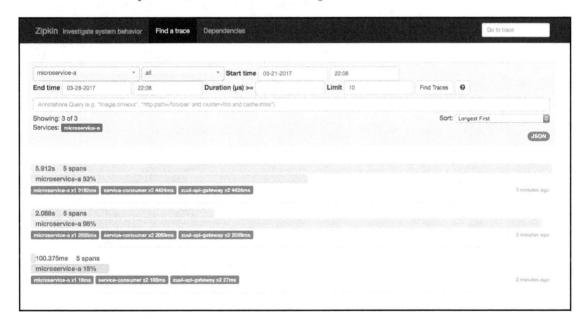

The first two rows show the failed requests. The third row shows the details of a successful request. We can further dig in by clicking on the successful row. The following screenshot shows the details displayed:

pent on each service. You can further dig in by clicking on the **service** bar. The following screenshot shows the details displayed:

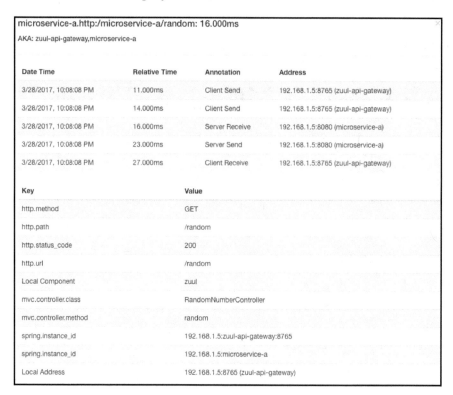

In this section, we added distributed tracing for our microservices. We will now be able to visually track everything that is happening with our microservices. This will make it easy to track down and debug issues.

Hystrix - fault tolerance

Microservice architectures are built with a number of microservice components. What if one microservice goes down? Would all dependent microservices fail and make the entire system collapse? Or would the error be gracefully handled and a degraded minimum functionality provided to the user? These questions decide the success of microservice architectures.

Microservice architectures should be resilient and be able to handle service errors gracefully. Hystrix provides fault-tolerant capabilities to microservices.

Implementation

We will add Hystrix to our service consumer microservice and enhance the add service to return a basic response even when Microservice A is down.

We will start with adding Hystrix Starter to the pom.xml file of service consumer microservice. The following snippet shows the dependency details:

```
<dependency>
  <groupId>org.springframework.cloud</groupId>
  <artifactId>spring-cloud-starter-hystrix</artifactId>
</dependency>
```

Next, we would enable Hystrix auto-configuration by adding the @EnableHystrix annotation to the ServiceConsumerApplication class. The following snippet shows the details:

```
@SpringBootApplication
@EnableFeignClients("com.mastering.spring.consumer")
@EnableHystrix
@EnableDiscoveryClient
public class ServiceConsumerApplication {
```

`NumberAdderController` exposes a service with request mapping `/add`. This uses `RandomServiceProxy` to fetch random numbers. What if this service fails? Hystrix provides a fallback. The following snippet shows how we can add a fallback method to a request mapping. All we need to do is add the `@HystrixCommand` annotation to the `fallbackMethod` attribute, defining the name of the fallback method--in this example, `getDefaultResponse`:

```
@HystrixCommand(fallbackMethod = "getDefaultResponse")
@RequestMapping("/add")
public Long add() {
   //Logic of add() method
}
```

Next, we define the `getDefaultResponse()` method with the same return type as the `add()` method. It returns a default hardcoded value:

```
public Long getDefaultResponse() {
   return 10000L;
 }
```

Let's bring down Microservice A and invoke `http://localhost:8100/add`. You will get the following response:

```
10000
```

When `Microservice A` fails, the service consumer microservice handles it gracefully and offers reduced functionality.

Summary

Spring Cloud makes it easy to add Cloud-Native features to your microservices. In this chapter, we looked at some of the important patterns in developing Cloud-Native applications and implemented them using various Spring Cloud projects.

It is important to remember that the field of developing Cloud-Native applications is still in its inception phase--in its first few years. It would need more time to mature. Expect some evolution in patterns and frameworks in the years to come.

In the next chapter, we will shift our attention to Spring Data Flow. Typical use cases on the cloud include real-time data analytics and data pipelines. These use cases involve the flow of data between multiple microservices. Spring Data Flow provides patterns and best practices for distributed streaming and data pipelines.

10
Spring Cloud Data Flow

Spring Data Flow brings the microservices architecture into typical data flow and event flow scenarios. We will discuss more about these scenarios later in this chapter. Building on top of other Spring Projects, such as Spring Cloud Stream, Spring Integration, and Spring Boot, Spring Data Flow makes it easy to define and scale use cases involving data and event flows using message-based integration.

In this chapter, we will discuss the following topics:

- Why do we need asynchronous communication?
- What is Spring Cloud Stream? How does it build on top of Spring Integration?
- Why do we need Spring Data Flow?
- What are the important concepts in Spring Data Flow you would need to understand?
- What are the use cases where Spring Data Flow is useful?

We will also implement a simple event flow scenario with three microservices acting as the source (application generating the events), processor, and sink (application consuming events). We will implement the microservices using Spring Cloud Stream and establish connections between them over the message broker using Spring Cloud Data Flow.

Message-based asynchronous communication

There are two options when integrating applications:

- **Synchronous**: Service consumer invokes the service provider and waits for a response.

- **Asynchronous**: Service consumer invokes the service provider by putting the message on the message broker but does not wait for the response.

The services that we built with Spring Boot in Chapter 5, *Building Microservices with Spring Boot*, (random service, add service) are examples of synchronous integration. These are typical web services that are exposed over HTTP. The service consumer calls the service and waits for a response. The next call is made only on the completion of the previous service call.

One important disadvantage of this approach is the expectation that the service provider is always available. The service consumer will need to re-execute the service again if the service provider is down or, for some reason, the service fails in execution.

An alternate approach is to use message-based asynchronous communications. Service consumer puts a message on the message broker. The service provider listens on the message broker and as soon as a message is available, it processes it.

An advantage here is that even if the service provider is down for a while, it can process the messages on the message broker whenever it comes back up. The service provider does not need to be available all the time. While there is a possibility of a lag, data would eventually be consistent.

The following figure shows an example of asynchronous message-based communication:

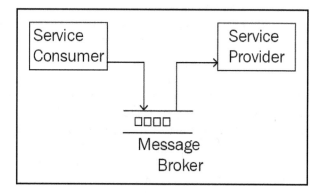

There are two kinds of scenarios where asynchronous communication improves reliability:

- If the service provider is down, then the messages will be queued in the message broker. When service provider is back up, it will process these messages. So, the messages will not be lost even if service provider is down.

- If there is an error in processing the message, the service provider will put the message in an error channel. When the error is analyzed and fixed, the message can be moved from the error channel to the input channel and queued for reprocessing.

The important thing to note is that in both the preceding scenarios, service consumer does not need to worry if the service provider is down or message processing has failed. Service consumer sends a message and forgets about it. The messaging architecture ensures that the message is eventually processed successfully.

Message-based asynchronous communication is typically used in event flows and data flows:

- **Event flows**: This involve processing logic based on an event. For example, a new customer event or a stock price change event or a currency change event. Downstream applications will be listening on the message broker for events and will react to them.
- **Data flows**: This involve data that is enhanced through multiple applications and finally stored down to a data store.

Functionally, the content of the message exchanged between data flow architectures is different from that of event flow architectures. However, technically, it is a just another message that is sent from one system to another. In this chapter, we will not differentiate between event and data flows. Spring Cloud Data Flow can handle all these flows--in spite of having only data flow in the name. We use event flow, data flow, or message flow interchangeably to indicate a flow of messages between different applications.

Complexities of asynchronous communication

While the preceding example is a simple communication between two applications, typical flows in real-world applications can be much more complex.

The following figure shows an example scenario involving the message flow across three different applications. The source application generates the event. The processor application processes the event and generates another message that will be processed by the sink application:

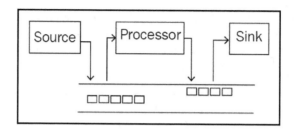

Another example scenario involves an event that is consumed by multiple applications. For example, when a customer is registered, we would want to send them an e-mail, a welcome kit, and a mail. A simple messaging architecture for this scenario is shown in the following figure:

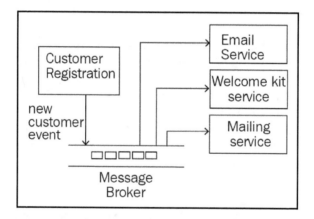

To implement the preceding scenarios, a number of different steps are involved:

1. Configuring the message broker.
2. Creating different channels on the message broker.
3. Writing application code to connect to a specific channel on the message broker.
4. Installing necessary binders in the applications to connect to the message brokers.
5. Setting up the connection between the applications and the message broker.
6. Building and deploying the applications.

Consider a scenario where some of these applications in the flow have to process a huge load of messages. We would need to create multiple instances of such applications based on the load. The implementation complexity becomes multifold. These are the challenges that Spring Cloud Data Flow and Spring Cloud Stream aim to solve.

In the next section, we will look at how different Spring projects--Spring Cloud Stream (built on top of Spring Integration) and Spring Cloud Data Flow enable us to do message-based integrations with little configuration.

Spring projects for asynchronous messages

In this section, we will look at different projects provided by Spring to enable message-based communication between applications. We will start with Spring Integration and then move on to projects that enable message-based integration even on the Cloud--Spring Cloud Stream and Spring Cloud Data Flow.

Spring Integration

Spring Integration helps integrate microservices seamlessly over a message broker. It allows programmers to focus on business logic and give control of the technical infrastructure (what message format to use? How to connect to message broker?) to the framework. Spring Integration provide a variety of configuration options through well-defined interfaces and message adapters. Spring Integration website (`https://projects.spring.io/spring-integration/`):

> *Extends the Spring programming model to support the well-known Enterprise Integration Patterns. Spring Integration enables lightweight messaging within Spring-based applications and supports integration with external systems via declarative adapters. Those adapters provide a higher-level of abstraction over Spring's support for remoting, messaging, and scheduling. Spring Integration's primary goal is to provide a simple model for building enterprise integration solutions while maintaining the separation of concerns that is essential for producing maintainable, testable code.*

Features provided by Spring Integration include the following:

- Simple implementations for enterprise integration patterns
- Aggregation of responses from multiple services
- Filtering results from the service

- Service message transformation
- Multiple protocol support--HTTP, FTP/SFTP, TCP/UDP, JMS
- Support for different styles of Webservices (SOAP and REST)
- Support for multiple message brokers, for example, RabbitMQ

In the previous chapter, we used Spring Cloud to make our microservices Cloud-Native--to be deployed in the Cloud and utilize all the benefits of Cloud deployment.

However, applications built with Spring Integration, especially those that interact with message brokers, need a lot of configuration to be deployed into the Cloud. This prevents them from taking advantage of the typical benefits of the Cloud, such as automatic scaling.

We would want to extend the features provided by Spring Integration and make them available on the Cloud. We would want new instances of our microservice cloud instances to be able to automatically integrate with message brokers. We would want to be able to scale our microservice cloud instances automatically without manual configuration. That's where Spring Cloud Stream and Spring Cloud Data Flow come in.

Spring Cloud Stream

Spring Cloud Stream is the framework of choice to build message-driven microservices for the Cloud.
Spring Cloud Stream allows programmers to focus on building microservices around the business logic of event processing, leaving infrastructure concerns, listed here, to the framework(s):

- Message broker configuration and channel creation
- Message-broker-specific conversions for message
- Creating binders to connect to the message broker

Spring Cloud Stream fits hand in glove into the microservices architecture. The typical microservices needed in use cases of event processing or data streaming can be designed with a clear separation of concerns. Individual microservices can handle business logic, define the input/output channels and leave the infrastructure concerns to the framework.

Typical stream applications involve the creation of events, processing of events, and storing down to a data store. Spring Cloud Stream provides three simple kinds of applications to support typical stream flows:

- **Source**: Source is the creator of events, for example, the application that triggers a stock price change event.

- **Processor**: Processor consumes an even, that is, processes a message, does some processing around it, and creates an event with the result.
- **Sink**: Sink consumes events. It listens on to a message broker and stores the event to a persistent data store.

> Spring Cloud Stream is used to create individual microservices in the data flow. Spring Cloud Stream microservices define business logic and the connection points, the inputs and/or outputs. Spring Cloud Data Flow helps in defining the flow, that is, connecting different applications.

Spring Cloud Data Flow

Spring Cloud Data Flow helps in establishing message flows between different kinds of microservices created using Spring Cloud Stream.

> Built on top of popular open source projects, **Spring XD** simplifies the creation of data pipelines and workflows--especially for Big Data use cases. However, Spring XD has challenges adapting to newer requirements (canary deployments and distributed tracing, for example) related to data pipelines. Spring XD architecture is based on a run-time dependent on a number of peripherals. This makes sizing the cluster a challenging exercise. Spring XD is now resigned as Spring Cloud Data Flow. The architecture of Spring Cloud Data Flow is based on composable microservice applications.

Important features in Spring Cloud Data Flow are as follows:

- Configuring a stream, that is, how data or events flow from one application to another. Stream DSL is used to define the flow between applications.
- Establishing a connection between the applications and the message broker.
- Providing analytics around applications and streams.
- Deploying applications defined in streams to the target runtime.
- Support for multiple target runtimes. Almost every popular cloud platform is supported.
- Scaling up applications on the Cloud.
- Creating and invoking tasks.

Sometimes, the terminology can get a little confusing. A stream is an alternate terminology for a flow. It's important to remember that Spring Cloud Stream actually does not define the entire stream. It only helps in creating one of the microservices involved in the entire stream. As we will see in the next sections, streams are actually defined using Stream DSL in Spring Cloud Data Flow.

Spring Cloud Stream

Spring Cloud Stream is used to create individual microservices involved in a stream and define the connection points to a message broker.
Spring Cloud Stream is built on top of two important Spring Projects:

- **Spring Boot**: To enable the creation of production-ready microservices
- **Spring Integration**: To enable microservices to communicate over message brokers

Some of the important features of Spring Cloud Stream are as follows:

- Bare minimum configuration to connect a microservice to a message broker.
- Support for a variety of message brokers--RabbitMQ, Kafka, Redis, and GemFire.
- Support for persistence of messages--in case a service is down, it can start processing the messages once it is back up.
- Support for consumer groups--in cases of heavy loads, you need multiple instances of the same microservice. You can group all these microservice instances under a single consumer group so that the message is picked up only by one of the available instances.
- Support for partitioning--there can be situations where you would want to ensure that a specific set of messages are addressed by the same instance. Partitioning allows you to configure the criteria to identify messages to be handled by the same partition instance.

Spring Cloud Stream architecture

The following figure shows an architecture of a typical Spring Cloud Stream microservice. A source would only have an input channel, the processor would have both the input and output channel, and a sink would have only an output channel:

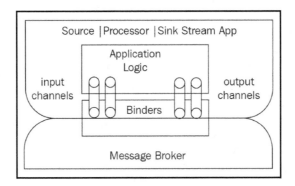

Applications declare what kind of connection they would want--an input and/or an output. Spring Cloud Stream will establish all that would be needed to connect applications over the message broker.

Spring Cloud Stream would do the following:

- Inject the input and/or output channels into the application
- Establish connections with the message broker through a message=broker-specific binder

 Binders bring configurability to Spring Cloud Stream applications. A String Cloud Stream application only declares the channels. Deployment team can configure, at runtime, which message broker (Kafka or RabbitMQ) the channels connect to. Spring Cloud Stream uses auto-configuration to detect the binder available on the classpath. To connect to a different message broker, all that we need to do is change the dependency for the project. Another option is to include multiple binders in the classpath and choose the one to use at runtime.

Event processing - stock trading example

Let's imagine a scenario. A stock trader is interested in significant stock price changes of stocks that he/she has invested in. The following figure shows a simple architecture of such an application built with Spring Cloud Stream:

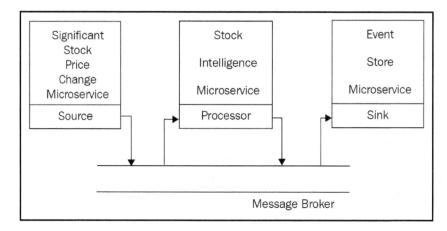

Important things to note are as follows:

- **Significant stock price change microservice**: This triggers an event on the message broker whenever there is a significant change in the price of any stock listed on the exchange. This is the **Source** application.
- **Stock intelligence microservice**: This listens to the message brokers for stock price change events. When there is a new message, it checks the stock against inventory and adds information on the user's current holdings to the message and puts another message on the message broker. This is the **Processor** application.
- **Event store microservice**: This listens on the message broker for stock price change on an invested stock alert. When there is a new message, it stores it down in data store. This is the **Sink** application.

The preceding architecture gives us the flexibility to enhance our systems without major changes:

- E-mail microservice and SMS microservice listens on the message broker for stock price change on an invested stock alert and sends an e-mail/SMS alert.
- A stock trader might want to make significant changes in other stocks they have not invested in. Stock intelligence microservice can be enhanced further.

As we discussed earlier, Spring Cloud Stream helps us build the basic building blocks of a stream, that is, the microservices. We will create three microservices using Spring Cloud Stream. We will later use these three microservices and create a stream, that is, a flow between the applications using Spring Cloud Data Flow.

We will start with creating the microservices using Spring Cloud Stream in the next section. Before we start with source, processor, and sink stream applications, we will set up a simple model project:

Model for stock trading example

The `StockPriceChangeEvent` class contains the ticker of the stock, the old price of the stock, and the new prices of the stock:

```
public class StockPriceChangeEvent {
  private final String stockTicker;
  private final BigDecimal oldPrice;
  private final BigDecimal newPrice;
  //Setter, Getters and toString()
}
```

The `StockPriceChangeEventWithHoldings` class extends `StockPriceChangeEvent`. It has one additional property--`holdings`. The `holdings` variable is used to store the number of stocks the trader currently owns:

```
public class StockPriceChangeEventWithHoldings
extends StockPriceChangeEvent {
  private Integer holdings;
  //Setter, Getters and toString()
}
```

The `StockTicker` enum stores list of stocks that the application supports:

```
public enum StockTicker {
  GOOGLE, FACEBOOK, TWITTER, IBM, MICROSOFT
}
```

The source application

The source application will be the producer of stock price change events. It will define an output channel and put a message on the message broker.

Let's use Spring Initializr (`https://start.spring.io`) to set up the application. Provide the details listed here and click on **Generate Project**:

- **Group**: `com.mastering.spring.cloud.data.flow`
- **Artifact**: `significant-stock-change-source`
- **Dependencies**: `Stream Rabbit`

Listed here are some of the important dependencies from the `pom.xml` file:

```
<dependency>
  <groupId>org.springframework.cloud</groupId>
  <artifactId>spring-cloud-starter-stream-rabbit</artifactId>
</dependency>
```

Update the `SpringBootApplication` file with the following code:

```
@EnableBinding(Source.class)
@SpringBootApplication
public class SignificantStockChangeSourceApplication {
  private static Logger logger = LoggerFactory.getLogger
  (SignificantStockChangeSourceApplication.class);
// psvm - main method
  @Bean
  @InboundChannelAdapter(value = Source.OUTPUT,
  poller = @Poller(fixedDelay = "60000", maxMessagesPerPoll = "1"))
  public MessageSource<StockPriceChangeEvent>
  stockPriceChangeEvent()        {
    StockTicker[] tickers = StockTicker.values();
    String randomStockTicker =
    tickers[ThreadLocalRandom.current().nextInt(tickers.length)]
  .name();
    return () - > {
      StockPriceChangeEvent event = new
      StockPriceChangeEvent(randomStockTicker,
      new BigDecimal(getRandomNumber(10, 20)), new
      BigDecimal(getRandomNumber(10, 20)));
      logger.info("sending " + event);
      return MessageBuilder.withPayload(event).build();
      };
    }
  private int getRandomNumber(int min, int max) {
    return ThreadLocalRandom.current().nextInt(min, max + 1);
  }
}
```

A few important things to note are as follows:

- `@EnableBinding(Source.class)`: The `EnableBinding` annotation enables binding a class with the respective channel it needs--an input and/or an output. The source class is used to register a Cloud Stream with one output channel.
- `@Bean @InboundChannelAdapter(value = Source.OUTPUT, poller = @Poller(fixedDelay = "60000", maxMessagesPerPoll = "1"))`: The `InboundChannelAdapter` annotation is used to indicate that this method can create a message to be put on a message broker. The value attribute is used to indicate the name of the channel where the message is to be put. `Poller` is used to schedule the generation of messages. In this example, we are using `fixedDelay` to generate messages every minute (60 * 1000 ms).
- `private int getRandomNumber(int min, int max)`: This method is used to create a random number in the range passed as parameters.

The `Source` interface defines an output channel, as shown in the following code:

```
public abstract interface
org.springframework.cloud.stream.messaging.Source {
    public static final java.lang.String OUTPUT = "output";
    @org.springframework.cloud.stream.
    annotation.Output(value="output")
    public abstract org.springframework.
    messaging.MessageChannel    output();
}
```

Processor

The processor application will pick up the message from the input channel on the message broker. It will process the message and put it out on the output channel of the message broker. In this specific example, processing involves adding the position of current holdings to the message.

Let's use Spring Initializr (`https://start.spring.io`) to set up the application. Provide the details listed here and click on **Generate Project**:

- **Group**: `com.mastering.spring.cloud.data.flow`
- **Artifact**: `stock-intelligence-processor`
- **Dependencies**: `Stream Rabbit`

Update the `SpringBootApplication` file with the following code:

```
@EnableBinding(Processor.class)@SpringBootApplication
public class StockIntelligenceProcessorApplication {
  private static Logger logger =
  LoggerFactory.getLogger
  (StockIntelligenceProcessorApplication.class);
  private static Map < StockTicker, Integer > holdings =
    getHoldingsFromDatabase();
    private static Map < StockTicker,
    Integer > getHoldingsFromDatabase() {
      final Map < StockTicker,
      Integer > holdings = new HashMap < >();
      holdings.put(StockTicker.FACEBOOK, 10);
      holdings.put(StockTicker.GOOGLE, 0);
      holdings.put(StockTicker.IBM, 15);
      holdings.put(StockTicker.MICROSOFT, 30);
      holdings.put(StockTicker.TWITTER, 50);
      return holdings;
  }
  @Transformer(inputChannel = Processor.INPUT,
  outputChannel = Processor.OUTPUT)
  public Object addOurInventory(StockPriceChangeEvent event) {
    logger.info("started processing event " + event);
    Integer holding =  holdings.get(
      StockTicker.valueOf(event.getStockTicker()));
    StockPriceChangeEventWithHoldings eventWithHoldings =
      new StockPriceChangeEventWithHoldings(event, holding);
    logger.info("ended processing eventWithHoldings "
      + eventWithHoldings);
    return eventWithHoldings;
  }
  public static void main(String[] args) {
    SpringApplication.run(
      StockIntelligenceProcessorApplication.class,args);
  }
}
```

A few important things to note are as follows:

- `@EnableBinding(Processor.class)`: The `EnableBinding` annotation enables binding a class with the respective channel it needs--an input and/or an output. The `Processor` class is used to register a Cloud Stream with one input channel and one output channel.

- `private static Map<StockTicker, Integer>`
  `getHoldingsFromDatabase()`: This method processes a message, updates the holdings, and return a new object, which will be put as a new message into the output channel.
- `@Transformer(inputChannel = Processor.INPUT, outputChannel = Processor.OUTPUT)`: The `Transformer` annotation is used to indicate a method that is capable of transforming/enhancing one message format into another.

As shown in the following code, the `Processor` class extends the `Source` and `Sink` classes. Hence, it defines both the output and input channels:

```
public abstract interface
org.springframework.cloud.stream.messaging.Processor extends
org.springframework.cloud.stream.messaging.Source,
org.springframework.cloud.stream.messaging.Sink {
}
```

Sink

Sink will pick the message from the message broker and process it. In this example, we will pick the message and log it. A Sink will define an input channel only.

Let's use Spring Initializr (`https://start.spring.io`) to set up the application. Provide the details listed here and click on **Generate Project**:

- **Group**: `com.mastering.spring.cloud.data.flow`
- **Artifact**: `event-store-sink`
- **Dependencies**: `Stream Rabbit`

Update the `SpringBootApplication` file with the following code:

```
@EnableBinding(Sink.class)@SpringBootApplication
public class EventStoreSinkApplication {
  private static Logger logger =
  LoggerFactory.getLogger(EventStoreSinkApplication.class);
  @StreamListener(Sink.INPUT)
  public void loggerSink(StockPriceChangeEventWithHoldings event) {
  logger.info("Received: " + event);
  }
  public static void main(String[] args) {
    SpringApplication.run(EventStoreSinkApplication.class, args);
  }
}
```

A few important things to note are as follows:

- `@EnableBinding(Sink.class)`: The `EnableBinding` annotation enables binding a class with the respective channel it needs--an input and/or an output. The `Sink` class is used to register a Cloud Stream with one input channel.
- `public void loggerSink(StockPriceChangeEventWithHoldings event)`: This method typically contains the logic to store a message to the data store. In this example, we are printing the message to the log.
- `@StreamListener(Sink.INPUT)`: The `StreamListener` annotation is used to listen on a channel for incoming messages. In this example, `StreamListener` is configured to listen on the default input channel.

As shown in the following snippet, the `Sink` interface defines an input channel:

```
public abstract interface
org.springframework.cloud.stream.messaging.Sink {
  public static final java.lang.String INPUT = "input";
  @org.springframework.cloud.stream.annotation.Input(value="input")
  public abstract org.springframework.messaging.SubscribableChannel
  input();
}
```

Now that we have the three stream applications ready, we will need to connect them. In the next section, we will cover how Spring Cloud Data Flow helps in connecting different streams.

Spring Cloud Data Flow

Spring Cloud Data Flow helps in establishing message flows between different kinds of microservices created using Spring Cloud Stream. All the microservices that are deployed through the Spring Cloud Data Flow server should be Spring Boot microservices that define appropriate channels.

Spring Cloud Data Flow provides interfaces to define applications and define flows between them using Spring DSL. Spring Data Flow Server understands the DSL and establishes the flow between applications.

Typically, this involves multiple steps:

- Using a mapping between the application name and the deployable unit of the application to download the application artifacts from repositories. Spring Data Flow Server supports Maven and Docker repositories.
- Deploying the applications to the target runtime.
- Creating channels on the message broker.
- Establishing connections between the applications and the message broker channels.

Spring Cloud Data Flow also provides options for the scaling of the applications involved when needed. A deployment manifest maps applications to target runtime. A couple of questions that a deployment manifest answers are as follows:

- How many instances of an application need to be created?
- How much memory is needed by each instance of an application?

Data Flow Server understands the deployment manifests and creates the target runtime as specified. Spring Cloud Data Flow supports a variety of runtimes:

- Cloud Foundry
- Apache YARN
- Kubernetes
- Apache Mesos
- Local server for development

We will use the local server in our examples in this chapter.

High-level architecture

In the preceding example, we have three microservices that need to be connected in a data flow. The following figure represents the high-level architecture of implementing the solution with Spring Cloud Data Flow:

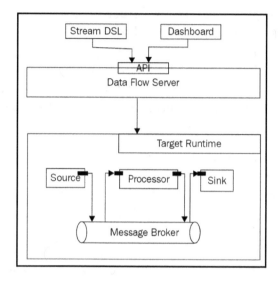

In the preceding figure, source, sink, and processor are Spring Boot microservices created using Spring Cloud Stream:

- The source microservice defines an output channel
- The processor microservice defines both input and output channels
- The sink microservice defines an input channel

Implementing Spring Cloud Data Flow

Implementing Spring Cloud Data Flow involves five steps:

1. Setting up Spring Cloud Data Flow server.
2. Setting up the Data Flow Shell project.
3. Configuring the apps.
4. Configuring the stream.
5. Running the stream.

Setting up Spring Cloud Data Flow server

Let's use Spring Initializr (`https://start.spring.io`) to set up the application. Provide the details listed here and click on **Generate Project**:

- **Group**: `com.mastering.spring.cloud.data.flow`
- **Artifact**: `local-data-flow-server`
- **Dependencies**: `Local Data Flow Server`

Listed here are some of the important dependencies from the `pom.xml` file:

```
<dependency>
  <groupId>org.springframework.cloud</groupId>
  <artifactId>spring-cloud-starter-dataflow-server-
  local</artifactId>
</dependency>
```

Update the `SpringBootApplication` file with the following code:

```
@EnableDataFlowServer
@SpringBootApplication
public class LocalDataFlowServerApplication {
  public static void main(String[] args) {
    SpringApplication.run(LocalDataFlowServierApplication.class,
    args);
  }
}
```

The `@EnableDataFlowServer` annotation is used to activate a Spring Cloud Data Flow Server implementation.

Before you run the Local Data Flow Server, ensure that the message broker RabbitMQ is up and running.

The following is an important extract from the start up log when `LocalDataFlowServerApplication` is launched:

```
Tomcat initialized with port(s): 9393 (http)
Starting H2 Server with URL: jdbc:h2:tcp://localhost:19092/mem:dataflow
Adding dataflow schema classpath:schema-h2-common.sql for h2 database
Adding dataflow schema classpath:schema-h2-streams.sql for h2 database
Adding dataflow schema classpath:schema-h2-tasks.sql for h2 database
Adding dataflow schema classpath:schema-h2-deployment.sql for h2 database
Executed SQL script from class path resource [schema-h2-common.sql] in 37
ms.
Executed SQL script from class path resource [schema-h2-streams.sql] in 2
```

```
ms.
Executed SQL script from class path resource [schema-h2-tasks.sql] in 3 ms.
Executing SQL script from class path resource [schema-h2-deployment.sql]
Executed SQL script from class path resource [schema-h2-deployment.sql] in
3 ms.
Mapped "{[/runtime/apps/{appId}/instances]}" onto public
org.springframework.hateoas.PagedResources
Mapped "{[/runtime/apps/{appId}/instances/{instanceId}]}" onto public
Mapped "{[/streams/definitions/{name}],methods=[DELETE]}" onto public void
org.springframework.cloud.dataflow.server.controller.StreamDefinitionContro
ller.delete(java.lang.String)
Mapped "{[/streams/definitions],methods=[GET]}" onto public
org.springframework.hateoas.PagedResources
Mapped "{[/streams/deployments/{name}],methods=[POST]}" onto public void
org.springframework.cloud.dataflow.server.controller.StreamDeploymentContro
ller.deploy(java.lang.String,java.util.Map<java.lang.String,
java.lang.String>)
Mapped "{[/runtime/apps]}" onto public
org.springframework.hateoas.PagedResources<org.springframework.cloud.datafl
ow.rest.resource.AppStatusResource>
org.springframework.cloud.dataflow.server.controller.RuntimeAppsController.
list(org.springframework.data.domain.Pageable,org.springframework.data.web.
PagedResourcesAssembler<org.springframework.cloud.deployer.spi.app.AppStatu
s>) throws
java.util.concurrent.ExecutionException,java.lang.InterruptedException
Mapped "{[/tasks/executions],methods=[GET]}" onto public
org.springframework.hateoas.PagedResources
```

A few important things to note are as follows:

- The default port for Spring Cloud Data Flow server is `9393`. This can be changed by specifying a different port as `server.port` in `application.properties`.
- Spring Cloud Data Flow Server uses an internal schema to store all the configuration of applications, tasks, and streams. In this example, we have not configured any database. So, by default, the `H2` in-memory database is used. Spring Cloud Data Flow Server supports a variety of databases, including MySql and Oracle, to store the configuration.
- Since `H2` in-memory database is used, you can see that different schemas are set up during start up and also the different SQL scripts to set up data are executed.
- Spring Cloud Data Flow Server exposes a number of APIs around its configuration, applications, tasks, and streams. We will discuss more about these APIs in a later section.

The following screenshot shows the launch screen of Spring Cloud Data Flow at
`http://localhost:9393/dashboard`:

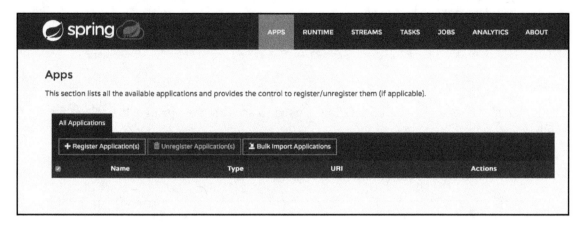

There are different tabs that can be used to view and modify applications, streams, and tasks. In the next step, we will use the command-line interface--the Data Flow Shell to set up applications and streams.

Setting up Data Flow Shell project

Data Flow Shell provides options to use commands to configure streams and other things in Spring Data Flow Server.

Let's use Spring Initializr (`https://start.spring.io`) to set up the application. Provide the details listed here and click on **Generate Project**:

- **Group**: `com.mastering.spring.cloud.data.flow`
- **Artifact**: `data-flow-shell`
- **Dependencies**: `Data Flow Shell`

Listed here are some of the important dependencies from the `pom.xml` file:

```
<dependency>
  <groupId>org.springframework.cloud</groupId>
  <artifactId>spring-cloud-dataflow-shell</artifactId>
</dependency>
```

Update the `SpringBootApplication` file with the following code:

```
@EnableDataFlowShell
@SpringBootApplication
public class DataFlowShellApplication {
  public static void main(String[] args) {
  SpringApplication.run(DataFlowShellApplication.class, args);
  }
}
```

The `@EnableDataFlowShell` annotation is used to activate the Spring Cloud Data Flow shell.

The following screenshot shows the message shown when Data Flow Shell application is launched. We can type in commands at command prompt:

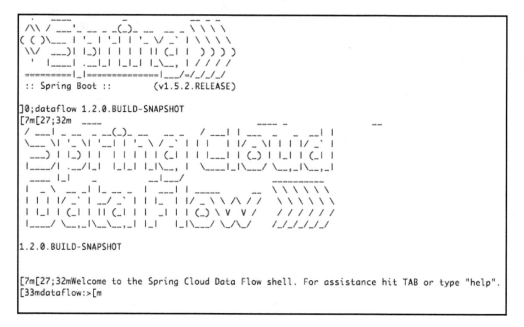

You can try the "help" command to get the list of the commands supported. The following screenshot shows some of the commands that are printed when the `help` command is executed:

```
 Properties  Servers  Data Source Explorer   Console    Progress  JUnit

DataFlowShellApplication [Java Application] /Library/Java/JavaVirtualMachines/jdk1.8.0_31.jdk/Contents/Hom
help

[7m[27;32m* ! - Allows execution of operating system (OS) commands
* // - Inline comment markers (start of line only)
* ; - Inline comment markers (start of line only)
* aggregate-counter delete - Delete an aggregate counter
* aggregate-counter display - Display aggregate counter values by chosen interval
* aggregate-counter list - List all available aggregate counter names
* app import - Register all applications listed in a properties file
* app info - Get information about an application
* app list - List all registered applications
* app register - Register a new application
* app unregister - Unregister an application
* clear - Clears the console
* cls - Clears the console
* counter display - Display the value of a counter
* counter list - List all available counter names
* counter reset - Reset the counter with the given name
* dataflow config info - Show the Dataflow server being used
* dataflow config server - Configure the Spring Cloud Data Flow REST server to use
* date - Displays the local date and time
* exit - Exits the shell
* field-value-counter display - Display the value of a field value counter
* field-value-counter list - List all available field value counter names
* field-value-counter reset - Reset the field value counter with the given name
* help - List all commands usage
* http get - Make GET request to http endpoint
* http post - POST data to http endpoint
* job execution display - Display the details of a specific job execution
* job execution list - List created job executions filtered by jobName
* job execution step display - Display the details of a specific step execution
* job execution step list - List step executions filtered by jobExecutionId
* job execution step progress - Display the details of a specific step progress
* job instance display - Display the job executions for a specific job instance.
* quit - Exits the shell
* runtime apps - List runtime apps
* script - Parses the specified resource file and executes its commands
* stream all destroy - Destroy all existing streams
* stream all undeploy - Un-deploy all previously deployed stream
* stream create - Create a new stream definition
* stream deploy - Deploy a previously created stream
* stream destroy - Destroy an existing stream
* stream list - List created streams
* stream undeploy - Un-deploy a previously deployed stream
* system properties - Shows the shell's properties
* task create - Create a new task definition
```

You will see that when you executed any of the following commands, you would find empty lists printed, as we do not have any of these configured yet:

- `app list`
- `stream list`
- `task list`
- `runtime apps`

Configuring the apps

Before we would start configuring the stream, we would need to register the applications that constitute the stream. We have three applications to register--source, processor, and sink.

To register an application in Spring Cloud Data Flow, you would need to access the application deployable. Spring Cloud Data Flow gives the option of picking up the application deployable from a Maven repository. To keep things simple, we will pick up the applications from a local Maven repository.

Run `mvn clean install` on all the three applications that we created using Spring Cloud Stream:

- `significant-stock-change-source`
- `stock-intelligence-processor`
- `event-store-sink`

This will ensure that all these applications are built and stored in your local Maven repository.

The syntax of the command to register an app from a Maven repository is shown here:

```
app register --name {{NAME_THAT_YOU_WANT_TO_GIVE_TO_APP}} --type source --
uri maven://{{GROUP_ID}}:{{ARTIFACT_ID}}:jar:{{VERSION}}
```

The Maven URIs for the three applications are listed as follows:

```
maven://com.mastering.spring.cloud.data.flow:significant-stock-change-
source:jar:0.0.1-SNAPSHOT
maven://com.mastering.spring.cloud.data.flow:stock-intelligence-
processor:jar:0.0.1-SNAPSHOT
maven://com.mastering.spring.cloud.data.flow:event-store-sink:jar:0.0.1-
SNAPSHOT
```

The commands to create the apps are listed here. These commands can be executed on the Data Flow Shell application:

```
app register --name significant-stock-change-source --type source --uri
maven://com.mastering.spring.cloud.data.flow:significant-stock-change-
source:jar:0.0.1-SNAPSHOT

app register --name stock-intelligence-processor --type processor --uri
maven://com.mastering.spring.cloud.data.flow:stock-intelligence-
processor:jar:0.0.1-SNAPSHOT

app register --name event-store-sink --type sink --uri
maven://com.mastering.spring.cloud.data.flow:event-store-sink:jar:0.0.1-
SNAPSHOT
```

You will see the messages shown here when the app is successfully registered:

```
Successfully registered application 'source:significant-stock-change-
source'

Successfully registered application 'processor:stock-intelligence-
processor'

Successfully registered application 'sink:event-store-sink'
```

You can also see the registered apps on the Spring Cloud Data Flow Dashboard at `http://localhost:9393/dashboard`, as shown in the following screenshot:

We can also register an app using the dashboard, as shown in the following screenshot:

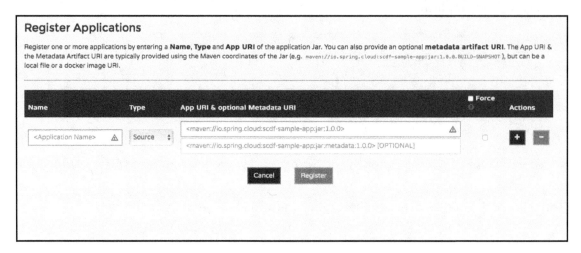

Configuring the stream

Stream DSL can be used to configure a stream--a simple example has been shown here to connect `app1` to `app2`. The messages put on the output channel by `app1` will be received on the input channel of `app2`:

```
app1 | app2
```

We would want to connect the three applications. The following snippet shows an example of a DSL used to connect the preceding applications:

```
#source | processor | sink

significant-stock-change-source|stock-intelligence-processor|event-store-
sink
```

This indicates the following:

- The output channel of the source should be linked to the input channel of processor
- The output channel of the processor should be linked to the input channel of sink

The entire command to create a stream is shown as follows:

```
stream create --name process-stock-change-events --definition significant-
stock-change-source|stock-intelligence-processor|event-store-sink
```

You should see the following output if the stream is successfully created:

```
Created new stream 'process-stock-change-events'
```

You can also see the registered stream on the **Streams** tab of Spring Cloud Data Flow dashboard at `http://localhost:9393/dashboard`, as shown in the following screenshot:

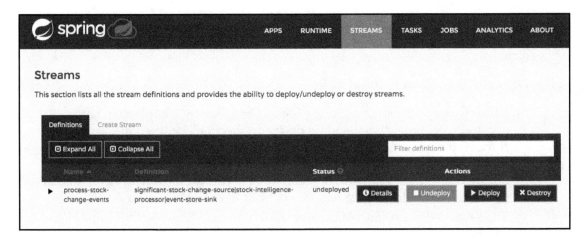

Deploying the stream

To deploy the stream, we can execute the following command on the Data Flow Shell:

```
stream deploy --name process-stock-change-events
```

You will see the message shown here when the request is sent for the creation of stream:

```
Deployment request has been sent for stream 'process-stock-change-events'
```

The following extract shows an extract from the Local Data Flow Server log:

```
o.s.c.d.spi.local.LocalAppDeployer : deploying app process-stock-change-
events.event-store-sink instance 0

Logs will be in /var/folders/y_/x4jdvdkx7w94q5qsh745gzz00000gn/T/spring-
cloud-dataflow-3084432375250471462/process-stock-change-
events-1492100265496/process-stock-change-events.event-store-sink

o.s.c.d.spi.local.LocalAppDeployer : deploying app process-stock-change-
events.stock-intelligence-processor instance 0
```

```
Logs will be in /var/folders/y_/x4jdvdkx7w94q5qsh745gzz00000gn/T/spring-
cloud-dataflow-3084432375250471462/process-stock-change-
events-1492100266448/process-stock-change-events.stock-intelligence-
processor

o.s.c.d.spi.local.LocalAppDeployer : deploying app process-stock-change-
events.significant-stock-change-source instance 0

Logs will be in /var/folders/y_/x4jdvdkx7w94q5qsh745gzz00000gn/T/spring-
cloud-dataflow-3084432375250471462/process-stock-change-
events-1492100267242/process-stock-change-events.significant-stock-change-
source
```

A few important things to note are as follows:

- When we deploy a stream, Spring Cloud Data Flow will deploy all the applications in the stream and set up the connections between the applications through the message broker. The application code is independent of the message broker. Kafka has a different message broker setup compared to RabbitMQ. Spring Cloud Data Flow will take care of it. If you want to switch from RabbitMQ to Kafka, the application code does not need to change.
- The Local Data Flow Server log contains the path to logs of all the applications-- source, processor, and sink.

Log messages - setting up connections to the message factory

The following snippet shows extracts related to setting up the message broker from the `Source`, `Transformer`, and `Sink` applications:

```
#Source Log
CachingConnectionFactory : Created new connection:
SimpleConnection@725b3815 [delegate=amqp://guest@127.0.0.1:5672/,
localPort= 58373]

#Transformer Log
o.s.i.endpoint.EventDrivenConsumer : Adding
{transformer:stockIntelligenceProcessorApplication.addOurInventory.transfor
mer} as a subscriber to the 'input' channel

o.s.integration.channel.DirectChannel : Channel 'application:0.input' has 1
subscriber(s).

o.s.i.endpoint.EventDrivenConsumer : started
```

```
stockIntelligenceProcessorApplication.addOurInventory.transformer

o.s.i.endpoint.EventDrivenConsumer : Adding {message-
handler:inbound.process-stock-change-events.significant-stock-change-
source.process-stock-change-events} as a subscriber to the 'bridge.process-
stock-change-events.significant-stock-change-source' channel

o.s.i.endpoint.EventDrivenConsumer : started inbound.process-stock-change-
events.significant-stock-change-source.process-stock-change-events

#Sink Log

c.s.b.r.p.RabbitExchangeQueueProvisioner : declaring queue for inbound:
process-stock-change-events.stock-intelligence-processor.process-stock-
change-events, bound to: process-stock-change-events.stock-intelligence-
processor

o.s.a.r.c.CachingConnectionFactory : Created new connection:
SimpleConnection@3de6223a [delegate=amqp://guest@127.0.0.1:5672/,
localPort= 58372]
```

A few things to note are as follows:

- `Created new connection: SimpleConnection@725b3815 [delegate=amqp://guest@127.0.0.1:5672/, localPort= 58373]`: Since we added `spring-cloud-starter-stream-rabbit` into the classpath of all three applications, the message broker used is RabbitMQ.
- `Adding {transformer:stockIntelligenceProcessorApplication.addOurInventory.transformer} as a subscriber to the 'input' channel`: Similar to this, the input and/or output channels of each application are set up on the message broker. Source and processor applications listen on the channels for incoming messages.

Log messages - the flow of events

Extracts related to processing of the message are shown as follows:

```
#Source Log
SignificantStockChangeSourceApplication : sending StockPriceChangeEvent
[stockTicker=MICROSOFT, oldPrice=15, newPrice=12]

#Transformer Log
.f.StockIntelligenceProcessorApplication : started processing event
StockPriceChangeEvent [stockTicker=MICROSOFT, oldPrice=18, newPrice=20]

.f.StockIntelligenceProcessorApplication : ended processing
eventWithHoldings StockPriceChangeEventWithHoldings [holdings=30,
toString()=StockPriceChangeEvent [stockTicker=MICROSOFT, oldPrice=18,
newPrice=20]]

#Sink Log
c.m.s.c.d.f.EventStoreSinkApplication : Received:
StockPriceChangeEventWithHoldings [holdings=30,
toString()=StockPriceChangeEvent [stockTicker=MICROSOFT, oldPrice=18,
newPrice=20]]
```

The source application sends `StockPriceChangeEvent`. The `Transformer` application receives the event, adds the holdings to the message, and creates a new `StockPriceChangeEventWithHoldings` event. The sink application receives and logs this message.

Spring Cloud Data Flow REST APIs

Spring Cloud Data Flow offers RESTful APIs around applications, streams, tasks, jobs, and metrics. A complete list can be obtained by sending a GET request to `http://localhost:9393/`.

The following screenshot shows the response for the `GET` request:

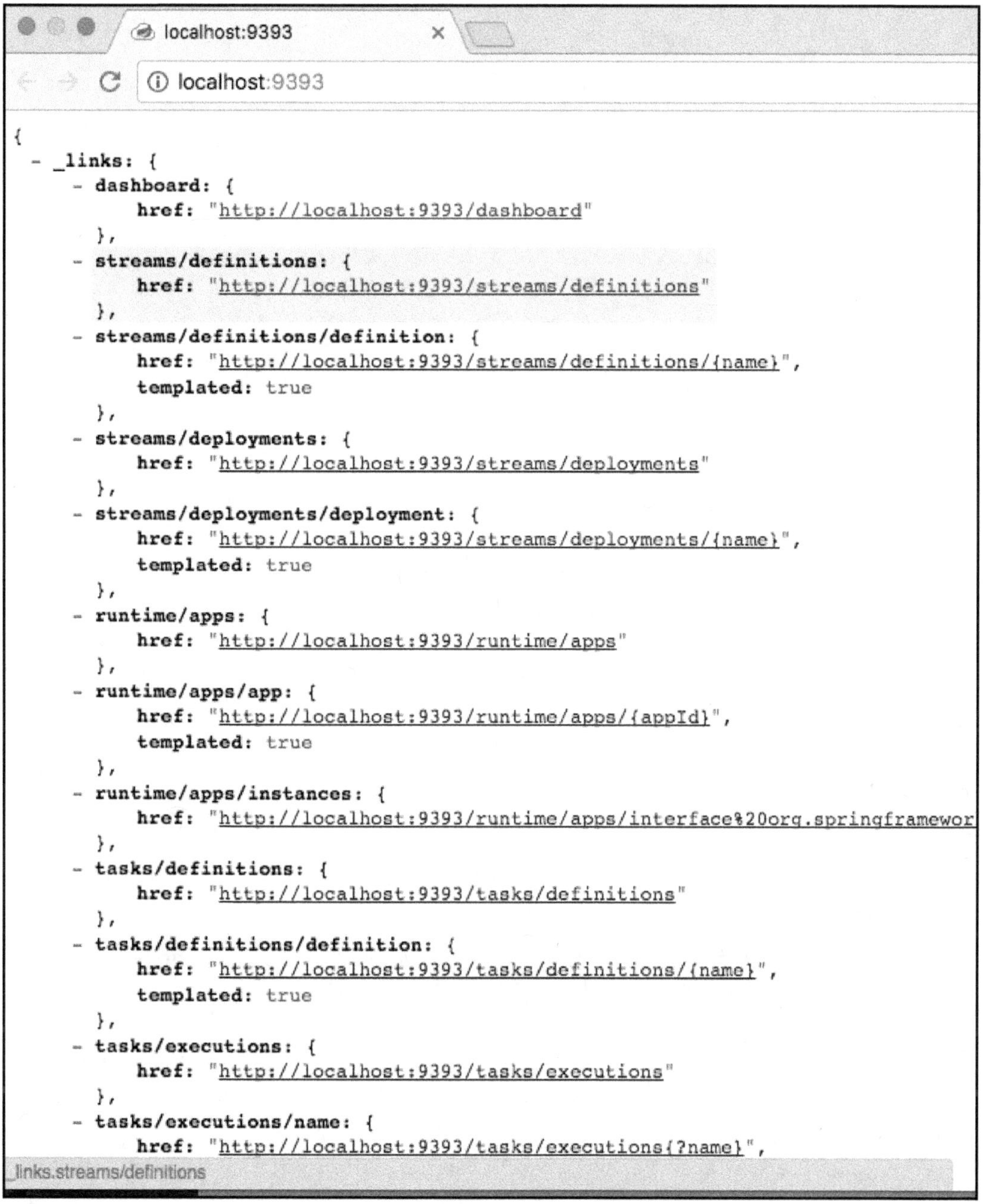

localhost:9393
localhost:9393
{
- _links: {
- dashboard: {
href: "http://localhost:9393/dashboard"
},
- streams/definitions: {
href: "http://localhost:9393/streams/definitions"
},
- streams/definitions/definition: {
href: "http://localhost:9393/streams/definitions/{name}",
templated: true
},
- streams/deployments: {
href: "http://localhost:9393/streams/deployments"
},
- streams/deployments/deployment: {
href: "http://localhost:9393/streams/deployments/{name}",
templated: true
},
- runtime/apps: {
href: "http://localhost:9393/runtime/apps"
},
- runtime/apps/app: {
href: "http://localhost:9393/runtime/apps/{appId}",
templated: true
},
- runtime/apps/instances: {
href: "http://localhost:9393/runtime/apps/interface%20org.springframewor
},
- tasks/definitions: {
href: "http://localhost:9393/tasks/definitions"
},
- tasks/definitions/definition: {
href: "http://localhost:9393/tasks/definitions/{name}",
templated: true
},
- tasks/executions: {
href: "http://localhost:9393/tasks/executions"
},
- tasks/executions/name: {
href: "http://localhost:9393/tasks/executions{?name}",
_links.streams/definitions

All the APIs are self-explanatory. Let's look at an example of sending a GET request to
`http://localhost:9393/streams/definitions`:

```
{
    "_embedded":{
    "streamDefinitionResourceList":[
            {
                "name":"process-stock-change-events"
                "dslText":"significant-stock-change-source|stock-
                intelligence-processor|event-store-sink",
                "status":"deployed",
                "statusDescription":"All apps have been successfully
                deployed",
                "_links":{
                    "self":{
                        "href":"http://localhost:9393/streams/definitions/
                        process-stock-change-events"
                    }
                }
            }
        ]
    },
    "_links":{
        "self":{
            "href":"http://localhost:9393/streams/definitions"
        }
    },
    "page":{
        "size":20,
        "totalElements":1,
        "totalPages":1,
        "number":0
    }
}
```

Important things to note are as follows:

- The API is RESTful. _embedded element contains the data for the request.
  _links element contains HATEOAS links. The page element contains pagination
  information.
- _embedded.streamDefinitionResourceList.dslText contains the
  definition of the stream "significant-stock-change-source|stock-
  intelligence-processor|event-store-sink".
- _embedded.streamDefinitionResourceList.status

Spring Cloud Task

Spring Cloud Data Flow can also be used to create and schedule batch applications. For the last decade, Spring Batch has been the framework of choice to develop batch applications. Spring Cloud Task extends this and enables execution of batch programs on the Cloud.

Let's use Spring Initializr (`https://start.spring.io`) to set up the application. Provide the details listed here and click on **Generate Project**:

- **Group**: `com.mastering.spring.cloud.data.flow`
- **Artifact**: `simple-logging-task`
- **Dependencies**: `Cloud Task`

Update the `SimpleLoggingTaskApplication` class with the following code:

```
@SpringBootApplication
@EnableTask

public class SimpleLoggingTaskApplication {

@Bean
public CommandLineRunner commandLineRunner() {
  return strings -> System.out.println(
  "Task execution :" + new SimpleDateFormat().format(new Date()));
  }
public static void main(String[] args) {
  SpringApplication.run(SimpleLoggingTaskApplication.class, args);
  }
}
```

This code simply puts a sysout with the current timestamp. The `@EnableTask` annotation enables the task features in a Spring Boot application.

We can register the task on the data flow shell using the following commands:

```
app register --name simple-logging-task --type task --uri
maven://com.mastering.spring.cloud.data.flow:simple-logging-task:jar:0.0.1-
SNAPSHOT
task create --name simple-logging-task-definition --definition "simple-
logging-task"
```

The commands are very similar to those used to register the stream apps we created earlier. We are adding a task definition to be able to execute the task.

The task can be launched using the following command:

```
task launch simple-logging-task-definition
```

Task executions can be triggered and monitored on the Spring Cloud Flow dashboard as well.

Summary

Spring Cloud Data Flow brings Cloud-Native features to data flow and event flow streams. It makes it easy to create and deploy streams on the Cloud. In this chapter, we covered how individual applications in event-driven flows can be set up using Spring Cloud Stream. We took a 1000 feet view on creating tasks with Spring Cloud Task. We used Spring Cloud Data Flow to set up streams and also execute simple tasks.

In the next chapter, we will start understanding a new way of building web applications--the reactive style. We will understand why nonblocking applications are being hyped up and how reactive applications can be built using Spring Reactive.

11

Reactive Programming

In the previous chapter, we discussed implementing typical data flow use cases with microservices using Spring cloud data flow.

Functional Programming marks a shift from traditional imperatives to a more declarative style of programming. Reactive programming builds on top of functional programming to provide an alternative style.

In this chapter, we will discuss the basics of reactive programming.

The microservice architecture promotes message-based communication. One important tenet of reactive programming is building applications around events (or messages). Some of the important questions we need to answer include the following:

- What is reactive programming?
- What are the typical use cases?
- What kind of support does Java provide for it?
- What are the reactive features in Spring WebFlux?

The Reactive Manifesto

Most applications from a few years back had the luxury of the following:

- Multi-second response times
- Multiple hours of offline maintenance
- Smaller volumes of data

Times have changed. New devices (mobiles, tablets, and so on) and newer approaches (cloud-based) have emerged. In today's world, we are talking about:

- Sub-second response times
- 100% availability
- An exponential increase in data volumes

Different approaches have emerged during the last few years to meet these emerging challenges. While reactive programming is not really a new phenomenon, it is one of the approaches that have been successful in dealing with these challenges.

The Reactive Manifesto (`http://www.reactivemanifesto.org`) aims to capture common themes.

> *We believe that a coherent approach to systems architecture is needed, and we believe that all necessary aspects are already recognised individually: we want systems that are Responsive, Resilient, Elastic and Message Driven. We call these Reactive Systems.*
>
> *Systems built as Reactive Systems are more flexible, loosely coupled, and scalable. This makes them easier to develop and amenable to change. They are significantly more tolerant of failure, and when failure does occur, they meet it with elegance rather than disaster. Reactive Systems are highly responsive, giving users effective interactive feedback.*

While the Reactive Manifesto clearly states the characteristics of responsive systems, it is not as clear on how Reactive Systems are built.

Characteristics of Reactive Systems

The following figure shows the important characteristics of Reactive Systems:

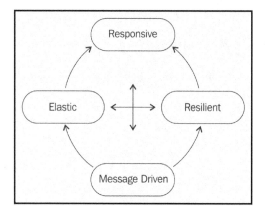

The important characteristics are as follows:

- **Responsive**: Systems respond in a timely manner to their users. Clear response time requirements are set, and the system meets them in all situations.
- **Resilient**: Distributed systems are built using multiple components. Failures can occur in any of these components. Reactive Systems should be designed to contain failures within a localized space, for example, within each component. This prevents the entire system from going down in cases of local failure.
- **Elastic**: Reactive Systems stay responsive under varying loads. When under heavy load, these systems can add additional resources while releasing them when the load goes down. Elasticity is achieved using commodity hardware and software.
- **Message driven**: Reactive Systems are driven by messages (or events). This ensures low coupling between components. This guarantees that the different components of the system can be scaled independently. Using non-blocking communication ensures that threads are alive for a shorter period of time.

Reactive Systems are responsive to different kinds of stimulus. A few examples are as follows:

- **React to events**: Built based on message passing, Reactive Systems respond quickly to events.
- **React to load**: Reactive Systems stay responsive under varying loads. They use more resources under high loads and release them under lesser loads.
- **React to failures**: Reactive Systems can handle failures gracefully. Components of Reactive Systems are built to localize failures. External components are used to monitor the availability of components and have the capability to replicate components when needed.
- **React to users**: Reactive Systems are responsive to users. They do not waste time performing additional processing when consumers are not subscribed to specific events.

Reactive use case - a stock price page

While the Reactive Manifesto helps us understand the characteristics of a Reactive System, it does not really help with understanding how Reactive Systems are built. To understand this, we will consider the traditional approach to building a simple use case and compares it with the reactive approach.

The use case we want to build is a stock price page that displays the price of a specific stock. As long as the page remains open, we want to update the latest price of the stock on the page.

The traditional approach

The traditional approach uses polling to check whether the stock price has changed. The following sequence diagram shows the traditional approach of building such a use case:

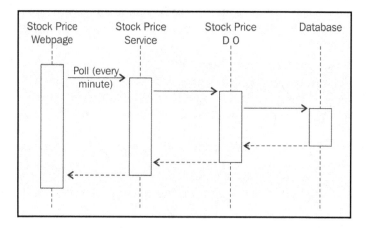

Once the page is rendered, it sends AJAX requests to the stock price service for the latest price at regular intervals. These calls have to be done irrespective of whether the stock price has changed since the web page does not have any knowledge of the stock price change.

The reactive approach

Reactive approaches involve connecting the different components involved to be able to react to events as they occur.

When the stock price web page is loaded, the web page registers for events from the stock price service. When the stock price change event occurs, an event is triggered. The latest stock price is updated on the web page. The following sequence diagram shows the reactive approach of building the stock price page:

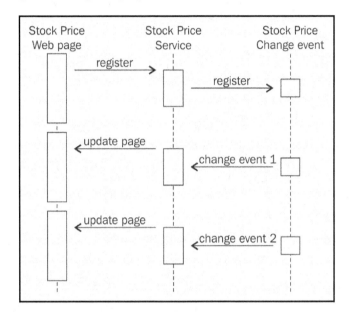

The reactive approach typically involves three steps:

1. Subscribing to events.
2. Occurrence of events.
3. Unregistering.

When the stock price web page is initially loaded, it will subscribe to the stock price change event. The way you subscribe is different based on the reactive framework and/or the message broker (if any) that you use.

When the stock price change event for a specific stock occurs, a new event is triggered for all the subscribers of the event. The listener ensures that the web page is updated with the latest stock price.

Once the web page is closed (or refreshed), an unregister request is sent out by the subscriber.

Comparison between the traditional and reactive approaches

The traditional approach is very simple. The reactive approach needs to implement a reactive subscribe and event chain. If the event chain involves a message broker, it becomes even more complex.

In the traditional approach, we poll for changes. This means that the entire sequence is triggered every minute (or the specified interval) irrespective of whether there is a change in the stock price. In the reactive approach, once we register for the event, the sequence is triggered only when the stock price changes.

The lifetime of the threads in the traditional approach is longer. All resources used by the thread are locked for a longer duration. Considering the big picture of a server serving multiple requests at the same time, there will be more contention for threads and their resources. In the reactive approach, threads live for a short span and hence there is less contention for resources.

Scaling in the traditional approach involves scaling up the database and creating more web servers. Because of the small lifetime of threads, the same infrastructure can handle more users in the reactive approach. While the reactive approach has all the options of scaling of the traditional approach, it provides more distributed options. For example, the triggering of the stock price change event can be communicated to the application through a message broker, as shown in the following figure:

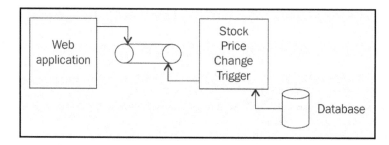

This means that the web application and the stock price change-triggered application can be scaled independently of each other. This gives more options in scaling up quickly when the need arises.

Reactive programming in Java

Java 8 does not have any built-in support for reactive programming. A number of frameworks provide reactive features. We will discuss Reactive Streams, Reactor, and Spring WebFlux in subsequent sections.

Reactive streams

> *Reactive Streams is an initiative to provide a standard for asynchronous stream processing with non-blocking back pressure. This encompasses efforts aimed at runtime environments (JVM and JavaScript) as well as network protocols.*

A few important things to note are as follows:

- Reactive streams aim to define a minimal set of interfaces, methods, and protocols to enable reactive programming
- Reactive streams aim to be a language-neutral approach with implementation in the Java (JVM-based) and JavaScript languages
- Multiple transport streams (TCP, UDP, HTTP, and WebSockets) are supported

Maven dependencies for Reactive Streams are shown as follows:

```
<dependency>
  <groupId>org.reactivestreams</groupId>
  <artifactId>reactive-streams</artifactId>
  <version>1.0.0</version>
</dependency>

<dependency>
  <groupId>org.reactivestreams</groupId>
  <artifactId>reactive-streams-tck</artifactId>
  <version>1.0.0</version>
  <scope>test</scope>
</dependency>
```

A few of the important interfaces defined in Reactive Streams are shown as follows:

```
public interface Subscriber<T> {
  public void onSubscribe(Subscription s);
  public void onNext(T t);
  public void onError(Throwable t);
  public void onComplete();
}
```

```
public interface Publisher<T> {
  public void subscribe(Subscriber<? super T> s);
}
public interface Subscription {
  public void request(long n);
  public void cancel();
}
```

A few important things to note are as follows:

- **Interface Publisher**: `Publisher` provides a stream of elements in response to the demand received from its Subscriber(s). A Publisher can serve any number of subscribers. The subscriber count might vary with time.
- **Interface Subscriber** : `Subscriber` registers to listen to the stream of events. Subscribing is a two-step process. The first step is calling Publisher.subscribe(Subscriber). The second step involves making a call to Subscription.request(long). Once these steps are completed, the subscriber can start processing notifications using the `onNext(T t)` method. The `onComplete()` method signals the end of notifications. Demand can be signaled via Subscription.request(long) whenever the `Subscriber` instance is capable of handling more.
- **Interface Subscription** : `Subscription` represents the link between one `Subscriber` and its `Publisher`. A subscriber can request more data using `request(long n)`. It can cancel the subscription to notifications using the `cancel()` method.

Reactor

Reactor is a reactive framework from the Spring Pivotal team. It builds on top of Reactive Streams. As we will discuss later in this chapter, Spring Framework 5.0 uses the Reactor framework to enable reactive web features.

Dependencies for Reactor are shown as follows:

```
<dependency>
  <groupId>io.projectreactor</groupId>
  <artifactId>reactor-core</artifactId>
  <version>3.0.6.RELEASE</version>
</dependency>
<dependency>
  <groupId>io.projectreactor.addons</groupId>
```

```
      <artifactId>reactor-test</artifactId>
      <version>3.0.6.RELEASE</version>
   </dependency>
```

Reactor adds in a couple of important things on top of the `Subscriber`, `Consumer`, and `Subscriptions` terminology introduced by Reactive Streams.

- **Flux**: Flux represents a Reactive Stream that emits 0 to *n* element
- **Mono**: Mono represents a Reactive Stream that emits either no elements or one element

In subsequent examples, we will create stub Mono and Flux objects, which would be pre-configured to emit elements at specific intervals. We will create Consumers (or Observers) to listen to these events and react to them.

Mono

Creating a Mono is very simple. The following Mono emits one element after a delay of 5 seconds.

```
Mono<String> stubMonoWithADelay =
Mono.just("Ranga").delayElement(Duration.ofSeconds(5));
```

We want to listen to the events from Mono and log them to the console. We can do that using the statement specified here:

```
stubMonoWithADelay.subscribe(System.out::println);
```

However, if you run the program with the two preceding statements in a `Test` annotation as shown in the following code, you would see that nothing is printed to the console:

```
@Test
public void monoExample() throws InterruptedException {
  Mono<String> stubMonoWithADelay =
  Mono.just("Ranga").delayElement(Duration.ofSeconds(5));
  stubMonoWithADelay.subscribe(System.out::println);
}
```

Nothing is printed to the console because the `Test` execution ends before the Mono emits the element after 5 seconds. To prevent this, let's delay the execution of `Test` using `Thread.sleep`:

```
@Test
public void monoExample() throws InterruptedException {
  Mono<String> stubMonoWithADelay =
```

```
    Mono.just("Ranga").delayElement(Duration.ofSeconds(5));
    stubMonoWithADelay.subscribe(System.out::println);
    Thread.sleep(10000);
}
```

When we create a subscriber using
stubMonoWithADelay.subscribe(System.out::println), we are using the functional
programming feature introduced in Java 8. System.out::println is a method definition.
We are passing the method definition as a parameter to a method.

This is possible because of a specific functional interface called Consumer. A functional
interface is an interface with only one method. The Consumer functional interface is used to
define an operation that accepts a single input argument and returns no result. An outline
of the Consumer interface is shown in the following snippet:

```
@FunctionalInterface
public interface Consumer<T> {
  void accept(T t);
}
```

Instead of using a lambda expression, we can explicitly define Consumer as well. The
following code snippet shows the important details:

```
class SystemOutConsumer implements Consumer<String> {
  @Override
  public void accept(String t) {
    System.out.println("Received " + t + " at " + new Date());
  }
}
@Test
public void monoExample() throws InterruptedException {
  Mono<String> stubMonoWithADelay =
  Mono.just("Ranga").delayElement(Duration.ofSeconds(5));
  stubMonoWithADelay.subscribe(new SystemOutConsumer());
  Thread.sleep(10000);
}
```

A couple of important things to note are as follows:

- class SystemOutConsumer implements Consumer<String>: We create a
  SystemOutConsumer class that implements the functional interface Consumer.
  The type of input is String.
- public void accept(String t): We define the accept method to print the
  content of the string to the console.

- stubMonoWithADelay.subscribe(new SystemOutConsumer()): We create an instance of SystemOutConsumer to subscribe the events.

The output is shown in the following screenshot:

```
Markers   Properties   Servers   Data Source Explorer   Snippets   Console ⊠   Progress   JUnit
<terminated> SpringReactiveTest.monoExample [JUnit] /Library/Java/JavaVirtualMachines/jdk1.8.0_31.jdk/Contents/Home/bin
19:30:17.803 [main] DEBUG reactor.util.Loggers$LoggerFactory - Using Slf4j logging framework
Received Ranga at Thu Apr 27 19:30:22 IST 2017
```

We can have multiple subscribers listening on events from a Mono or Flux. The following snippet shows how we can create an additional subscriber:

```
class WelcomeConsumer implements Consumer<String> {
  @Override
  public void accept(String t) {
    System.out.println("Welcome " + t);
  }
}
@Test
public void monoExample() throws InterruptedException {
  Mono<String> stubMonoWithADelay =
  Mono.just("Ranga").delayElement(Duration.ofSeconds(5));
  stubMonoWithADelay.subscribe(new SystemOutConsumer());
  stubMonoWithADelay.subscribe(new WelcomeConsumer());
  Thread.sleep(10000);
}
```

A couple of important things to note are as follows:

- class WelcomeConsumer implements Consumer<String>: We are creating another Consumer class, WelcomeConsumer
- stubMonoWithADelay.subscribe(new WelcomeConsumer()): We are adding an instance of WelcomeConsumer as a subscriber to the events from Mono

The output is shown in the following screenshot:

```
19:29:36.538 [main] DEBUG reactor.util.Loggers$LoggerFactory - Using Slf4j logging framework
Welcome Ranga
Received Ranga at Thu Apr 27 19:29:41 IST 2017
```

Flux

Flux represents a reactive stream emitting 0 to *n* elements. The following snippet shows a simple Flux example:

```
@Test
public void simpleFluxStream() {
  Flux<String> stubFluxStream = Flux.just("Jane", "Joe");
  stubFluxStream.subscribe(new SystemOutConsumer());
}
```

A couple of important things to note are as follows:

- `Flux<String> stubFluxStream = Flux.just("Jane", "Joe")`: We are creating a Flux using the `Flux.just` method. It can create simple streams with hardcoded elements.
- `stubFluxStream.subscribe(new SystemOutConsumer())`: We are registering an instance of `SystemOutConsumer` as a subscriber on Flux.

The output is shown in the following screenshot:

```
<terminated> SpringReactiveTest.simpleFluxStream [JUnit] /Library/Java/JavaVirtualMachines/jdk1.8.0_31.jdk/Contents/Hom
19:19:47.896 [main] DEBUG reactor.util.Loggers$LoggerFactory - Using Slf4j logging framework
Received Jane at Thu Apr 27 19:19:47 IST 2017
Received Joe at Thu Apr 27 19:19:47 IST 2017
```

The following snippet shows a more complex example of a Flux with two subscribers:

```
private static List<String> streamOfNames =
Arrays.asList("Ranga", "Adam", "Joe", "Doe", "Jane");
@Test
public void fluxStreamWithDelay() throws InterruptedException {
  Flux<String> stubFluxWithNames =
  Flux.fromIterable(streamOfNames)
  .delayElements(Duration.ofMillis(1000));
  stubFluxWithNames.subscribe(new SystemOutConsumer());
  stubFluxWithNames.subscribe(new WelcomeConsumer());
  Thread.sleep(10000);
}
```

A few important things to note are as follows:

- `Flux.fromIterable(streamOfNames).delayElements(Duration.ofMilli s(1000))`: Creates a Flux from the specified list of strings. Elements are emitted at the specified delay of 1000 milliseconds.
- `stubFluxWithNames.subscribe(new SystemOutConsumer())` and `stubFluxWithNames.subscribe(new WelcomeConsumer())`: We are registering two subscribers on Flux.
- `Thread.sleep(10000)`: Similar to the first Mono example, we introduce sleep to make the program wait until all elements from the Flux are emitted.

The output is shown in the following screenshot:

```
<terminated> SpringReactiveTest.fromAList [JUnit] /Library/Java/JavaVirtualMachines/jdk1.8.0_31.jdk/Contents/Home/bin/ja
19:32:49.795 [main] DEBUG reactor.util.Loggers$LoggerFactory - Using Slf4j logging framework
Welcome Ranga
Received Ranga at Thu Apr 27 19:32:50 IST 2017
Welcome Adam
Received Adam at Thu Apr 27 19:32:51 IST 2017
Welcome Joe
Received Joe at Thu Apr 27 19:32:52 IST 2017
Welcome Doe
Received Doe at Thu Apr 27 19:32:53 IST 2017
Welcome Jane
Received Jane at Thu Apr 27 19:32:54 IST 2017
```

Spring Web Reactive

Spring Web Reactive is one of the important new features in Spring Framework 5. It brings in reactive capabilities for web applications.

Spring Web Reactive is based on the same fundamental programming model as Spring MVC. The following table provides a quick comparison of the two frameworks:

	Spring MVC	Spring Web Reactive
Use	Traditional web application	Reactive web applications
Programming Model	`@Controller` with `@RequestMapping`	The same as Spring MVC
Base API	The Servlet API	Reactive HTTP
Runs on	Servlet Containers	Servlet Containers(>3.1), Netty, and Undertow

In the subsequent steps, we want to implement a simple use case for Spring Web Reactive.

The following are the important steps involved:

- Creating a project using Spring Initializr
- Creating a Reactive Controller returning an event stream (Flux)
- Creating an HTML view

Creating a project using Spring Initializr

Let's start with creating a new project using Spring Initializr (`http://start.spring.io/`). The following screenshot shows the details:

A few things to note are as follows:

- **Group**: `com.mastering.spring.reactive`
- **Artifact**: `spring-reactive-example`
- **Dependencies** : `ReactiveWeb` (to build a reactive web application) and `DevTools` (for auto-reload when the application code is changed)

Download the project and import it into your IDE as a Maven project.

Important dependencies in the `pom.xml` file are shown as follows:

```
<dependency>
  <groupId>org.springframework.boot</groupId>
  <artifactId>spring-boot-starter</artifactId>
</dependency>

<dependency>
  <groupId>org.springframework.boot</groupId>
  <artifactId>spring-boot-devtools</artifactId>
</dependency>

<dependency>
  <groupId>org.springframework.boot</groupId>
  <artifactId>spring-boot-starter-webflux</artifactId>
</dependency>

<dependency>
  <groupId>org.springframework.boot</groupId>
  <artifactId>spring-boot-starter-test</artifactId>
  <scope>test</scope>
</dependency>
```

The `spring-boot-starter-webflux` dependency is the most important dependency for Spring Web Reactive. A quick look at the `pom.xml` file of `spring-boot-starter-webflux` reveals the building blocks of Spring Reactive--`spring-webflux`, `spring-web`, and `spring-boot-starter-reactor-netty`.

Netty is the default embedded reactive server. The following snippet shows the dependencies:

```
<dependency>
  <groupId>org.springframework.boot</groupId>
  <artifactId>spring-boot-starter</artifactId>
</dependency>

<dependency>
  <groupId>org.springframework.boot</groupId>
  <artifactId>spring-boot-starter-reactor-netty</artifactId>
</dependency>

<dependency>
  <groupId>com.fasterxml.jackson.core</groupId>
  <artifactId>jackson-databind</artifactId>
</dependency>

<dependency>
```

```
      <groupId>org.hibernate</groupId>
      <artifactId>hibernate-validator</artifactId>
   </dependency>

   <dependency>
      <groupId>org.springframework</groupId>
      <artifactId>spring-web</artifactId>
   </dependency>

   <dependency>
      <groupId>org.springframework</groupId>
      <artifactId>spring-webflux</artifactId>
   </dependency>
```

Creating a Reactive Controller

Creating a Spring Reactive Controller is very similar to creating a Spring MVC Controller. The basic constructs are the same: `@RestController` and the different `@RequestMapping` annotations. The following snippet shows a simple reactive controller named `StockPriceEventController`:

```
@RestController
public class StockPriceEventController {
   @GetMapping("/stocks/price/{stockCode}")
   Flux<String> retrieveStockPriceHardcoded
   (@PathVariable("stockCode") String stockCode) {
      return Flux.interval(Duration.ofSeconds(5))
      .map(l -> getCurrentDate() + " : "
      + getRandomNumber(100, 125))
      .log();
   }
   private String getCurrentDate() {
      return (new Date()).toString();
   }
   private int getRandomNumber(int min, int max) {
      return ThreadLocalRandom.current().nextInt(min, max + 1);
   }
}
```

A few important things to note are as follows:

- `@RestController` and `@GetMapping("/stocks/price/{stockCode}")`: Basic constructs are the same as Spring MVC. We are creating a mapping to the specified URI.

- `Flux<String>`
  `retrieveStockPriceHardcoded(@PathVariable("stockCode") String`
  `stockCode)`: Flux represents a stream of 0 to *n* elements. The return type
  `Flux<String>` indicates that this method returns a stream of values representing
  the current price of a stock.
- `Flux.interval().map(l -> getCurrentDate() + " : " +`
  `getRandomNumber(100, 125))`: We are creating a hardcoded Flux returning a
  stream of random numbers.
- `Duration.ofSeconds(5)`: Stream elements are returned every 5 seconds.
- `Flux.<<*****>>.log()`: Invoking the `log()` method on Flux helps observe all
  Reactive Streams signals and trace them using Logger support.
- `private String getCurrentDate()`: Returns the current time as a string.
- `private int getRandomNumber(int min, int max)`: Returns a random
  number between `min` and `max`.

Creating an HTML view

In the previous step, Creating a Reactive Controller, we mapped a Flux stream to the
`"/stocks/price/{stockCode}"` URL. In this step, let's create a view to show the current
value of the stock on the screen.

We will create a simple static HTML page (`resources/static/stock-price.html`) with
a button to start retrieving from the stream. The following snippet shows the HTML:

```
<p>
  <button id="subscribe-button">Get Latest IBM Price</button>
  <ul id="display"></ul>
</p>
```

We want to create a JavaScript method to register with the stream and append new
elements to a specific div. The following snippet shows the JavaScript method:

```
function registerEventSourceAndAddResponseTo(uri, elementId) {
  var stringEvents = document.getElementById(elementId);
  var stringEventSource = new (uri);
  stringEventSource.onmessage = function(e) {
    var newElement = document.createElement("li");
    newElement.innerHTML = e.data;
    stringEvents.appendChild(newElement);
  }
}
```

The EventSource interface is used to receive server-sent events. It connects to a server over HTTP and receives events in a text/event-stream format. When it receives an element, the onmessage method is called.

The following snippet shows the code to register the onclick event for the get latest IBM price button:

```
addEvent("click", document.getElementById('subscribe-button'),
function() {
        registerEventSourceAndAddResponseTo("/stocks/price/IBM",
        "display");
    }
);
function addEvent(evnt, elem, func) {
    if (typeof(EventSource) !== "undefined") {
      elem.addEventListener(evnt,func,false);
    }
    else { // No much to do
      elem[evnt] = func;
    }
}
```

Launching SpringReactiveExampleApplication

Launch the application class SpringReactiveExampleApplication as a Java application. One of the last messages you would see in the startup log is Netty started on port(s): 8080. Netty is the default embedded server for Spring Reactive.

The following screenshot shows the browser when you navigate to the localhost:8080/static/stock-price.html URL:

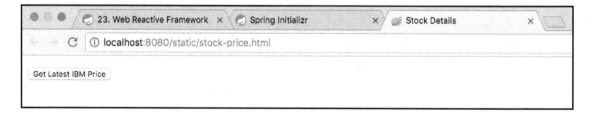

When the **Get Latest IBM Price** button is clicked, EventSource kicks in and registers for events from "/stocks/price/IBM". As soon as an element is received, it is shown on the screen.

The following screenshot shows the screen after a few events are received. You can observe that an event is received every 5 seconds:

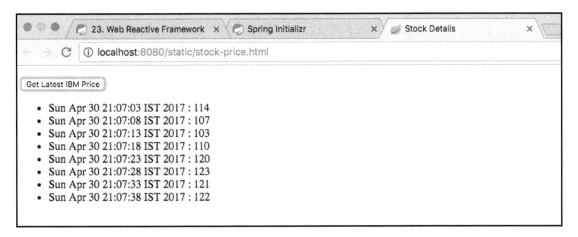

The next screenshot shows an extract from the log after the browser window is closed:

```
[ctor-http-nio-2] reactor.Flux.OnAssembly.1           : | onSubscribe([Fuseable] FluxOnAssembly.OnAssemblySubscriber)
[ctor-http-nio-2] reactor.Flux.OnAssembly.1           : | request(1)
[     parallel-1] reactor.Flux.OnAssembly.1           : | onNext(Sun Apr 30 21:07:03 IST 2017 : 114)
[ctor-http-nio-2] reactor.Flux.OnAssembly.1           : | request(31)
[     parallel-1] reactor.Flux.OnAssembly.1           : | onNext(Sun Apr 30 21:07:08 IST 2017 : 107)
[     parallel-1] reactor.Flux.OnAssembly.1           : | onNext(Sun Apr 30 21:07:13 IST 2017 : 103)
[     parallel-1] reactor.Flux.OnAssembly.1           : | onNext(Sun Apr 30 21:07:18 IST 2017 : 110)
[     parallel-1] reactor.Flux.OnAssembly.1           : | onNext(Sun Apr 30 21:07:23 IST 2017 : 120)
[     parallel-1] reactor.Flux.OnAssembly.1           : | onNext(Sun Apr 30 21:07:28 IST 2017 : 123)
[     parallel-1] reactor.Flux.OnAssembly.1           : | onNext(Sun Apr 30 21:07:33 IST 2017 : 121)
[     parallel-1] reactor.Flux.OnAssembly.1           : | onNext(Sun Apr 30 21:07:38 IST 2017 : 122)
[     parallel-1] reactor.Flux.OnAssembly.1           : | onNext(Sun Apr 30 21:07:43 IST 2017 : 119)
[     parallel-1] reactor.Flux.OnAssembly.1           : | onNext(Sun Apr 30 21:07:48 IST 2017 : 100)
[     parallel-1] reactor.Flux.OnAssembly.1           : | onNext(Sun Apr 30 21:07:53 IST 2017 : 109)
[     parallel-1] reactor.Flux.OnAssembly.1           : | onNext(Sun Apr 30 21:07:58 IST 2017 : 123)
[     parallel-1] reactor.Flux.OnAssembly.1           : | onNext(Sun Apr 30 21:08:03 IST 2017 : 123)
[     parallel-1] reactor.Flux.OnAssembly.1           : | onNext(Sun Apr 30 21:08:08 IST 2017 : 124)
[     parallel-1] reactor.Flux.OnAssembly.1           : | onNext(Sun Apr 30 21:08:13 IST 2017 : 120)
[     parallel-1] reactor.Flux.OnAssembly.1           : | onNext(Sun Apr 30 21:08:18 IST 2017 : 108)
[     parallel-1] reactor.Flux.OnAssembly.1           : | onNext(Sun Apr 30 21:08:23 IST 2017 : 107)
[     parallel-1] reactor.Flux.OnAssembly.1           : | onNext(Sun Apr 30 21:08:28 IST 2017 : 122)
[     parallel-1] reactor.Flux.OnAssembly.1           : | onNext(Sun Apr 30 21:08:33 IST 2017 : 104)
[     parallel-1] reactor.Flux.OnAssembly.1           : | onNext(Sun Apr 30 21:08:38 IST 2017 : 118)
[     parallel-1] reactor.Flux.OnAssembly.1           : | onNext(Sun Apr 30 21:08:43 IST 2017 : 102)
[     parallel-1] reactor.Flux.OnAssembly.1           : | onNext(Sun Apr 30 21:08:48 IST 2017 : 102)
[     parallel-1] reactor.Flux.OnAssembly.1           : | onNext(Sun Apr 30 21:08:53 IST 2017 : 103)
[     parallel-1] reactor.Flux.OnAssembly.1           : | onNext(Sun Apr 30 21:08:58 IST 2017 : 117)
[     parallel-1] reactor.Flux.OnAssembly.1           : | request(24)
[     parallel-1] reactor.Flux.OnAssembly.1           : | onNext(Sun Apr 30 21:09:03 IST 2017 : 104)
[ctor-http-nio-2] reactor.Flux.OnAssembly.1           : | cancel()
```

You can observe a sequence of `onNext` method calls, which are triggered as soon as the element is available. When the browser window is closed, the `cancel()` method is called to terminate the stream.

In this example, we created a controller returning an event stream (as `Flux`) and a web page registering to the event stream using `EventSource`. In the next example, let's take a look at extending the reach of an event stream to the database.

Reactive databases

All normal databases operations are blocking; that is, the thread waits until a response is received from the database.

To fully benefit from Reactive Programming, end-to-end communication has to be reactive, that is, based on event streams.

ReactiveMongo is designed to be reactive and avoid blocking operations. All operations, including select, update, or delete, return immediately. Data can be streamed into and out of the database using event streams.

In this section, we will use the Spring Boot Reactive MongoDB starter to create a simple example connecting to ReactiveMongo.

The following steps are involved:

1. Integrating Spring Boot Reactive MongoDB Starter.
2. Creating a model object the stock document.
3. Creating `reactiveCrudRepository`.
4. Initialising stock data using Command-line Runner.
5. Creating Reactive methods in Rest Controller.
6. Updating the view to subscribe to the event stream.

Integrating Spring Boot Reactive MongoDB Starter

To connect to the ReactiveMongo database, Spring Boot provides a starter project--Spring Boot Reactive MongoDB Starter. Let's add this to our the `pom.xml` file:

```
<dependency>
  <groupId>org.springframework.boot</groupId>
  <artifactId>spring-boot-starter-data-mongodb-
    reactive</artifactId>
</dependency>
```

The `spring-boot-starter-data-mongodb-reactive` starter brings in the `spring-data-mongodb`, `mongodb-driver-async`, and `mongodb-driver-reactivestreams` dependencies. The following snippet shows the important dependencies in the `spring-boot-starter-data-mongodb-reactive` starter:

```
<dependency>
  <groupId>org.springframework.data</groupId>
  <artifactId>spring-data-mongodb</artifactId>
  <exclusions>
   <exclusion>
     <groupId>org.mongodb</groupId>
     <artifactId>mongo-java-driver</artifactId>
   </exclusion>
   <exclusion>
     <groupId>org.slf4j</groupId>
     <artifactId>jcl-over-slf4j</artifactId>
   </exclusion>
  </exclusions>
</dependency>
<dependency>
 <groupId>org.mongodb</groupId>
 <artifactId>mongodb-driver</artifactId>
</dependency>
<dependency>
 <groupId>org.mongodb</groupId>
 <artifactId>mongodb-driver-async</artifactId>
</dependency>
<dependency>
 <groupId>org.mongodb</groupId>
 <artifactId>mongodb-driver-reactivestreams</artifactId>
</dependency>
<dependency>
 <groupId>io.projectreactor</groupId>
 <artifactId>reactor-core</artifactId>
</dependency>
```

The `EnableReactiveMongoRepositories` annotation enables ReactiveMongo features. The following snippet shows it being added to the `SpringReactiveExampleApplication` class:

```
@SpringBootApplication
@EnableReactiveMongoRepositories
public class SpringReactiveExampleApplication {
```

Creating a model object - a stock document

We will create the `Stock` document class, as shown in the following code. It contains three member variables--`code`, `name`, and `description`:

```
@Document
public class Stock {
  private String code;
  private String name;
  private String description;
    //Getters, Setters and Constructor
}
```

Creating a ReactiveCrudRepository

Traditional Spring Data Repositories are blocking. Spring Data introduces a new repository for interaction with reactive databases. The following code shows some of the important methods declared in the `ReactiveCrudRepository` interface:

```
@NoRepositoryBean
public interface ReactiveCrudRepository<T, ID extends Serializable>
extends Repository<T, ID> {
  <S extends T> Mono<S> save(S entity);
  Mono<T> findById(ID id);
  Mono<T> findById(Mono<ID> id);
  Mono<Boolean> existsById(ID id);
  Flux<T> findAll();
  Mono<Long> count();
  Mono<Void> deleteById(ID id);
  Mono<Void> deleteAll();
  }
```

All the methods in the preceding interface are non-blocking. They return either Mono or Flux, which can be used to retrieve elements when events are triggered.

We want to create a Repository for the Stock Document object. The following snippet shows the definition of `StockMongoReactiveCrudRepository`. We extend `ReactiveCrudRepository` with `Stock` as the document being managed and a key of type `String`:

```
public interface StockMongoReactiveCrudRepository
extends ReactiveCrudRepository<Stock, String> {
}
```

Initialising stock data using the Command Line Runner

Let's use the Command-line Runner to insert some data into ReactiveMongo. The following snippet shows the details added to `SpringReactiveExampleApplication`:

```
@Bean
CommandLineRunner initData(
StockMongoReactiveCrudRepository mongoRepository) {
  return (p) -> {
  mongoRepository.deleteAll().block();
  mongoRepository.save(
  new Stock("IBM", "IBM Corporation", "Desc")).block();
  mongoRepository.save(
  new Stock("GGL", "Google", "Desc")).block();
  mongoRepository.save(
  new Stock("MST", "Microsoft", "Desc")).block();
  };
}
```

The `mongoRepository.save()` method is used to save the `Stock` document to ReactiveMongo. The `block()` method ensures that the save operation is completed before the next statement is executed.

Creating Reactive methods in Rest Controller

We can now add in the controller methods to retrieve details using `StockMongoReactiveCrudRepository`:

```
@RestController
public class StockPriceEventController {
  private final StockMongoReactiveCrudRepository repository;
  public StockPriceEventController(
  StockMongoReactiveCrudRepository repository) {
    this.repository = repository;
  }
```

```
@GetMapping("/stocks")
Flux<Stock> list() {
  return this.repository.findAll().log();
}

@GetMapping("/stocks/{code}")
Mono<Stock> findById(@PathVariable("code") String code) {
  return this.repository.findById(code).log();
}
}
```

A few important things to note are as follows:

- private final StockMongoReactiveCrudRepository repository: StockMongoReactiveCrudRepository is injected in using the constructor injection.
- @GetMapping("/stocks") Flux<Stock> list(): Exposes a GET method to retrieve a list of stocks. Returns a Flux indicating that this would be a stream of stocks.
- @GetMapping("/stocks/{code}") Mono<Stock> findById(@PathVariable("code") String code): findById returns a Mono, indicating that it would return 0 or 1 stock element(s).

Updating the view to subscribe to the event stream

We want to update the view with new buttons to trigger events to list all stocks and show the details of a specific stock. The following snippet shows the code to be added to resources\static\stock-price.html:

```
<button id="list-stocks-button">List All Stocks</button>
<button id="ibm-stock-details-button">Show IBM Details</button>
```

The following snippet enables click events on the new buttons, trigger connection with their respective events:

```
<script type="application/javascript">
addEvent("click",
document.getElementById('list-stocks-button'),
function() {
  registerEventSourceAndAddResponseTo("/stocks","display");
 }
);
addEvent("click",
document.getElementById('ibm-stock-details-button'),
```

```
function() {
  registerEventSourceAndAddResponseTo("/stocks/IBM","display");
}
);
</script>
```

Launching SpringReactiveExampleApplication

Launch MongoDB and the `SpringReactiveExampleApplication` class. The following screenshot shows the screen loading the page at
`http://localhost:8080/static/stock-price.html`:

The following screenshot shows the screen when the stock list is clicked on:

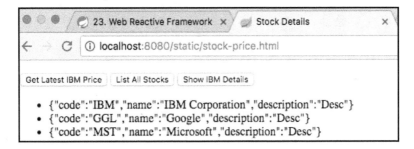

The following screenshot shows the screen when the `Show IBM Details` button is clicked on:

Summary

In this chapter, we took a quick peek into the world of Reactive Programming. We discussed the important frameworks in the Java Reactive world--Reactive Streams, Reactor, and Spring Web Flux. We implemented a simple web page using event streams.

Reactive Programming is not a silver bullet. While it might not be the correct option for all use cases, it is a possible option you should evaluate. Its language, framework support, and the use of Reactive Programming are in the initial stages of evolution.

In the next chapter, we will move on to discuss best practices in developing applications using Spring Framework.

12
Spring Best Practices

In the previous chapters, we discussed a number of Spring Projects--Spring MVC, Spring Boot, Spring Cloud, Spring Cloud Data Flow, and Spring Reactive. The challenges with enterprise application development do not end with choosing the right framework. One of the biggest challenges is the appropriate use of the frameworks.

In this chapter, we will discuss the best practices of enterprise application development with the Spring Framework. We talk about best practices related to the following:

- The structure of enterprise applications
- Spring configuration
- Managing dependency versions
- Exception handling
- Unit testing
- Integration testing
- Session management
- Caching
- Logging

Maven standard directory layout

Maven defines a standard directory layout for all projects. Once all projects adopt this layout, it allows developers to switch between projects with ease.

The following screenshot shows an example directory layout for a web project:

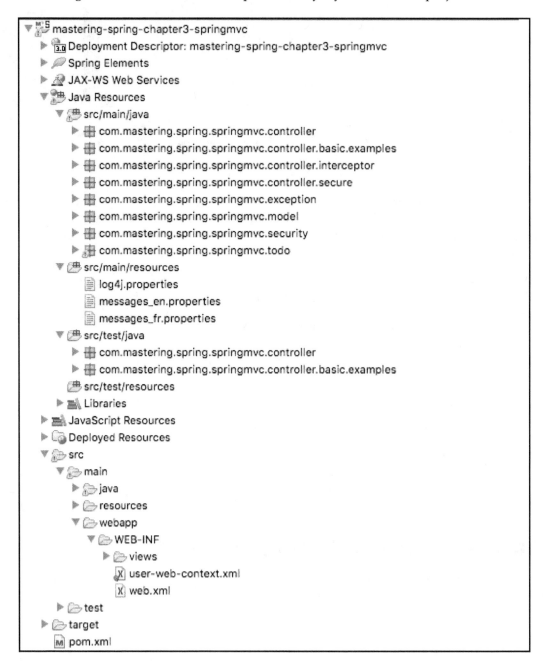

The following are some of the important standard directories:

- `src/main/java`: All application-related source code
- `src/main/resources`: All application-related resources--Spring context files, property files, logging configuration, and so on
- `src/main/webapp`: All resources related to the web application--view files (JSP, view templates, static content, and so on)
- `src/test/java`: All unit testing code
- `src/test/resources`: All resources related to unit testing

Layered architecture

One of the core design aims is **Separation of Concerns** (**SoC**). One of the good practices, irrespective of the size of an application or microservice, is to create a layered architecture.

Each layer in a layered architecture has one concern, and it should implement it well. Layering the applications also helps in simplifying unit tests. The code in each layer can be completely unit tested by mocking out the following layer. The following figure shows some of the important layers in a typical microservice/web application:

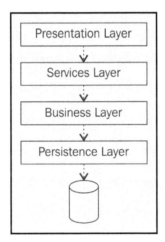

The layers shown in the previous diagram are as follows:

- **Presentation layer**: In a microservice, the presentation layer is where the Rest Controllers reside. In a typical web application, this layer would also contain the view-related content--JSPs, templates, and static content. The presentation layer talks to the services layer.
- **Services layer**: This acts a facade to the business layer. Different views--mobile, web, and tablets, this might need different kinds of data. The Services layer understands their needs and provides the right data based on the presentation layer.
- **Business layer**: This is where all the business logic is. Another best practice is to the put most of the business logic into the Domain Model. The business layer talks to data layer to get the data and add business logic on top of it.
- **Persistence layer**: This takes care of retrieving and storing data to the database. This layer typically contains the JPA mappings or the JDBC code.

Recommended practices

It is recommended that you have different Spring contexts for each of the layers. This helps in separating concerns of each layer. This also helps in unit testing code for the specific layer.

An application `context.xml` can be used to import contexts from all the layers. This can be context that is loaded when an application is run. Some of the possible spring context names are listed as follows:

- `application-context.xml`
- `presentation-context.xml`
- `services-context.xml`
- `business-context.xml`
- `persistence-context.xml`

Separate API and impl for important layers

Another best practice to ensure loosely coupled application layers is to have separate API and implementation modules in each layer. The following screenshot shows the data layer with two submodules--API and impl:

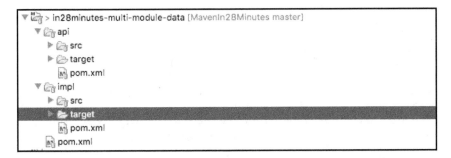

The data `pom.xml` defines two child modules:

```
<modules>
  <module>api</module>
  <module>impl</module>
</modules>
```

The `api` module is used to define the interface that the data layer offers. The `impl` module is used to create the implementation.

The business layer should be built using the API from the data layer. The business layer should not depend on the implementation (the `impl` module) of the data layer. This helps in creating a clear separation between the two layers. The implementation of the data layer can be changed without affecting the business layer.

The following snippet shows an extract from the `pom.xml` file of the business layer:

```
<dependency>
  <groupId>com.in28minutes.example.layering</groupId>
  <artifactId>data-api</artifactId>
</dependency>

<dependency>
  <groupId>com.in28minutes.example.layering</groupId>
  <artifactId>data-impl</artifactId>
  <scope>runtime</scope>
</dependency>
```

While the `data-api` dependency has the default scope--compile--the `data-impl` dependency has a scope runtime. This ensures that the `data-impl` module is not available during the compilation of business layer.

While separate `API` and `impl` can be implemented for all layers, it is recommended that you use it at least for the business layer.

Exception handling

There are two types of exceptions:

- **Checked exceptions**: When a service method throws this exception, all the consumer methods should either handle or throw the exception
- **Unchecked exceptions**: The consumer method is not required to handle or throw the exception thrown by the service method

`RuntimeException` and all its subclasses are unchecked exceptions. All other exceptions are checked exceptions.

Checked exceptions can make your code cumbersome to read. Take a look at the following example:

```
PreparedStatement st = null;
try {
    st = conn.prepareStatement(INSERT_TODO_QUERY);
    st.setString(1, bean.getDescription());
    st.setBoolean(2, bean.isDone());
    st.execute();
    } catch (SQLException e) {
      logger.error("Failed : " + INSERT_TODO_QUERY, e);
      } finally {
        if (st != null) {
          try {
            st.close();
            } catch (SQLException e) {
            // Ignore - nothing to do..
            }
        }
      }
    }
```

The declaration of the execute method in the `PreparedStatement` class is shown as follows:

```
boolean execute() throws SQLException
```

`SQLException` is a checked exception. So, any method that calls the `execute()` method should either handle the exception or throw it. In the preceding example, we are handling the exception using a `try-catch` block.

Spring's approach to exception handling

Spring takes a different approach to this problem. It makes most of the exceptions unchecked. The code becomes simple:

```
jdbcTemplate.update(INSERT_TODO_QUERY,
bean.getDescription(),bean.isDone());
```

The update method in `JDBCTemplate` does not declare throwing any exception.

The recommended approach

We recommend an approach very similar to the one used by Spring Framework. When deciding what exceptions to throw from a method, always think about the consumer of the method.

Can the consumer of the method do something about the exception?

In the preceding example, if the execution of the query failed, the `consumer` method would not be able to do anything except show an error page to the user. In that kind of a scenario, we should not complicate things and force the consumer to handle the exception.

We recommend the following approach to exception handling in applications:

- Think about the consumer. If the consumer of the method cannot do anything useful (except logging or showing an error page) about the exception, make it unchecked.
- In the topmost layer, typically the presentation layer, have `catch all` exception handling to display an error page or to send an error response to the consumer. Refer to `@ControllerAdvice` in `Chapter 3`, *Building Web Application with Spring MVC* for more details about implementing catch all exception handling.

Keeping your Spring configuration light

One of the problems with Spring before annotations was the size of the application context XML files. Application context XML files ran into hundreds of lines (sometimes, even thousands of lines). However, with annotations, there is no need for such long application context XML files anymore.

We recommend that you use component scans to locate and autowire the beans instead of manually wiring the beans in XML files. Keep your application context XML files very small. We recommend that you use Java `@Configuration` whereever some framework-related configuration is needed.

Using the basePackageClasses attribute in ComponentScan

When using component scan, we recommend that you use the `basePackageClasses` attribute. The following snippet shows an example:

```
@ComponentScan(basePackageClasses = ApplicationController.class)
public class SomeApplication {
```

The `basePackageClasses` attribute is the type-safe alternative to `basePackages()` in order to specify the packages to scan for the annotated components. The package of each specified class will be scanned.

This will ensure that even when the package is renamed or moved, the component scan would work as expected.

Not using version numbers in schema references

Spring can recognize the correct version of the schemas from the dependencies. Hence, it is not necessary to use version numbers in the schema references anymore. The class snippet shows an example:

```
<?xml version="1.0" encoding="UTF-8"?>
<beans xmlns="http://www.springframework.org/schema/beans"
  xmlns:xsi="http://www.w3.org/2001/XMLSchema-instance"
  xmlns:context="http://www.springframework.org/schema/context"
  xsi:schemaLocation="http://www.springframework.org/schema/beans
  http://www.springframework.org/schema/beans/spring-beans.xsd
  http://www.springframework.org/schema/context/
```

```
http://www.springframework.org/schema/context/spring-
context.xsd">
<!-- Other bean definitions-->
</beans>
```

Preferring constructor injection over setter injection for mandatory dependencies

There are two kinds of dependencies for beans:

- **Mandatory dependencies**: These are dependencies that you want to be available for the bean. If the dependency is not available, you would want the context to fail loading up.
- **Optional dependencies**: These are dependencies that are optional. They are not always available. It's fine to load the context even if these are not available.

We recommend that you wire mandatory dependencies using constructor injection instead of setter injection. This would ensure that the context would fail to load if the mandatory dependency is missing. The following snippet shows an example:

```
public class SomeClass {
  private MandatoryDependency mandatoryDependency
  private OptionalDependency optionalDependency;
  public SomeClass(MandatoryDependency mandatoryDependency) {
    this.mandatoryDependency = mandatoryDependency;
}
public void setOptionalDependency(
OptionalDependency optionalDependency) {
  this.optionalDependency = optionalDependency;
}
//All other logic
}
```

An extract from the Spring documentation (`https://docs.spring.io/spring/docs/curre nt/spring-framework-reference/htmlsingle/#beans-constructor-injection`) is presented as follows:

> *The Spring team generally advocates constructor injection as it enables one to implement application components as immutable objects and ensure that the required dependencies are not null. Furthermore, constructor-injected components are always returned to the client (calling) code in a fully initialized state. As a side note, a large number of constructor arguments is a bad code smell, implying that the class likely has too many responsibilities and should be refactored to better address proper Separation of Concerns. Setter injection should primarily only be used for optional dependencies that can be assigned reasonable default values within the class. Otherwise, not-null checks must be performed everywhere the code uses the dependency. One benefit of setter injection is that setter methods make objects of that class amenable to reconfiguration or re-injection later. Management through* JMX MBeans *is therefore a compelling use case for setter injection.*

Managing dependency versions for Spring Projects

If you are using Spring Boot, then the simplest option to manage dependency versions is to use `spring-boot-starter-parent` as the parent POM. This is the option we used in all our project examples in this book:

```
<parent>
  <groupId>org.springframework.boot</groupId>
  <artifactId>spring-boot-starter-parent</artifactId>
  <version>${spring-boot.version}</version>
  <relativePath /> <!-- lookup parent from repository -->
</parent>
```

Versions of more than 200 dependencies are managed by `spring-boot-starter-parent`. Before a Spring Boot release, it is ensured that all the versions of these dependencies play well together. The following are some of the dependency versions that are managed:

```
<activemq.version>5.14.3</activemq.version>
 <ehcache.version>2.10.3</ehcache.version>
 <elasticsearch.version>2.4.4</elasticsearch.version>
 <h2.version>1.4.193</h2.version>
 <jackson.version>2.8.7</jackson.version>
 <jersey.version>2.25.1</jersey.version>
```

```
<junit.version>4.12</junit.version>
<mockito.version>1.10.19</mockito.version>
<mongodb.version>3.4.2</mongodb.version>
<mysql.version>5.1.41</mysql.version>
<reactor.version>2.0.8.RELEASE</reactor.version>
<reactor-spring.version>2.0.7.RELEASE</reactor-spring.version>
<selenium.version>2.53.1</selenium.version>
<spring.version>4.3.7.RELEASE</spring.version>
<spring-amqp.version>1.7.1.RELEASE</spring-amqp.version>
<spring-cloud-connectors.version>1.2.3.RELEASE</spring-cloud-
connectors.version>
<spring-batch.version>3.0.7.RELEASE</spring-batch.version>
<spring-hateoas.version>0.23.0.RELEASE</spring-hateoas.version>
<spring-kafka.version>1.1.3.RELEASE</spring-kafka.version>
<spring-restdocs.version>1.1.2.RELEASE</spring-restdocs.version>
<spring-security.version>4.2.2.RELEASE</spring-security.version>
<thymeleaf.version>2.1.5.RELEASE</thymeleaf.version>
```

It is recommended that you do not override any of the versions of the managed dependencies in the project POM file. This ensures that when we upgrade our Spring Boot version, we would get the latest version upgrades of all the dependencies.

Sometimes, you have to use a custom corporate POM as a parent POM. The following snippet shows how to manage dependency versions in this scenario:

```
<dependencyManagement>
  <dependencies>
    <dependency>
      <groupId>org.springframework.boot</groupId>
      <artifactId>spring-boot-dependencies</artifactId>
      <version>${spring-boot.version}</version>
      <type>pom</type>
      <scope>import</scope>
    </dependency>
  </dependencies>
</dependencyManagement>
```

If you are not using Spring Boot, then you can manage all basic Spring dependencies using Spring BOM:

```
<dependencyManagement>
  <dependencies>
    <dependency>
      <groupId>org.springframework</groupId>
      <artifactId>spring-framework-bom</artifactId>
      <version>${org.springframework-version}</version>
      <type>pom</type>
      <scope>import</scope>
```

```
        </dependency>
      </dependencies>
    </dependencyManagement>
```

Unit testing

While the basic aim of unit testing is to find defects, approaches for writing unit tests for each of the layers are different. In this section, we will take a quick look at unit testing examples and best practices for different layers.

The business layer

When writing tests for the business layer, we recommend that you avoid using Spring Framework in the unit tests. This will ensure that your tests are framework independent and will run faster.

The following is an example of a unit test written without using Spring Framework:

```
@RunWith(MockitoJUnitRunner.class)
public class BusinessServiceMockitoTest {
  private static final User DUMMY_USER = new User("dummy");
  @Mock
  private DataService dataService;
  @InjectMocks
  private BusinessService service = new BusinessServiceImpl();
  @Test
  public void testCalculateSum() {
    BDDMockito.given(dataService.retrieveData(
    Matchers.any(User.class)))
    .willReturn(Arrays.asList(
    new Data(10), new Data(15), new Data(25)));
    long sum = service.calculateSum(DUMMY_USER);
    assertEquals(10 + 15 + 25, sum);
  }
}
```

Spring Framework is used to wire dependencies in the running application. However, in your unit tests, using the @InjectMocks Mockito annotation in combination with @Mock is the best option.

Web layer

Unit tests for web layers involve testing the Controllers--REST and otherwise.

We recommend the following:

- Using Mock MVC for web layers built on Spring MVC
- Jersey Test Framework is a good choice for REST Services built using Jersey and JAX-RS

A quick example of setting up the Mock MVC framework is shown as follows:

```
@RunWith(SpringRunner.class)
@WebMvcTest(TodoController.class)
public class TodoControllerTest {
   @Autowired
   private MockMvc mvc;
   @MockBean
   private TodoService service;
   //Tests
}
```

Using `@WebMvcTest` will allow us to use autowire `MockMvc` and execute web requests. A great feature of `@WebMVCTest` is that it only instantiates the controller components. All other Spring components are expected to be mocked and can be autowired using `@MockBean`.

The data layer

Spring Boot offers a simple annotation `@DataJpaTest` for data layer unit tests. A simple example is listed as follows:

```
@DataJpaTest
@RunWith(SpringRunner.class)
public class UserRepositoryTest {
   @Autowired
   UserRepository userRepository;
   @Autowired
   TestEntityManager entityManager;
  //Test Methods
}
```

`@DataJpaTest` may also inject a `TestEntityManager` bean, which provides an alternative to the standard JPA `entityManager` specifically designed for tests.

If you want to use `TestEntityManager` outside of `@DataJpaTest`, you can also use the `@AutoConfigureTestEntityManager` annotation.

Data JPA tests are run against an embedded database by default. This ensures that tests can be run as many times as you would want without affecting the database.

Other best practices

We recommend that you follow the Test-Driven Development (TDD) approach to develop code. Writing tests before code results in a clear understanding of the complexity and dependencies of the code unit being written. In my experience, this leads to better design and better code.

The best projects that I worked on recognize that unit tests are more important than the source code. Applications evolve. Architectures of a few years back are legacy today. By having great unit tests, we can continuously refactor and improve our projects.

A few guidelines are listed as follows:

- Unit tests should be readable. Other developers should be able to understand the test in less than 15 seconds. Aim for tests that serve as documentation for code.
- Unit tests should fail only when there is a defect in the production code. This seems simple. However, if unit tests use external data, they can fail when external data changes. Over a period of time, developers lose confidence in unit tests.
- Unit tests should run fast. Slow tests are run infrequently, losing all benefits associated with unit testing.
- Unit tests should be run as part of Continuous Integration. As soon as there is a commit in the version control, the build (with unit tests) should run and notify developers in case of failures.

Integration testing

While unit tests test a specific layer, integration tests are used to test the code in multiple layers. To keep the tests repeatable, we recommend that you use an embedded database instead of a real database for integration tests.

We recommend that you create a separate profile for integration tests using an embedded database. This ensures that each developer has their own database to run the tests against. Let's look at few simple examples.

The `application.properties` file:

```
app.profiles.active: production
```

The `application-production.properties` file:

```
app.jpa.database: MYSQL
app.datasource.url: <<VALUE>>
app.datasource.username: <<VALUE>>
app.datasource.password: <<VALUE>>
```

The `application-integration-test.properties` file:

```
app.jpa.database: H2
app.datasource.url=jdbc:h2:mem:mydb
app.datasource.username=sa
app.datasource.pool-size=30
```

We would need to include the H2 driver dependency in the test scope, as shown in the following snippet:

```
<dependency>
  <groupId>mysql</groupId>
  <artifactId>mysql-connector-java</artifactId>
  <scope>runtime</scope>
</dependency>

<dependency>
  <groupId>com.h2database</groupId>
  <artifactId>h2</artifactId>
  <scope>test</scope>
</dependency>
```

An example integration test using the `@ActiveProfiles("integration-test")` is shown as follows. The integration tests will now run using an embedded database:

```
@ActiveProfiles("integration-test")
@RunWith(SpringRunner.class)
@SpringBootTest(classes = Application.class, webEnvironment =
SpringBootTest.WebEnvironment.RANDOM_PORT)
public class TodoControllerIT {
  @LocalServerPort
  private int port;
  private TestRestTemplate template = new TestRestTemplate();
  //Tests
}
```

Integration tests are critical to be able to continuously deliver working software. The features Spring Boot provides make it easy to implement integration tests.

Spring Session

Managing the session state is one of the important challenges in distributing and scaling web applications. HTTP is a stateless protocol. The state of the user interactions with web applications is typically managed in HttpSession.

It is important to have as little data as possible in a session. Focus on identifying and removing data that is not needed in the session.

Consider a distributed application with three instances, as shown here. Each of these instances has its own local session copy:

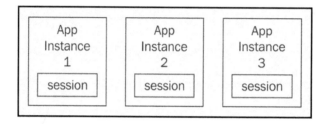

Imagine a user is being currently served from App Instance 1. Imagine if App Instance 1 goes down and the load balancer sends the user to App Instance 2. App Instance 2 is not aware of the session state that was available with App Instance 1. The user has to log in and start off again. That's not a good user experience.

Spring Session provides features to externalize your session store. Instead of using the local HttpSession, Spring Session provides alternatives to store the session state to different data stores:

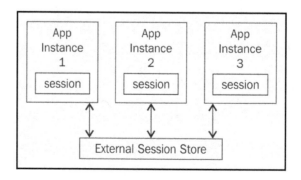

Spring Session also provides a clear Separation of Concerns. The application code remains the same irrespective of the session data store being used. We can switch between session data stores through configuration.

Example

In this example, we will connect Spring Session to use a Redis session store. While the code to put data into session remains the same, the data would be stored to Redis instead of HTTP Session.

There are three simple steps involved:

1. Add dependencies for Spring Session.
2. Configure Filter to replace HttpSession with Spring Session.
3. Enable filtering for Tomcat by extending `AbstractHttpSessionApplicationInitializer`.

Adding dependencies for Spring Session

The dependencies needed for Spring Session connecting to a Redis store are `spring-session-data-redis` and `lettuce-core`:

```
<dependency>
  <groupId>org.springframework.session</groupId>
  <artifactId>spring-session-data-redis</artifactId>
  <type>pom</type>
</dependency>

<dependency>
  <groupId>io.lettuce</groupId>
  <artifactId>lettuce-core</artifactId>
</dependency>
```

Configuring Filter to replacing HttpSession with Spring Session

The following configuration creates a Servlet Filter to replace HTTPSession with a Session implementation from Spring Session--Redis Data Store in this example:

```
@EnableRedisHttpSession
public class ApplicationConfiguration {
  @Bean
  public LettuceConnectionFactory connectionFactory() {
    return new LettuceConnectionFactory();
  }
}
```

Enabling filtering for Tomcat by extending AbstractHttpSessionApplicationInitializer

In the previous step, Servlet Filter needs to be enabled on every request to the Servlet Container (Tomcat). The following snippet shows the code involved:

```
public class Initializer
extends AbstractHttpSessionApplicationInitializer {
  public Initializer() {
    super(ApplicationConfiguration.class);
  }
}
```

That's all the configuration you would need. The great thing with Spring Session is the fact that your application code talking to HTTPSession does not change! You can continue using the HttpSession interface, but in the background, Spring Session ensures that the session data is stored to an external data store - Redis in this example:

```
req.getSession().setAttribute(name, value);
```

Spring Session provides simple options to connect to an external session store. Backing up your session on an external session store ensures that your user can fail over even when one of your application instances goes down.

Caching

Caching is essential in order to build a performant application. You would not want to hit the external service or the database all the time. Data that does not change frequently can be cached.

Spring provides transparent mechanisms to connect and use a Cache. The following steps are involved in enabling a cache on an application:

1. Add the Spring Boot Starter Cache dependency.
2. Add caching annotations.

Let's discuss these in detail.

Adding the Spring Boot Starter Cache dependency

The following snippet shows the `spring-boot-starter-cache` dependency. Itt brings in all the dependencies and auto-configuration needed to configure a cache:

```
<dependency>
  <groupId>org.springframework.boot</groupId>
  <artifactId>spring-boot-starter-cache</artifactId>
</dependency>
```

Adding caching annotations

The next step is to add the caching annotations, indicating when something needs to be added or removed from the cache. The following snippet shows an example:

```
@Component
public class ExampleRepository implements Repository {
  @Override
  @Cacheable("something-cache-key")
  public Something getSomething(String id) {
      //Other code
  }
}
```

Some of the annotations that are supported are as follows:

- `Cacheable`: Used to cache the result of a method invocation. The default implementation constructs the key based on the parameters passed to the method. The method will not be invoked if the value is found in the cache.
- `CachePut`: Similar to `@Cacheable`. A significant difference is that the method is always invoked and the result is put in a cache.
- `CacheEvict`: Triggers an evict for a specific element from the cache. Typically done when an element is deleted or updated.

A few other important things to note about Spring Caching are as follows:

- The default cache used is ConcurrentHashMap
- The Spring Caching abstraction is JSR-107-compliant
- Other caches that can be auto-configured include EhCache, Redis, and Hazelcast

Logging

Spring and Spring Boot depend on the Commons Logging API. They are not dependent on any other logging frameworks. Spring Boot provides starters to simplify the configuration of specific logging frameworks.

Logback

Starter `spring-boot-starter-logging` is all that you need to use the Logback framework. This dependency is the default logging included in most of the starters, including `spring-boot-starter-web`. The dependency is shown as follows:

```xml
<dependency>
  <groupId>org.springframework.boot</groupId>
  <artifactId>spring-boot-starter-logging</artifactId>
</dependency>
```

The following snippet shows logback and related dependencies included in `spring-boot-starter-logging`:

```xml
<dependency>
  <groupId>ch.qos.logback</groupId>
  <artifactId>logback-classic</artifactId>
</dependency>
```

```xml
<dependency>
  <groupId>org.slf4j</groupId>
  <artifactId>jcl-over-slf4j</artifactId>
</dependency>

<dependency>
  <groupId>org.slf4j</groupId>
  <artifactId>jul-to-slf4j</artifactId>
</dependency>

<dependency>
  <groupId>org.slf4j</groupId>
  <artifactId>log4j-over-slf4j</artifactId>
</dependency>
```

Log4j2

To use Log4j2, we need to use the starter `spring-boot-starter-log4j2`. When we use starters such as `spring-boot-starter-web`, we need to ensure that we exclude the dependency in `spring-boot-starter-logging`. The following snippet shows the details:

```xml
<dependency>
  <groupId>org.springframework.boot</groupId>
  <artifactId>spring-boot-starter</artifactId>
  <exclusions>
    <exclusion>
      <groupId>org.springframework.boot</groupId>
      <artifactId>spring-boot-starter-logging</artifactId>
    </exclusion>
  </exclusions>
</dependency>

<dependency>
  <groupId>org.springframework.boot</groupId>
  <artifactId>spring-boot-starter-log4j2</artifactId>
</dependency>
```

The following snippet shows the dependencies used in the `spring-boot-starter-log4j2` starter:

```xml
<dependency>
  <groupId>org.apache.logging.log4j</groupId>
  <artifactId>log4j-slf4j-impl</artifactId>
</dependency>

<dependency>
```

```
    <groupId>org.apache.logging.log4j</groupId>
    <artifactId>log4j-api</artifactId>
  </dependency>

  <dependency>
    <groupId>org.apache.logging.log4j</groupId>
    <artifactId>log4j-core</artifactId>
  </dependency>

<dependency>
  <groupId>org.slf4j</groupId>
  <artifactId>jul-to-slf4j</artifactId>
</dependency>
```

Framework independent configuration

Irrespective of the logging framework used, Spring Boot allows a few basic configuration options in application properties. A few examples are shown as follows:

```
logging.level.org.springframework.web=DEBUG
logging.level.org.hibernate=ERROR
logging.file=<<PATH_TO_LOG_FILE>>
```

In the age of microservices, irrespective of the framework you use for logging, we recommend that you log to the console (instead of a file) and use a centralized logging store tool to capture logs from all microservice instances.

Summary

In this chapter, we looked at some of the best practices in developing Spring-based applications. We covered best practices in structuring our projects--layering, following the Maven standard directory layout, and using api and implementation modules. We also discussed how to keep our Spring configuration to a minimum. We looked at best practices related to logging, caching, session management, and exception handling.

13
Working with Kotlin in Spring

Kotlin is a statically-typed JVM language, enabling code that is expressive, short, and readable. Spring Framework 5.0 has good support for Kotlin.

In this chapter, we will explore some of the important features of Kotlin and learn how to create a basic REST service with Kotlin and Spring Boot.

By the end of this chapter, you will understand the following:

- What is Kotlin?
- How does it compare with Java?
- How to create a Kotlin project in Eclipse?
- How to create a Spring Boot project with Kotlin?
- How to implement and unit test a simple Spring Boot REST service using Kotlin?

Kotlin

Kotlin is an open source, statically-typed language that can be used to build applications that run on the JVM, Android, and JavaScript platforms. Kotlin is developed by JetBrains under the Apache 2.0 license and the source code is available on GitHub (`https://github.com/jetbrains/kotlin`).

A couple of quotes from Andrey Breslav, the lead language designer for Kotlin, are listed as follows. These help us understand the thought process behind Kotlin:

The primary purpose of Project Kotlin is to create for developers a general-purpose language that can serve as a useful tool that is safe, concise, flexible, and 100 percent Java-compatible.

Kotlin is designed to be an industrial-strength object-oriented language, and a "better language" than Java, but still be fully interoperable with Java code, allowing companies to make a gradual migration from Java to Kotlin.

Kotlin is one of the official languages supported by Android. The official Android developer page for Kotlin (`https://developer.android.com/kotlin/index.html`) highlights the important reasons why Kotlin is quickly becoming popular with developers:

Kotlin is expressive, concise, extensible, powerful, and a joy to read and write. It has wonderful safety features in terms of nullability and immutability, which aligns with our investments to make Android apps healthy and performant by default. Best of all, it's interoperable with our existing Android languages and runtime.

Some of the important things about Kotlin include the following:

- Complete compatibility with Java. You can call Java code from Kotlin and vice-versa.
- Concise and readable language. Kotlin FAQ (`http://kotlinlang.org/docs/reference/faq.html`) estimates a 40% reduction in the number of lines of code.
- Support for both functional and object-oriented programming.
- IntelliJ IDEA, Android Studio, Eclipse, and NetBeans are the IDE that have support for Kotlin. While the support is not as good as that for Java, it is improving by the day.
- All major build tools--Gradle, Maven and Ant--have support for building Kotlin projects.

Kotlin versus Java

Java was developed by James Gosling at Sun Microsystems and released in 1995. It has remained a popular language for more than two decades now.

One of the important reasons for the popularity of Java is the Java platform including the Java Virtual Machine (JVM). The Java platform provides security and portability for the Java language. A number of languages emerged in the last few years that aimed to leverage the advantages of the Java platform. They compile to the bytecode and can run on the JVM. These languages include the following frameworks:

- Clojure
- Groovy
- Scala
- JRuby
- Jython

Kotlin aims to address some of the important issues in the Java language and provide a concise alternative. Some of the important differences with the Java language are as follows.

Variables and type inference

Kotlin infers the type of variable from the value assigned to it. In the following example, `intVariable` is assigned a type of `Int`:

```
//Type Inference
var intVariable = 10
```

Since Kotlin is type-safe, the following snippet will result in a compilation error if uncommented:

```
//intVariable = "String"
//If uncommented -> Type mismatch:
//inferred type is String but Int was expected
```

Variables and immutability

Typically, like all other programming languages, the values of variables can be changed. The following snippet shows an example:

```
var variable = 5
variable = 6 //You can change value
```

However, if `val` (instead of `var`) is used to define a variable, then the variable is immutable. The value of the variable cannot be changed. This is similar to `final` variables in Java. Consider the following code:

```
val immutable = 6
//immutable = 7 //Val cannot be reassigned
```

Type system

In Kotlin, everything is an object. There are no primitive variables.

The following are the important numeric types:

- Double--64 bit
- Float--32 bit
- Long--64 bit
- Int--32 bit
- Short--16 bit
- Byte--8 bit

Unlike Java, Kotlin does not treat characters as a numeric type. Any numeric operation on a character will result in a compilation error. Consider the following code:

```
var char = 'c'
//Operator '==' cannot be applied to 'Char' and 'Int'
//if(char==1) print (char);
Null safety
```

Java programmers are very familiar with `java.lang.NullPointerException`. Any operations performed on object variable referencing null will throw `NullPointerException`.

Kotlin's type system aims to eliminate `NullPointerException`. Normal variables cannot hold null. The following code snippet will not compile if uncommented:

```
var string: String = "abc"
//string = null //Compilation Error
```

To be able to store null in a variable, a special declaration needs to be used. That is, type followed by a ?. For example, consider the following `String?` :

```
var nullableString: String? = "abc"
nullableString = null
```

Once a variable is declared to be nullable, Only safe (?.) or non-null asserted (!!.) calls are allowed. Direct references will result in compilation errors:

```
//Compilation Error
//print(nullableString.length)
if (nullableString != null) {
  print(nullableString.length)
  }
print(nullableString?.length)
```

Functions

In Kotlin, functions are declared using the `fun` keyword. The following code snippet shows an example:

```
fun helloBasic(name: String): String {
  return "Hello, $name!"
}
```

Function arguments are specified in brackets after the function name. The `name` is an argument of type `String`. The function return type is specified after the arguments. The return type of the function is `String`.

The following line of code shows the invocation of the `helloBasic` function:

```
println(helloBasic("foo")) // => Hello, foo!
```

Kotlin also allows named parameters. The following line of code shows an example:

```
println(helloBasic(name = "bar"))
```

Function arguments can optionally have a default value.

```
fun helloWithDefaultValue(name: String = "World"): String {
  return "Hello, $name!"
}
```

The following line of code shows the invocation of the `helloWithDefaultValue` function without specifying any parameters. The default value of the name argument is used:

```
println(helloWithDefaultValue()) //Hello, World
```

If a function has just one expression, then it can be defined on a single line. The `helloWithOneExpression` function is a simplified version of the `helloWithDefaultValue` function. The return type is inferred from the value returned:

```
fun helloWithOneExpression(name: String = "world")
= "Hello, $name!"
```

Functions returning void and having only one expression can also be defined on a single line. The following code snippet shows an example:

```
fun printHello(name: String = "world")
= println("Hello, $name!")
```

Arrays

Arrays are represented by a Class `Array` in Kotlin. The following code snippet shows some of the important properties and methods in the `Array` class:

```
class Array<T> private constructor() {
  val size: Int
  operator fun get(index: Int): T
  operator fun set(index: Int, value: T): Unit
  operator fun iterator(): Iterator<T>
  // ...
}
```

An array can be created using the `intArrayOf` function:

```
val intArray = intArrayOf(1, 2, 10)
```

The following code snippet shows some of the important operations that can be performed on an array:

```
println(intArray[0])//1
println(intArray.get(0))//1
println(intArray.all { it > 5 }) //false
println(intArray.any { it > 5 }) //true
println(intArray.asList())//[1, 2, 10]
println(intArray.max())//10
println(intArray.min())//1
```

Collections

Kotlin has simple funtions to initialize collections. The following line of code shows an example of initializing a list:

```
val countries = listOf("India", "China", "USA")
```

The following code snippet shows some of the important operations that can be performed on a list:

```
println(countries.size)//3
println(countries.first())//India
println(countries.last())//USA
println(countries[2])//USA
```

Lists, created with `listOf`, are immutable in Kotlin. To be able to change the content of a list, the `mutableListOf` function needs to be used:

```
//countries.add("China") //Not allowed
val mutableContries = mutableListOf("India", "China", "USA")
mutableContries.add("China")
```

The `mapOf` function is used to initialize a map, as shown in the following code snippet:

```
val characterOccurances =
mapOf("a" to 1, "h" to 1, "p" to 2, "y" to 1)//happy
println(characterOccurances)//{a=1, h=1, p=2, y=1}
```

The following line of code shows the retrieval of a value for a specific key:

```
println(characterOccurances["p"])//2
```

A map can be destructured into its key value constituents in a loop. The following lines of code show the details:

```
for ((key, value) in characterOccurances) {
  println("$key -> $value")
}
```

No checked exceptions

Checked exceptions in Java have to be handled or rethrown. This results in a lot of unnecessary code. The following example shows the `try catch` block how to handle the checked exceptions thrown by `new FileReader("pathToFile")` – throws `FileNotFoundException` and `reader.read()` – throws `IOException`:

```
public void openSomeFileInJava(){
  try {
        FileReader reader = new FileReader("pathToFile");
        int i=0;
        while(i != -1){
          i = reader.read();
          //Do something with what was read
        }
    reader.close();
    } catch (FileNotFoundException e) {
        //Exception handling code
      } catch (IOException e) {
      //Exception handling code
    }
}
```

Kotlin does not have any checked exceptions. It's up to the client code if they want to handle the exception. Exception handling is not forced on the client.

Data class

Typically, we will create a number of bean classes to hold data. Kotlin introduces the concept of a data class. The following block of code show the declaration of a data class:

```
data class Address(val line1: String,
val line2: String,
val zipCode: Int,
val state: String,
val country: String)
```

Kotlin provides a primary constructor, `equals()`, `hashcode()`, and a few other utility methods for data classes. The following lines of code shows the creation of an object using the constructors:

```
val myAddress = Address("234, Some Apartments",
"River Valley Street", 54123, "NJ", "USA")
```

Kotlin also provides a `toString` method:

```
println(myAddress)
//Address(line1=234, Some Apartments, line2=River Valley
//Street, zipCode=54123, state=NJ, country=USA)
```

The `copy` function can be used to make a copy (clone) of an existing data class object. The following code snippet shows the details:

```
val myFriendsAddress = myAddress.copy(line1 = "245, Some Apartments")
println(myFriendsAddress)
//Address(line1=245, Some Apartments, line2=River Valley
//Street, zipCode=54123, state=NJ, country=USA)
```

An object of a data class can easily be destructured. The following line of code shows the details. The `println` makes use of string templates to print the value:

```
val (line1, line2, zipCode, state, country) = myAddress;

println("$line1 $line2 $zipCode $state $country");
//234, Some Apartments River Valley Street 54123 NJ USA
```

Creating a Kotlin project in Eclipse

Before we are able to use Kotlin in Eclipse, we will need to install the Kotlin plugin in Eclipse.

Kotlin plugin

The Kotlin plugin can be installed from `https://marketplace.eclipse.org/content/kot` `lin-plugin-eclipse`. Click on the **Install** button shown in the following screenshot:

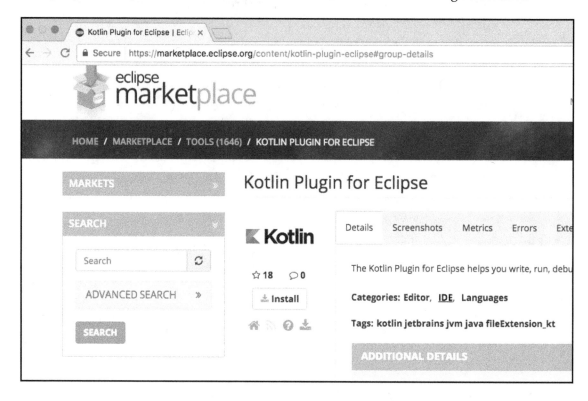

Choose **Kotlin Plugin for Eclipse** and click on the **Confirm** button, as shown in the following screenshot:

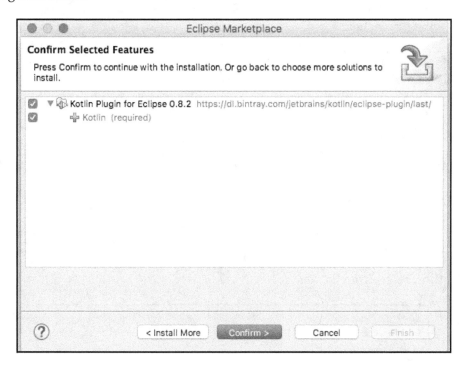

Accept defaults in the subsequent steps to install the plugin. The installation will take a little while. Restart Eclipse once the installation of the plugin is complete.

Creating a Kotlin project

Now let's create a new Kotlin Project. In Eclipse, click on **File** | **New** | **Project**..., as shown in the following screenshot:

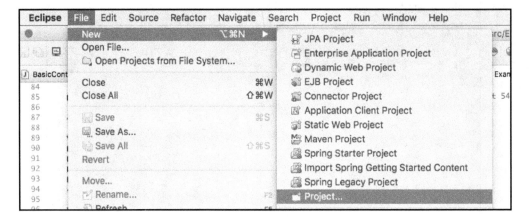

Choose **Kotlin Project** from the list.

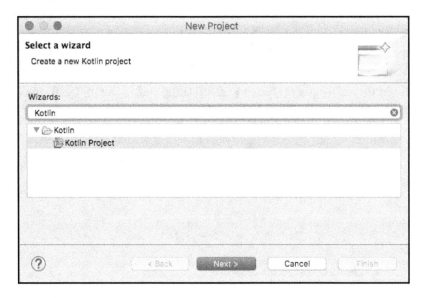

Provide `Kotlin-Hello-World` as the name of the project, accept all defaults, and click on **Finish**. Eclipse will create a new Kotlin project.

The following screenshot shows the structure of a typical Kotlin project. Both the `Kotlin Runtime Library` and `JRE System Library` are available in the project.

Creating a Kotlin class

To create a new Kotlin class, right-click on the **src** folder and choose **New | Other**, as shown in the following screenshot:

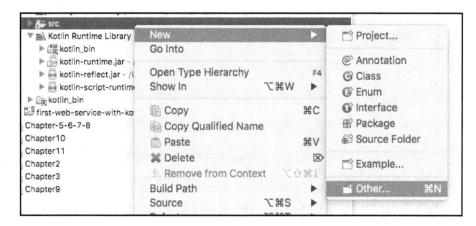

Choose **Kotlin class**, as shown in the following screenshot:

Give your new Kotlin class a name (`HelloWorld`) and a package
(`com.mastering.spring.kotlin.first`). Click on **Finish**.

Create a main function, as shown in the following lines of code:

```kotlin
fun main(args: Array<String>) {
  println("Hello, world!")
}
```

Running a Kotlin class

Right-click on the `HelloWorld.kt` file and click on **Run as | Kotlin** as shown in the following screenshot:

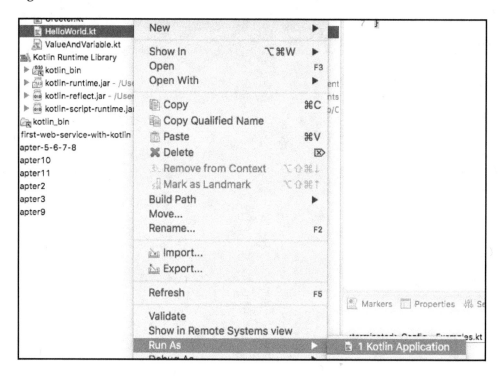

`Hello, World` is printed on the console, as shown here:

Creating a Spring Boot project using Kotlin

We will use Spring Initializr (`http://start.spring.io`) to initialize a Kotlin project. The following screenshot shows the **Group** and **ArtifactId** to choose from:

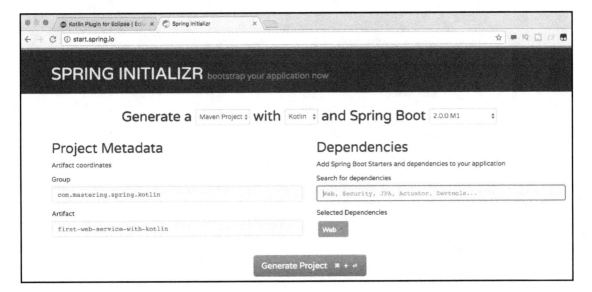

The following are a couple of important things to note:

- Choose **Web** as the dependency
- Choose **Kotlin** as the language (second drop-down at the top of the screenshot)
- Click on **Generate Project** and import the downloaded project into the eclipse as a Maven project

The following screenshot shows the structure of the generated project:

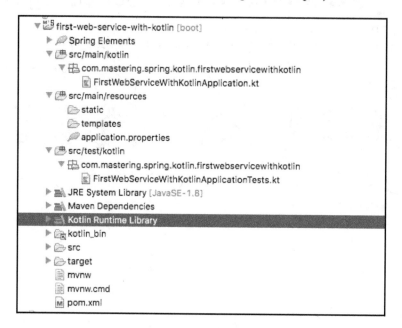

The following are some of the important things to note:

- src/main/kotlin: This is the folder where all the Kotlin source code is present. This is similar to src/main/java in a Java project.
- src/test/kotlin: This is the folder where all the Kotlin test code is present. This is similar to src/test/java in a Java project.
- Resource folders are the same as a typical Java project--src/main/resources and src/test/resources.
- Instead of JRE, **Kotlin Runtime Library** is used as the execution environment.

Dependencies and plugins

In addition to the normal dependencies in a Java Spring Boot project, there are two additional dependencies in the pom.xml

```
<dependency>
  <groupId>org.jetbrains.kotlin</groupId>
  <artifactId>kotlin-stdlib-jre8</artifactId>
  <version>${kotlin.version}</version>
</dependency>
```

```
<dependency>
  <groupId>org.jetbrains.kotlin</groupId>
  <artifactId>kotlin-reflect</artifactId>
  <version>${kotlin.version}</version>
</dependency>
```

The following are a couple of important things to note:

- `kotlin-stdlib-jre8` is the standard library supporting the new JDK APIs added in Java 8
- `kotlin-reflect` is the runtime component for using reflection features on a Java platform

In addition to `spring-boot-maven-plugin`, `kotlin-maven-plugin` is added in as a plugin in `pom.xml`. `kotlin-maven-plugin` compiles Kotlin sources and modules. This plugin is configured to be used during the `compile` and `test-compile` phases. The following piece of code shows the details:

```
<plugin>
 <artifactId>kotlin-maven-plugin</artifactId>
 <groupId>org.jetbrains.kotlin</groupId>
 <version>${kotlin.version}</version>
 <configuration>
   <compilerPlugins>
     <plugin>spring</plugin>
   </compilerPlugins>
   <jvmTarget>1.8</jvmTarget>
 </configuration>
 <executions>
 <execution>
   <id>compile</id>
   <phase>compile</phase>
   <goals>
     <goal>compile</goal>
   </goals>
 </execution>
 <execution>
   <id>test-compile</id>
   <phase>test-compile</phase>
   <goals>
     <goal>test-compile</goal>
   </goals>
  </execution>
 </executions>
 <dependencies>
   <dependency>
```

```
      <groupId>org.jetbrains.kotlin</groupId>
      <artifactId>kotlin-maven-allopen</artifactId>
      <version>${kotlin.version}</version>
    </dependency>
  </dependencies>
</plugin>
```

Spring Boot application class

The following code block shows the generated `SpringBootApplication` class, `FirstWebServiceWithKotlinApplication`. We made the class open to enable Spring Boot to override it:

```
@SpringBootApplication
open class FirstWebServiceWithKotlinApplication
fun main(args: Array<String>) {
  SpringApplication
  .run(
     FirstWebServiceWithKotlinApplication::class.java,
     *args)
}
```

The following are a few important things to note:

- Package, import, and annotations are the same as that of a Java class.
- The declaration of the main function in Java was `public static void main(String[] args)`. In the preceding example, we are using the Kotlin function syntax. Kotlin does not have static methods. Any function declared outside of a class can be called without needing a class reference.
- Launching `SpringApplication` in Java is done using `SpringApplication.run(FirstWebServiceWithKotlinApplication.class, args)`.
- `::` is used to obtain a Kotlin class runtime reference. So, `FirstWebServiceWithKotlinApplication::class` gives us a runtime reference to the Kotlin class. To obtain a Java class reference, we need to use the `.java` property on the reference. So, in Kotlin, the syntax is `FirstWebServiceWithKotlinApplication::class.java`.

- In Kotlin, `*` is called a spread operator. It is used when passing an array to a function accepting variable arguments. So, we will use `*args` to pass the array to the `run` method.

The application can be launched up by running
`FirstWebServiceWithKotlinApplication` as a Kotlin application.

Spring Boot application test class

The following code snippet shows the generated `SpringBootApplicationTest` class,
`FirstWebServiceWithKotlinApplicationTests`:

```
@RunWith(SpringRunner::class)
@SpringBootTest
class FirstWebServiceWithKotlinApplicationTests {
  @Test
  fun contextLoads() {
  }
}
```

The following are a few important things to note:

- Package, import, and annotations are the same as that of a Java class.
- `::` is used to obtain a Kotlin class runtime reference. Compared to `@RunWith(SpringRunner.class)` in Java, the Kotlin code uses `@RunWith(SpringRunner::class)`.
- The declaration of the test class uses the Kotlin function syntax.

Implementing a REST service using Kotlin

We will start with creating a service returning a hardcoded string. After that, we will discuss an example returning a proper JSON response. We will also look at an example of passing a path parameter.

Simple method returning a string

Let's start with creating a simple REST service returning a `welcome` message:

```
@RestController
class BasicController {
  @GetMapping("/welcome")
  fun welcome() = "Hello World"
}
```

A comparable Java method is shown as follows. A major difference is how we are able to define a function in one line in Kotlin--`fun welcome() = "Hello World"`:

```
@GetMapping("/welcome")
public String welcome() {
  return "Hello World";
}
```

If we run `FirstWebServiceWithKotlinApplication.kt` as a Kotlin application, it will start up the embedded Tomcat container. We can launch up the URL (`http://localhost:8080/welcome`) in the browser, as shown in the following screenshot:

Unit testing

Let's quickly write a unit test to test the preceding controller method:

```
@RunWith(SpringRunner::class)
@WebMvcTest(BasicController::class)
class BasicControllerTest {
  @Autowired
  lateinit var mvc: MockMvc;
  @Test
  fun `GET welcome returns "Hello World"`() {
    mvc.perform(
        MockMvcRequestBuilders.get("/welcome").accept(
        MediaType.APPLICATION_JSON))
```

```
        .andExpect(status().isOk())
        .andExpect(content().string(equalTo("Hello World")));
    }
}
```

In the preceding unit test, we will launch up a Mock MVC instance with `BasicController`. A few quick things to note are as follows:

- The annotations `@RunWith(SpringRunner.class)` and `@WebMvcTest(BasicController::class)` are similar to Java, except for the class references.
- `@Autowired lateinit var mvc: MockMvc`: This autowires the `MockMvc` bean that can be used to make requests. Properties declared as non-null must be initialized in the constructor. For properties that are autowired through the dependency injection, we can avoid null checks by adding `lateinit` to the variable declaration.
- `fun ` ``GET welcome returns "Hello World"`` `()`: This is a unique feature of Kotlin. Instead of giving the test method a name, we are giving a description for the test. This is awesome because, ideally, the test method will not be called from another method.
- `mvc.perform(MockMvcRequestBuilders.get("/welcome").accept(Media Type.APPLICATION_JSON))`: This performs a request to `/welcome` with the Accept header value, `application/json`, which is similar to the Java code.
- `andExpect(status().isOk())`: This expects that the status of the response is `200` (success).
- `andExpect(content().string(equalTo("Hello World")))`: This expects that the content of the response is equal to `"Hello World"`.

Integration testing

When we integration testing, we will want to launch the embedded server with all the controllers and beans that are configured. The following block of code shows how we can create a simple integration test:

```
    @RunWith(SpringRunner::class)
    @SpringBootTest(webEnvironment =
SpringBootTest.WebEnvironment.RANDOM_PORT)
    class BasicControllerIT {
      @Autowired
      lateinit var restTemplate: TestRestTemplate
      @Test
```

```
fun `GET welcome returns "Hello World"`() {
  // When
  val body = restTemplate.getForObject("/welcome",
  String::class.java)
  // Then
  assertThat(body).isEqualTo("Hello World")
 }
}
```

A few important things to note are as follows:

- @RunWith(SpringRunner::class), @SpringBootTest(webEnvironment = SpringBootTest.WebEnvironment.RANDOM_PORT): SpringBootTest provides additional functionality on top of the Spring TestContext. It provides support to configure the port for fully running container and TestRestTemplate (to execute requests). This is similar to the Java code, except for the class reference.
- @Autowired lateinit var restTemplate: TestRestTemplate: TestRestTemplate is typically used in integration tests. It provides additional functionality on top of the RestTemplate, which is especially useful in the integration of the test context. It does not follow redirects so that we can assert the response location. lateinit allows us to avoid null checks for the autowired variables.

Simple REST method returning an object

We will create a simple POJO WelcomeBean with a member field called message and one argument constructor, as shown in the following line of code:

```
data class WelcomeBean(val message: String = "")
```

The corresponding Java class is listed as follows:

```java
public class WelcomeBean {
  private String message;
  public WelcomeBean(String message) {
    super();
    this.message = message;
  }
  public String getMessage() {
  return message;
  }
}
```

Kotlin automatically adds constructors and other utility methods to data classes.

In the previous method, we returned a string. Let's create a method that returns a proper JSON response. Take a look at the following method:

```kotlin
@GetMapping("/welcome-with-object")
fun welcomeWithObject() = WelcomeBean("Hello World")
```

The method returns a simple `WelcomeBean` initialized with an "`Hello World`" message.

Executing a request

Let's send a test request and see what response we get. The following screenshot shows the output:

The response for the `http://localhost:8080/welcome-with-object` URL is shown as follows:

```
{"message":"Hello World"}
```

Unit testing

Let's quickly write a unit test checking for the JSON response and then add the test to `BasicControllerTest`:

```
@Test
fun `GET welcome-with-object returns "Hello World"`() {
  mvc.perform(
  MockMvcRequestBuilders.get("/welcome-with-object")
  .accept(MediaType.APPLICATION_JSON))
  .andExpect(status().isOk())
  .andExpect(content().string(
  containsString("Hello World")));
}
```

This test is very similar to the earlier unit test, except that we are using `containsString` to check whether the content contains an `"Hello World"` substring.

Integration testing

Let's shift our focus to writing an integration test and then add a method to `BasicControllerIT`, as shown in the following code snippet:

```
@Test
fun `GET welcome-with-object returns "Hello World"`() {
  // When
  val body = restTemplate.getForObject("/welcome-with-object",
  WelcomeBean::class.java)
  // Then
  assertThat(body.message, containsString("Hello World"));
}
```

This method is similar to the earlier integration test, except that we are asserting for a substring in the `assertThat` method.

Get method with path variables

Let's shift our attention to path variables. Path variables are used to bind values from the URI to a variable on the controller method. In the following example, we want to parameterize the name so that we can customize the welcome message with a name:

```
@GetMapping("/welcome-with-parameter/name/{name}")
fun welcomeWithParameter(@PathVariable name: String) =
WelcomeBean("Hello World, $name")
```

The following are a few important things to note:

- `@GetMapping("/welcome-with-parameter/name/{name}")`: `{name}` indicates that this value will be the variable. We can have multiple variable templates in a URI.
- `welcomeWithParameter(@PathVariable String name)`: `@PathVariable` ensures that the variable value from the URI is bound to the variable name.
- `fun welcomeWithParameter(@PathVariable name: String) = WelcomeBean("Hello World, $name")`: We are using the Kotlin single expression function declaration to directly return the created `WelcomeBean`. `"Hello World, $name"` makes use of Kotlin string templates. `$name` will be replaced by the value of the path variable name.

Executing a request

Let's send a test request and see what response we get. The following screenshot shows the response:

The response for the `http://localhost:8080/welcome-with-parameter/name/Buddy` URL is as follows:

```
{"message":"Hello World, Buddy!"}
```

As expected, the name in the URI is used to form the message in the response.

Unit testing

Let's quickly write a unit test for the preceding method. We will want to pass a name as a part of the URI and check whether the response contains the name. The following code shows how we can do that:

```
@Test
fun `GET welcome-with-parameter returns "Hello World, Buddy"`() {
  mvc.perform(
  MockMvcRequestBuilders.get(
  "/welcome-with-parameter/name/Buddy")
 .accept(MediaType.APPLICATION_JSON))
 .andExpect(status().isOk())
 .andExpect(content().string(
 containsString("Hello World, Buddy")));
 }
```

A few important things to note are as follows:

- `MockMvcRequestBuilders.get("/welcome-with-parameter/name/Buddy")`: This matches against the variable template in the URI. We will pass in the name, .
- `.andExpect(content().string(containsString("Hello World, Buddy")))`: We expect the response to contain the message with the name.

Integration testing

The integration test for the preceding method is very simple. Take a look at the following `test` method:

```
@Test
fun `GET welcome-with-parameter returns "Hello World"`() {
  // When
  val body = restTemplate.getForObject(
  "/welcome-with-parameter/name/Buddy",
  WelcomeBean::class.java)
  // Then
  assertThat(body.message,
  containsString("Hello World, Buddy"));
 }
```

A few important things to note are as follows:

- `restTemplate.getForObject("/welcome-with-parameter/name/Buddy", WelcomeBean::class.java)`: This matches against the variable template in the URI. We are passing in the name, `Buddy`.
- `assertThat(response.getBody(), containsString("Hello World, Buddy"))`: We expect the response to contain the message with the name.

In this section, we looked at the basics of creating a simple REST service with Spring Boot. We also ensured that we have good unit tests and integration tests.

Summary

Kotlin helps a developer write concise, readable code. It fits hand in glove with the philosophy of Spring Boot to make application development easier and faster.

In this chapter, we started with understanding Kotlin and how it compares with Java. We built a couple of simple REST services with Spring Boot and Kotlin. We saw examples of how code with Kotlin for services and unit tests is concise.

Kotlin has made great strides in the last couple of years--becoming an officially supported language for Android was a great first step. Support for Kotlin in Spring Framework 5.0 is the icing on the cake. The future of Kotlin depends on how successful it is with the larger Java development community. It has the potential to be an important tool in your arsenal.

Index

C

caching annotations
  adding 427
caching
  about 229, 427
  data 230
  enabling 229
  JSR-107 caching annotations 230
  spring-boot-starter-cache 229
centralized microservice configuration
  about 306
  options 308
  problem statement 306
  solution 307
challenges, microservices
  boundaries of subsystems, defining 129
  eventual consistency 130
  fault tolerance 130
  increased need for automation 129
  increased need for operations teams 131
  monitoring 130
  visibility 129
challenges, monolithic applications
  about 118
  difficult to scale 119
  long release cycles 118
  modern development practices, adapting 119
  new methodologies, adapting 119
  new technologies, adapting 119
characteristics, microservices
  automated build 124
  capability-aligned microservices 123
  event-driven architecture 124
  independent teams 126
  independently deployable units 123
  interoperability, with message-based
    communication 123
  release process 124
  small and lightweight 122
  stateless 123
characteristics, Reactive Systems
  elastic 385
  message driven 385
  resilient 385

responsive 385
checked exceptions 414
client 160
client-side load balancing
  implementing, with Zuul 333
Cloud Foundry
  Java Build Pack, reference 267
  reference 266
Cloud Native applications
  about 131
  Twelve-Factor App 132
constraints, REST
  cacheable 161
  Client-Server 160
  Hypermedia as the engine of application state
    (HATEOAS) 161
  layered system 161
  resource manipulation 161
  stateless 161
  uniform interface 161
Container Managed Beans 42
Contexts and Dependency Injection (CDI)
  @Inject 49
  @Named 49
  @Qualifier 49
  @Singleton 49
  about 27
  example 49
contexts
  exploring 48
Continuous Integration 9
controller, redirecting to View with form
  about 69
  command, creating 69
  controller get method, creating to handle form
    72, 73
  controller method, creating to display form 70
  form backing object, creating 69
  unit testing 73
  View, creating with form 70, 71
controller, redirecting to View with Model
  about 65
  setting up, to test 66
  Spring MVC controller, creating 65
  Test method, writing 66

www.ingramcontent.com/pod-product-compliance
Lightning Source LLC
LaVergne TN
LVHW081327050326
832903LV00024B/1059